HOMICIDE AMONG BLACK AMERICANS

Edited by

Darnell F. Hawkins

UNIVERSITY
PRESS OF
AMERICA

LANHAM • NEW YORK • LONDON

Copyright © 1986 by

University Press of America,® Inc.

4720 Boston Way
Lanham, MD 20706

3 Henrietta Street
London WC2E 8LU England

Library of Congress Cataloging in Publication Data

Homicide among Black Americans.

Includes bibliographies.
1. Homicide—United States.   2. Afro-Americans
criminals—United States.   3. Afro-Americans—United
States—Crime against.   4. Discrimination in criminal
justice administration—United States.   I. Hawkins,
Darnell Felix, 1946-   .
HV6529.H66   1986   364.1'52'08996073   86-18952
ISBN 0-8191-5598-5 (alk. paper)
ISBN 0-8191-5599-3 (pbk. : alk. paper)

All University Press of America books are produced on acid-free
paper which exceeds the minimum standards set by the National
Historical Publications and Records Commission.

ACKNOWLEDGEMENTS

Homicide Trends in the United States by Reynolds Farley. *Demography,* 17: 2 (May, 1980), pp. 177-188. Reprinted by permission of the Population Association of America.

Black and White Homicide Differentials: Alternatives to an Inadequate Theory. *Criminal Justice and Behavior,* 10: 4 (December, 1983), pp. 407-440; and Black Homicide: The Adequacy of Existing Research for Devising Prevention Strategies. *Crime and Delinquency* 31: 1 (January, 1985), pp. 83-103. Reprinted by permission of Sage Publications, Inc.

The Masculine Way of Violence by Robert Staples. *Black Masculinity: The Black Male's Role in American Society.* Black Scholar Press, San Francisco, 1982. Selection is chapter 4, pp. 55-71. Reprinted by the permission of the author.

Race and Capital Punishment, by Michael L. Radelet and Margaret Vandiver. Reprinted by permission from issue #25 of *Crime and Social Justice,* P. O. Box 40601, San Francisco, CA 94140.

I thank Janet Szafran, Bonita Samuels, Brad Buchner, and Bibb Latane for their assistance in preparing the manuscript for this volume. Support for the book was also provided by the Institute for Research in Social Science at the University of North Carolina at Chapel Hill and by the National Science Foundation, Minority Research Initiation Program, Grant Number RII-8421196.

CONTENTS

LIST OF CONTRIBUTORS

Robert Davis is an Associate Professor of Sociology at North Carolina A & T State University, Greensboro.

Donald R. Deskins, Jr. is a Professor of Geography/Sociology at the University of Michigan, Ann Arbor.

Reynolds Farley is a Professor of Sociology at the University of Michigan, Ann Arbor.

William B. Harvey is an Associate Professor of Educational Leadership and Program Evaluation at North Carolina State University, Raleigh.

Darnell F. Hawkins is an Associate Professor of Sociology at the University of North Carolina, Chapel Hill.

John A. Humphrey is a Professor of Sociology at the University of North Carolina, Greensboro.

Henry P. Lundsgaarde is a Professor of Anthropology at the University of Kansas.

James A. Mercy is Chief of the Intentional Injury Section in the Division of Injury Epidemiology and Control at the Centers for Disease Control.

Patrick W. O'Carroll is an Epidemic Intelligence Service Officer in the Intentional Injury Section of the Division of Injury Epidemiology and Control at the Centers for Disease Control.

Stuart Palmer is Dean of Arts and Sciences and a Professor of Sociology at the University of New Hampshire.

Michael L. Radelet is an Associate Professor of Sociology at the University of Florida.

Harold Rose is a Professor of Urban Affairs and Geography at the University of Wisconsin, Milwaukee.

Robert Staples is a Professor of Sociology in the School of Nursing at the University of California, San Francisco.

Margaret Vandiver is a Ph.D. candidate in the School of Criminology at Florida State University.

William Wilbanks is a Professor of Criminal Justice at Florida International University.

PREFACE

In the view of many, homicide is the quintessential crime. It is likely that no other type of crime has been so frequently depicted within the folklore and literature of the various peoples of the world. Perhaps no other behavior has been the object of such universal legal regulation. The study of homicide has also been an integral part of pre- modern and modern social science. Although a wide variety of factors have been shown to be correlated with the incidence of homicide in modern industrial societies, the influence of minority or subordinate group status has been consistently reported. That is, the incidence of homicide is usually greater among minority group members. In the United States, blacks as compared to other nonwhite and white Americans, have been shown to have disproportionately higher rates of homicide during the fifty years since national crime data have been available. Some evidence points to higher rates among blacks than whites during earlier years.

The existence of a particularly brutal form of slavery and post-Civil War vigilantism directed at blacks have meant that the black who kills has been an especially troublesome figure for whites throughout American history. Fear of insurrections and of retaliatory violence by blacks against whites has characterized race relations in the United States and has greatly influenced the development of the law, both substantive and procedural. Such fear has also had the effect of producing exaggerated public perceptions of the threat to whites posed by black violence and a concomitant failure to appreciate the tragic dimensions and consequences of black-on-black homicide.

Today, homicide is the leading cause of death among young black males. In response to this fact the Department of Health and Human Services during 1980 specifically targeted black males between the ages of 15 and 24 for homicide reduction programs. Efforts are now underway to identify aspects of black homicide that may be susceptible to professional intervention aimed at its reduction. As a part of this effort the federal government has set up a Homicide Surveillance Unit at the Centers for Disease Control to monitor intervention strategies tha be fully evaluated in 1990.

These plans for intervention have made more apparent several major limitations of existing research on black homicide: (1) Despite the centrality of homicide in the public consciousness and in the social scientific study of crime and despite its disproportionate incidence among blacks, few well crafted studies of black homicide can be found in the literature. Data on homicide among blacks have generally been included within analyses aimed at showing the disproportionate rate of black involvement in crime of all types. That is, the focus has not been on homicide, per se. (2) Most investigations have been primarily comparative. Analysts have compared black rates of homicide to those of other racial groups. As a result they have seldom gone beyond the mere documentation of consistently high rates of black homicide to examine more fully the patterning of this form of aggression *within the black community*. (3) Finally, despite the well documented aggregate rate differences between blacks and nonblacks, researchers have offered a surprisingly limited range of explanations for these differences.

The purpose of this volume is to provide a systematic and detailed

ix

examination of homicide among black Americans which overcomes some of the limitations of previous works. Both previously published and unpublished materials are included. As is true of most edited volumes, much of the value of this collection results from the bringing together of manuscripts with a common theme but which would be (or are) published in a variety of scholarly journals or other sources. Although by no means conceptually distinct, the volume is divided into three sections. In the first section I include quantitative analyses of rates, trends and patterns of homicide in the United States. Some historical pattterns are reported but the focus is on late twentieth century developments. The second section looks at more substantive issues. Of particular interest is the attempt to provide theories and causal models to explain the disproportionately high rates of homicide among blacks. In the final section I include discussions of two major public policy-oriented issues- the differential punishment of homicide offenders on the basis of race and the need for systematic programs designed to reduce the incidence of homicide among blacks.

The articles included in this volume are sociological in their focus. I do not include works of other disciplines that have made significant contributions to the study of homicide, notably psychology and psychiatry. The perspectives presented instead focus on institutional and social structural factors. It is suggested that homicide among blacks, especially its disproportionate incidence, can best be understood by examining the larger social conditions that give rise to individual pathological behavior. This is not to say that these scholarly orientations are completely absent from the volume. Most of the essays in the second section provide structural and social psychological explanations for the incidence of homicide among blacks. All stress the need for subsequent researchers to contextualize psychological, psychoanalytic and social interactionist theories within structural interpretations. Because of the lack of systematic investigation in this area of research, the volume has the dual purpose of providing a theoretical grounding for the study of homicide among blacks while also updating earlier works.

PART I
TRENDS AND PATTERNS OF HOMICIDE

PART I

TRENDS AND PATTERNS OF HOMICIDE

INTRODUCTION

Studies of rates, trends and patterns of homicide, like such analyses of crime in general, have come from a variety of research traditions and disciplines. In fact, many predate the development of what we now call social science. Crime and the criminal justice system have been targets of various reform efforts over the centuries and many would-be reformers were among the first to provide quantitative data on the incidence of crime, including homicide. These latter works are sometimes sources of valuable information about crime but are largely excluded from the present volume. Rather I have selected articles representative of the various research traditions found within sociology and criminology during more recent years. A review of these research traditions illustrates both the need for the present volume and the problems encountered in the study of homicide among blacks.

While sociologists tend to be primarily associated with the study of crime rates and patterns today, geographers or researchers trained in geographical methods made some of the earliest contributions to the study of crime. What might be called a carto- demographic school of crime analysis developed during the 19th and early 20th centuries in Europe and the United States, and continues today. Vold (1958:164- 65) Voss and Petersen (1971:65-76); Reid (1979:81, 133-36); and Greenberg (1979) have noted that cartographic, geographic and ecological approaches to the measurement of crime and the study of its etiology contributed greatly to the development of criminology as a scientific discipline.[1]

In the United States the earliest studies of crime in this tradition noted its regional and racial distribution. One of the most consistent findings was higher rates of crime among blacks than whites, but there was considerable disagreement over the reasons for this difference. Some researchers also reported comparatively high rates of crime among other racial groups such as American Indians and also among various white ethnic groups. The study of crime, including homicide, among blacks was greatly affected by racism, especially during the nearly half-century after the Civil War. Many analysts of crime during the late 1800s and early 1900s were influenced by Social Darwinist thought and cited evidence of higher rates of crime among blacks as proof of their moral and physical depravity. Two early studies that echoed this theme were conducted by Otken (1894) and Hoffman (1896).

Among the conclusions reached by these late nineteenth century researchers were: (1) Crime rates among blacks were lower during slavery than after emancipation; (2) During the period prior to the Civil War, rates of crime among blacks were higher among free blacks of the North than among black slaves in the South; and (3) Black crime rates in both the North and South increased rapidly during the decades after the Civil War. Hoffman (1896: 217) said of black crime:

During slavery, the Negro committed fewer crimes than the white man, and only on rare occasions was he guilty of the more atrocious crimes, such as rape and murder of white females. Whether from cowardice or

3

respect and devotion to his master, he respected the persons of his master's household, and few, indeed, are the recorded attempts at insurrection and revolt on the part of the southern slave.

The conclusion of many of these early researchers was that slavery helped to suppress the criminal behavior of blacks; thus, under conditions of freedom black crime would increase.

Hoffman's view is representative of the sometimes paradoxical notions of black criminality that prevailed in the past and persists to some extent today. On the one hand, black slaves were described as bestial, showing little respect for human life or the property of others. Homicide was seen as normal behavior among them. On the other hand, the racist literature of this period also depicted blacks as child-like and dependent. Under this conception blacks were seen as lacking in aggression or at least easily controlled by the imposition of authority. This description of blacks as child-like was similarly used to argue that they lacked moral development and resorted to violence as a result of moral naivete rather than malice. The fact that such perceptions of the black homicide offender exist even today has been documented by Swigert and Farrell (1976, 1977) in their study of the "normal primitive." They conclude that the normal primitive label is used to diagnose and sentence black criminal homicide defendants. Their behavior is said to lie outside the controls of normative society. Their "propensity to violence is said to arise from a cultural proclivity to the spontaneous expression of rage in diverse interpersonal situations and from an intellectual capacity that precludes the choice of alternative expressions" (1976: 96).

Black and white critics of such views of black criminality also conducted investigations of black crime during the late 1800s and early 1900s. Among them were W. E. B. DuBois (1899) and Frank Sanborn (1904). While disagreeing with most of the propositions of Otken and Hoffman, DuBois and Sanborn also noted the significantly higher rates of crime among blacks than among whites in the United States during the two decades after the Civil War. A major argument of Sanborn and several other researchers was that the black crime rate showed a significant increase during the 1870s and 1880s but had begun to decrease toward the beginning of the 20th century. Sanborn (1904: 30-32) offered evidence that the homicide rate among blacks in several major cities of the country either remained stable or decreased between 1873 and 1901. DuBois, Sanborn and others also stressed the fact that minor property or public order offenses, not violent crime, accounted for much of the discrepancy between overall black and white rates of offending.

As noted, most of these early investigations considered homicide as merely one category of crime among many. That is, all crime types were aggregated and black-white comparisons made on this basis. This practice was largely the result of a lack of precision in record keeping during earlier periods and even today. Consequently, even those researchers who wanted to study homicide as a unique crime type were hampered by a lack of data. Of course, the conclusions reached by Hoffman and others regarding black crime *during* slavery were based on little, if any, data.

A recent historical study of crime in antebellum South Carolina by Hindus (1980) reports a low rate of black homicide in that state during the

4

early 1800s. However, he notes that his measure of crime (court adjudications) most likely involved only those offenses by blacks against whites. Black-on-black homicide, as today, was likely more leniently treated than offenses by slaves against whites and any punishment was administered informally by the slaveowners. Thus, we are not able to determine the extent of black homicide for most of the antebellum period, except perhaps in some local areas where more extensive records might have been kept.

A major obstacle that confronted the earliest (post-Civil War) scientific analysts of black-white crime was the unavailability of arrest and mortality data. Researchers most often used imprisonment statistics with the obvious bias inherent in such data. Therefore, despite the documentation of substantial racial differences in imprisonment rates for most crimes during this period there was still much debate over the question of the *extent* of black-white crime differences. By the 1920s researchers such as Sellin (1928) began to conclude that although black-white differences in arrests, prosecution and imprisonment may be partly due to racial discrimination, the actual rate of crime among blacks far exceeded that of whites.

The availability of national arrest and mortality data after 1930 allowed homicide researchers to examine for the first time the patterning of homicide for the entire country while using more reliable and consistent measures than earlier available. These data provided even more evidence of the racial imbalance in the distribution of homicide in the United States than prior investigations had done. As in the study of crime in general (Greenberg, 1979) the use of aggregated state or national statistics was also used for the study of homicide, at least by non- psychological researchers. This method may be adequate for providing summary measures of rates and trends, but it may conceal micro-level patterns that may be useful for studying homicide, including its distribution *within* racial groups. Some of the problems associated with the use of aggregate data are discussed in various contributions to this volume.[2]

Harries (1974) has reviewed spatial and ecological approaches to the study of crime in the United States that appeared after 1930. He cites the important regional analyses of crime by Lottier (1938) and Shannon (1954); and the Urban Studies-Chicago School researchers such as Shaw and McKay (1942). These studies were among the first to document the high rates of crime, including homicide, in core city areas and in the southern United States. These studies also continued to add to the evidence of the existence of high rates of homicide among blacks, although spatial rather than group differences in crime were emphasized by these researchers. A few analysts within this tradition used the carto- demographic approach to specifically study homicide in the United States and in local areas. For example, Brearley (1932) used national mortality data to document the distribution of homicide by states between 1918 and 1927. His work was replicated by numerous other researchers. In a chapter titled "The Negro and Homicide" Brearley (1932:97) reported that the homicide rate for colored persons (blacks and other nonwhites) was almost seven times the white rate. He also noted that the black rate varied substantially from state to state.[3]

About twenty years after Brearley the work of Henry and Short (1954) and Wolfgang (1958) began a somewhat different research tradition, although modeled after the earlier carto-demographic investigations. Henry and Short examined homicide rates and patterns and tended to emphasize the

5

importance of economic factors (the business cycle) for analyzing and explaining the incidence of homicide across time. Such efforts to correlate rates of homicide with other quantitative measures (poverty, etc.) were also characteristic of some of the earlier work of the Chicago school but Henry and Short and Wolfgang were among the first to limit their analysis to a single crime type-homicide. Suicide, also studied by Henry and Short, is generally not perceived as a criminal offense. Wolfgang's study was not longitudinal. Instead he emphasized spatial variations in the rate of homicide and also such dimensions of homicide patterning as time-of-day, victim-offender characteristics, weapon use, situational factors surrounding the homicide act, and the legal processing of the offender. Many of these factors were discussed in somewhat less detail by Brearley.

Because of problems of data availability for larger areas, Wolfgang's study and numerous follow-up studies in this tradition were case studies at the local level and emphasized the intracity patterning of homicide as opposed to an analysis of regional or national rates and trends. The work of Brearley (1932), Henry and Short (1954) and Wolfgang (1958), to a greater extent than the earlier carto-demographic studies, tended to emphasize the disproportionate rates of homicide among American blacks. On the other hand, these studies paid less attention to the specific problem of homicide among blacks than is warranted given the consistently high rates of this crime in the black community. One exception is Pettigrew and Spier (1962) who conducted an important ecological analysis of black homicide that covered the period between 1949 and 1951.

In summary, there have been numerous studies that have pointed to the high incidence of homicide among blacks. The problem with these studies has been a lack of *systematic, detailed* analysis of the phenomenon, including attention to the intra-group distribution and patterning of the crime among blacks. This problem stems partly from the use by researchers of aggregate-level statistics for large geographical areas. But that fact alone does not provide a full explanation for the absence of more rigorous investigations. The devalued status of black life in the United States, a theme explored in the second section of this volume, may also be a contributing factor. That is, persisting racism in American society has resulted in an inattention to homicide *among* blackAmericans despite its disproportionate incidence.

The six articles in this section are representative of the various research traditions described above. They were also selected because each author attempts to bridge the gap between traditional aggregate-level studies of homicide and the specific issues associated with the study of homicide among blacks. Despite the emphasis on black homicide the studies included in this section have some of the evidentiary and data-availability problems of past works. Several include data for all nonwhites rather than blacks. All are aggregate-level analyses. Their significance lies in the efforts of the authors to highlight black-white differences while also considering such issues as the age,sex, and regional distribution of homicide within the black population.

The first study provides a survey of homicide trends in the United States. Farley uses national mortality data to examine long term and more recent trends in the incidence of homicide among whites and nonwhites. The study also examines age and sex differences in homicide victimization, especially emphasizing the extremely high rates of homicide found among young black males. He analyzes such trends primarily between 1940 and the 1970s. His study partly replicates and extends an earlier study of homicide among blacks during roughly the same time period (Shin et al., 1977). The major conclusions reached in these two investigations are: (1) Prior to 1940 homicide rates among blacks tended to fluctuate but were far below levels found today (Shin et al); (2) The rate of homicide among blacks decreased between 1940 and 1960, but their rate increased substantially between 1965 and the early 1970s. During this entire period, (1940- 1970), the rate for blacks was consistently higher than that for whites, with little evidence of a major decrease in the gap between them; and (3) During a time when other causes of death are falling, homicide among young black males has increased to become the leading cause of death.

O'Carroll and Mercy provide an updating of these national trends by looking at both FBI homicide victim data and mortality statistics for the period between 1976 and 1984. They note that blacks experienced an overall decrease in homicide rates during these years while whites experienced an increase. Yet, in 1984 blacks were still more than five times more likely than whites to die from homicide. They also provide valuable information on weapon use, victim-assailant relationship, and the circumstances surrounding homicide, themes further explored in the last three essays in this section.

Wilbanks analyzes data for one year to conduct a Brearley-like study of national homicide rates. He uses data on all homicides reported to the FBI during 1980. A significant finding, and one reported in earlier investigations, is the extent to which the black homicide rate varies across states. The articles by Humphrey and Palmer, and Rose and Deskins represent studies of homicide in both the carto- geographic and the Wolfgang traditions. Although Wolfgang stressed the importance of victim-offender relationships in understanding the genesis of homicide, the study of such relationships has not been an integral part of later investigations. Humphrey and Palmer ask whether there are parallels in victim- offender relationships between blacks and whites in North Carolina. Although comparative in their approach, they stress the importance of examining possible black-white differences in order to better understand reasons for the high rate of homicide among blacks.

Rose and Deskins, geographers by training, add a decidedly carto-geographic slant to the usual Wolfgang-type analysis. They also provide an essentially intragroup analyses of black homicide. Their primary focus is on weapon use in a six city sample: Atlanta, Houston, Detroit, Los Angeles, Pittsburgh and St. Louis. In addition to weapon use, they consider other aspects of homicide patterning such as temporal variations, intensity of violence, and other dimensions of victimization and offending. Their data come from FBI monthly homicide reports and other official sources.

The latter four articles, O'Carroll and Mercy, Wilbanks, Humphrey and Palmer, and Rose and Deskins, all report important findings regarding the patterning of black homicide-- some of which have been reported in previous studies. Others have not been reported in previous investigations or have been deemphasized. They report that there are considerable similarities and some important differences in the patterning of homicide among blacks and whites, including victim-offender relationships, urban concentration, regional variation, and the use of firearms as a weapon of choice. The observations made by Wilbanks and Rose and Deskins regarding the

7

intra-race patterning of homicide among blacks are especially significant. There is substantial evidence that much could be learned about black homicide and other aspects of black life in the United States if more careful attention were paid to differences among blacks as well as between blacks and whites. The incidence of homicide among blacks, as among nonblacks, is significantly correlated with social class. Hill and Achiss suggested such an intragroup approach to the study of blacks in 1943 and Wilson (1978) has recently stressed the importance of social class for understanding black-white inequality. The studies in this section suggest that the study of homicide among blacks may benefit from a within-group as well as a between-group analytic framework. Such a framework may be especially useful for examining issues of etiology as is done in the articles included in Part II of this volume.

Notes

1. I use the term "carto-demographic" to include many earlier studies that were either primarily cartographic or demographic in their approaches to the study of homicide. The former studies were mainly focused on the geographical distribution of acts of crime. The latter emphasised socio-demographic traits of criminal offenders. Of course, most studies combined elements of each approach.

2. This is not to suggest that aggregate-level data and analyses are not valuable. Most of social scientific research, especially within criminology and sociology, can be so characterized. There are two major problems, however, with past studies of homicide. First, they are primarily comparative. Researchers have stressed black-white differences. Second, researchers have relied *exclusively* on aggregate-level data and have not followed-up on the findings from such studies. For example, sociologists and criminologists (as opposed to psychologists and psychiatrists) have not conducted detailed studies of small samples of homicide offenders or victims. Such studies could help more fully examine the social structural and social interactional factors that are correlated with homicide. Both of these characteristics of past investigations (comparative *and* aggregate-level) have resulted in few studies that examine homicide within the black population or which are useful for beginning to explain the disproportionate incidence of homicide among blacks.

3. In comparison to earlier studies the carto-demographic studies of the 1930s through 1950s were generally more "scientific" in their orientation. This means that there was an emphasis on quantification and less emphasis on "proving" that blacks were more criminal than whites.

REFERENCES

Brearley, H. C. 1932. **Homicide in the United States**. Chapel Hill : University of North Carolina Press.

DuBois, W. E. Burghardt. 1899. **The Philadelphia Negro: A Social Study**. New York: Benjamin Blom.

Greenberg, Keith D. 1979. **Mathematical Criminology**. New Brunswick: Rutgers University Press.

Harries, Keith D. 1968. "The Geography of American Crime, 1968," **Journal of Geography** 70:204-213.

. 1974. **The Geography of Crime and Justice**. New York: McGraw-Hill.

Henry, Andrew F. and James F. Short, Jr. 1954. **Suicide and Homicide**. Glencoe, Illinois: Free Press.

Hill, M. C. and T. D. Ackiss. 1943. "Social Classes: A Frame of Reference for the Study of Negro Society." **Social Forces** 22:92-98.

Hoffman, Frederick. 1896. **Race Traits and Tendencies of the American Negro**. New York: MacMillan.

Hindus, Michael S. 1980. **Prison and Plantation: Crime, Justice, and Authority in Massachusetts and South Carolina, 1767-1878**. Chapel Hill: University of North Carolina Press.

Lottier, Stuart. 1938. "Distribution of Criminal Offenses in Sectional Regions." **Journal of Criminal Law, Criminology, and Police Science** 29:330-.

Otken, Charles H. 1894. **The Ills of the South**. New York: G. P. Putnam's Sons.

Pettigrew, Thomas F. and Rosalind B. Spier. 1962. "The Ecological Structure of Negro Homicide." **American Journal of Sociology** 67 (May): 621-629.

Reid, Sue Titus. 1979. **Crime and Criminology**. New York: Holt, Rinehart and Winston.

Sanborn, Frank M. 1904. "Negro Crime" in W. E. B. DuBois (ed.), **Proceedings of the Ninth Atlanta Conference for the Study of Negro Problems. Number 9**. Atlanta: Atlanta University Press. Proceedings reprinted as **Some Notes on Negro Crime, Particularly in Georgia**, 1968, New York: Octagon.

Sellin Thorsten. 1928. "The Negro Criminal: A Statistical Note." **The Annals of the American Academy of Political Science** 140: 52-64.

Shannon, Lyle W. 1954. "The Spatial Distribution of Criminal Offenses by States," **Journal of Criminal Law, Criminology, and Police Science** 45:264-273.

10

Shaw, Clifford R. and Henry D. McKay. 1942, 1972. **Juvenile Delinquency and Urban Areas.** Chicago: University of Chicago Press.

Shin, Yongsock, Davor Jedlicka and Everett S. Lee. 1977. "Homicide Among Blacks." **Phylon** 38(December): 398-407.

Swigert, Victoria Lynn and Ronald A. Farrell. 1976. **Murder, Inequality and the Law.** Lexington, MA: D. C. Heath.

Swigert, Victoria and Ronald A. Farrell. 1977. "Normal Homicides and the Law." **American Sociological Review** 42 (February):16-32.

Vold, George B. 1958, 1979. **Theoretical Criminology.** New York: Oxford University Press.

Voss, Harwin L. and David M. Petersen. 1971. **Ecology, Crime and Delinquency.** New York: Appleton.

Wilson, William J. 1978. **The Declining Significance of Race.** Chicago: University of Chicago Press.

Wolfgang, Marvin E. 1958. **Patterns in Criminal Homicide.** New York: Wiley.

HOMICIDE TRENDS IN THE UNITED STATES

Reynolds Farley

INTRODUCTION

Discussions of mortality trends in the United States generally focus upon gains in life expectation. Few demographic analyses concern causes of death (other than cancer) which are increasing. Twenty-five years ago, Henry and Short began their book on homicide and suicide by noting that 8,000 people were murdered each year in the United States and 17,000 took their own lives (1954, p. 13). One death in 60, they observed, was attributable to those causes. Today the figures are much higher: in 1978, approximately 21,000 Americans were homicide victims and another 27,500 killed themselves. One death in 40 resulted from these types of violence (U. S. National Center for Health Statistics, 1979a, Table 9).

Although increases are evident for all groups, the effect of homicide and changes in homicide are greatest among nonwhite men. In the early 1940s, about 3 percent of the nonwhite men who died were murder victims, but by the 1970s this proportion exceeded 6 percent. Homicide is now the fourth most common cause of death for nonwhite men, after diseases of the heart, malignant neoplasms and cerebrovascular disease. More nonwhite men die of homicide than of all contagious ailments, tuberculosis, cirrhosis of the liver or automobile accidents (U. S. National Center for Health Statistics, 1977, Table 8).

This investigation describes trends in homicide mortality and compares them to trends for other causes of death. Components of change in homicide mortality--especially the increasing use of firearms to kill people--are examined. The basic data are the National Center for Health Statistics' annual tabulations of decedents by age, sex, color and cause of death. These data refer to the victims--not to the perpetrators--of homicide. Data for nonwhites are analyzed since detailed population and mortality figures for blacks are only available for the last few years.[1]

A COMPARISON OF DEATH RATES FROM HOMICIDE WITH THOSE FROM OTHER CAUSES

The difference between the trends in homicide and other causes of mortality is evident in Figure 1. This shows age-standardized death rates from homicide (deaths per 100,000) and from all other causes (deaths per 1,000) for the span 1940 and 1977, the most recent year for which these data are available. Age standardization removes the confounding effects of changes in the age distribution and permits a comparison of rates for different years, races and sexes.[2]

This figure illustrates that death rates from homicide rose while those from all other causes generally moved in the opposite direction. Among nonwhite men, for example, the mortality rate from all causes except homicide declined from about 17 deaths per 1,000 in 1940 to 10 deaths in 1977. The homicide rate decreased from 57 decedents per 100,000 in 1940 to a low in the 1950s and then attained an elevated level of 83 deaths per 100,000

13

nonwhite men in 1972. Similar trends are evident for the other race and sex groups and, for all of them, the age-standardized rates from homicide in the early 1970s exceeded those of all previous years since 1940.

The substantial effects of homicide may also be seen by comparing its impact upon the life span to that of other causes of death. Table 1 presents trends in life expectation at birth and indicates how much the life span would increase if various diseases were eliminated. We show the effects of several causes which either once were or are now common killers: the major cardiovascular diseases (including both diseases of the heart and cerebrovascular diseases), malignant neoplasms, tuberculosis, motor vehicle accidents and homicide.

Relatively little progress was made in mitigating heart disease between 1940 and the mid-1960s (Moriyama, Krueger and Stamler, 1971, Chapter 9) although reductions have been recorded since then, especially for the cerebrovascular ailments (U. S. National Center for Health Statistics, 1979a, p. 6). The cost of heart disease among nonwhite men, for instance, rose from about eight years in 1940 to ten years in 1950 and 1960 and then declined to eight years in 1975, the most recent year for which cause- sex-color-specific life tables may be calculated. For all groups except nonwhite men, the cost of cardiovascular disease in terms of shortening the life span was less in 1975 than at previous dates since 1940.

Death rates from many types of cancer have steadily risen and the aggregate effect of malignant neoplasms upon the life span increased throughout this period (Lilienfield, Levin and Kessler, 1972, Chapters 2 and 3; Klebba, Maurer and Glass, 1974, pp. 10-18; U. S. National Center for Health Statistics, 1979a, Table 8). For all groups except nonwhite men, the effects of homicide are small compared to those of cancer but, in 1975, the elimination of homicide would have added about half as many years to the life span of nonwhite men as the elimination of cancer deaths.

The greatest reductions in death rates were associated with infectious diseases. In 1940, for instance, tuberculosis had a much greater impact upon the life span than did homicide. Improved standards of living and the use of sulfa drugs drastically reduced tuberculosis (Lowell, Edwards and Palmer, 1969, Chapters 2 and 3) and, by 1970, the impact of homicide upon the life span became greater than that of tuberculosis among men and women of both races.

Mortality from motor vehicle accidents increased after 1940 although declines occurred during World War II when gasoline was rationed and after 1973 when speed limits were lowered (Grove and Hetzel, 1968, Table 62; U. S. National Center for Health Statistics, 1979a, Tables 8, 9, and 10). At all dates, motor vehicle accidents have had a much greater impact than homicide upon the life span among whites. That is not the case for nonwhites; the elimination of homicide would currently add more years to the life span of either nonwhite men or women than would the elimination of motor vehicle mortality.

Table 1 also shows the trends in life expectation at birth. Since 1940, improvements have been greater for nonwhites than for whites and much larger for women than for men. That is, in 1940, nonwhites had a life span approximately 11 years inferior to that of whites but by 1975, the racial gap

14

TABLE 1. Trends in Life Expectation at Birth and Gains in Life Expectation If Selected Causes Were Eliminated

		Life Expectation or Gain in Life Expectation (Years)				
	Race	1940	1950	1960	1970	1975
MEN						
Life Expectation	White	62.1	66.5	67.4	68.0	69.4
	Nonwhite	51.5	59.1	61.1	61.3	63.6
			Gain If Cause Were Eliminated			
Major Cardiovascular Diseases	White	8.07	9.70	9.06	8.98	7.42
	Nonwhite	7.67	10.01	9.98	8.77	7.92
Malignant Neoplasms	White	1.33	1.84	2.08	2.34	2.55
	Nonwhite	.60	1.38	1.92	2.36	2.83
Tuberculosis	White	.71	.37	.09	.04	.01
	Nonwhite	2.06	1.24	.28	.13	.08
Motor Vehicle Accidents	White	.74	.77	.77	.93	.77
	Nonwhite	.54	.59	.73	.93	.74
Homicide	White	.08	.07	.08	.16	.21
	Nonwhite	.83	.86	.78	1.38	1.44
WOMEN						
Life Expectation	White	66.6	72.2	74.1	75.6	77.2
	Nonwhite	54.9	62.9	66.3	69.4	72.3
			Gain If Cause Were Eliminated			
Major Cardiovascular Diseases	White	7.51	8.24	6.63	6.67	5.98
	Nonwhite	9.26	11.20	10.18	8.45	7.17
Malignant Neoplasms	White	1.98	2.38	2.38	2.49	2.61
	Nonwhite	1.31	1.96	2.16	2.27	2.56
Tuberculosis	White	.58	.23	.05	.01	.01
	Nonwhite	2.02	1.05	.18	.09	.05
Motor Vehicle Accidents	White	.26	.27	.30	.41	.32
	Nonwhite	.14	.22	.24	.35	.47
Homicide	White	.02	.03	.04	.06	.08
	Nonwhite	.20	.23	.25	.33	.38

SOURCE: Robert D. Grove and Alice M. Hetzel, Vital Statistics Rates in the United States: 1940-1960 (Washington: Government Printing Office, 1968), Tables 51 and 63; U.S. National Center for Health Statistics, Vital Statistics of the United States, 1970, Vol. II, Part A, Table 1-9; 1975, Vol. II, Part B, Table 1-8; U.S. Bureau of the Census, Current Population Reports, Series P-25, No. 721, Table 2.

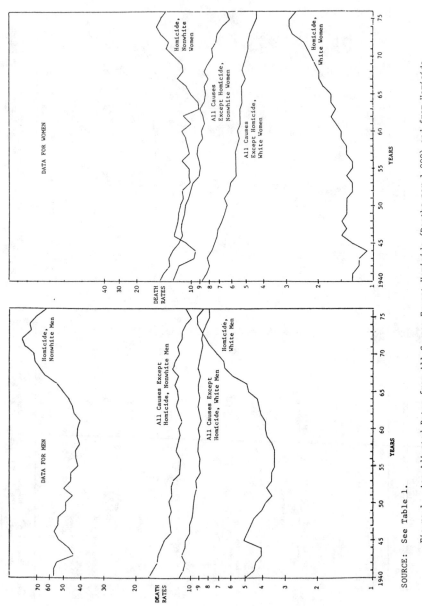

SOURCE: See Table 1.

Figure 1. Age-Adjusted Rates from All Causes Except Homicide (Deaths per 1,000) and from Homicide (Deaths per 100,000)

16

declined to about five years. In contrast to this racial convergence, the sexual disparity, which was only four years in 1940, widened to almost eight years in 1975 (U. S. National Center for Health Statistics, 1978, Table 5- 5).

Homicide accounts for a significant component of the current racial and sexual differences in life expectation. In 1975, a white man at birth could look forward to about six more years of life than a nonwhite man. Approximately one-fifth of that racial difference was accounted for by the higher homicide rates of nonwhites. A nonwhite woman in 1975 had a life expectation about eight and one-half years greater than a nonwhite man. Approximately one-eighth of that sexual difference in the life span resulted from the higher mortality rates of nonwhite men.

The recent increases in homicide have also retarded the rise in life expectation, especially among nonwhite men. Between 1960 and 1975, for instance, their life expectation rose by 2.3 years. Had there been no upturn in homicide mortality the gain would have been at least three years (for additional discussion of this point, see Dennis, 1979; Shin, Jedlicka and Lee, 1977).

DIFFERENCES IN HOMICIDE MORTALITY

Racial and sexual differences in homicide are evident in Figure 1 and Table 1. The consequences for the life span are much greater for nonwhites than for whites and larger for men than women. Eliminating homicide among nonwhite men would add about one-and- one-half years to their life span whereas among white women the advantage would be an addition of about one- tenth of a year of life.

The effects of age upon homicide rates-- independent of the secular trend--are summarized in Table 2. For each of the four groups, the age-specific death rates from homicide for 11 age intervals and for eight different years within the 1940 to 1975 interval were considered. The death rates were regressed upon age--that is, a series of 11 dichotomous variables indicating age groups--and upon year--also a series of dichotomous variables. The overall average mortality rates from homicide, 395 deaths per million nonwhite men and 48 per million white men, are shown at the bottom of each column. The regression coefficients are deviations from the overall mean and thus they assess the independent effects of a specific age category or a specific year. An effects coding procedure was used so that the age or year effects sum to zero. Adding the appropriate age and year effects to the grand mean provides an estimate of homicide mortality for a given age group and year.

The age effects demonstrate that homicide mortality rates sink to their minimum at ages 1 to 14, attain a peak at ages 25 to 44 and then decline at older ages. Among men at the ages of maximum risk of homicide, the rates of nonwhites are 11 times those of whites while among women, homicide rates for nonwhites exceed those of whites by a factor of eight. Homicide is currently the leading cause of death among black men and women aged 25 to 34. It accounts for about one-third of all the deaths occurring to black men at these ages and one-sixth of the deaths of black women (U. S. National Center for Health Statistics, 1979b, Tables 1-9). Among white men 25 to 34, homicide deaths are more numerous than deaths from heart disease,

17

TABLE 2. Age and Year Effects on the Homicide Mortality Rate by
          Sex and Color, 1940 to 1975

	Nonwhite Men	White Men	Nonwhite Women	White Women
Age Effects				
1-1	-305	- 4	- 2	+20
1-4	-371	-39	- 68	-10
5-14	-374	-42	- 81	-13
15-24	+237	+ 8	+ 62	+ 1
25-34	+733	+38	+147	+ 6
35-44	+492	+34	+ 99	+ 6
45-54	+242	+21	+ 23	+ 1
55-64	- 22	+ 9	- 33	- 3
65-74	-144	- 5	- 51	- 5
75-84	-227	- 8	- 56	- 1
85+	-261	-12	- 40	- 2
Year Effects				
1940	- 9	- 2	- 8	- 2
1945	- 19	- 2	-19	- 3
1950	- 50	-12	-10	- 2
1955	- 85	-15	- 8	- 5
1960	- 84	-13	- 5	- 2
1965	- 20	- 5	- 2	- 1
1970	+130	+16	+21	+ 4
1975	+137	+33	+31	+11
Overall Average Homicide Rate Per Million	395	48	93	18
R^2	.96	.87	.93	.81

SOURCE: Robert D. Grove and Alice M. Hetzel, Vital Statistics
         Rates in the United States: 1940-1960 (Washington:
         Government Printing Office, 1968), Table 63
         U.S. National Center for Health Statistics, Vital
         Statistics of the United States: 1965, Vol. II, Part A,
         Table 1-9; 1970, Vol. II, Part A, Table 1-8, Vol. II,
         Part B, Table 7-5; U.S. Bureau of the Census, Current
         Population Reports, Series P-24, No. 721, Table 2.

cerebrovascular ailments or malignant neoplasms but they are less common than accidental deaths. Even at the older ages, homicide continues to be a frequent cause of death among black men. For example, at ages 45 to 54 the only causes more commonly reported than homicide are cancer and diseases of the heart (U. S. National Center for Health Statistics, 1979b, Tables 1-9).

The coefficients associated with the year variables in Table 2, as well as the chronological trends illustrated in Figure 1, show the pattern of change over time in homicide independent of changes in age composition. Death rates from this cause declined after 1940.3 and reached a minimum during the 1945-1955 decade. This was followed by, first a modest rise, and then in the late 1960s a rapid increase in homicide. The identical pattern of change is found among men and women of both racial groups.

WHAT EXPLAINS THE RISE IN HOMICIDE?

During a period when many causes of death are falling, it is puzzling to find a major cause which is rising. Investigators who recount the previous mortality declines frequently try to assess the relative impacts of environmental changes, alterations in life style or diet and the consequences of specific medical technologies and public health measures. Such an analysis has not been attempted with homicide. Demograhic data, however, may be used to examine some of the possible trends, that is, constant or moderately falling homicide rates for some years after 1940 followed by a rise which was especially sharp after the mid-1960s (see Figure 1 and Table 2).

There are two popular but competing models which seek to explain differentials or trends in homicide. The first is the deterrence model which argues that the certainty of punishment, especially capital punishment, minimizes homicide. Using state data concerning murder rates and the conditional probabilities of conviction and execution, Ehrlich (1975) argued that capital punishment has a negative effect upon the incentive to commit homicide. His investigation suggested that the elimination of capital punishment was related to the rise in homicide.

Second, there are models which use social structural and cultural variables to account for differentials in homicide. Death rates from this cause have been shown to be highest in states where a high proportion of the population is poor, where there is a dense urban population, where many are unemployed or have low incomes and where racial minorities are numerous (for summaries, see Loftin and Hill, 1974; Parker and Smith, 1979).

Several investigators have used both indicators of punishment and of social structure in models which were fitted to time series data for homicide (Bechdolt, 1977; Yunker, 1977; Kleck, 1979). Although the findings depend upon the variables used in the models and time periods, the incorporation of social structural variables appears to reduce or eliminate the effects attributable to the punishment variables.

Both the deterrence and social structural models contribute to an understanding of trends in homicide but they may overlook a technological change which may account for the rise in murders--the increasing availability of firearms. Ethnographic accounts of homicide, such as

19

Lundsgaarde's (1977) study of the murders occurring in Houston in 1960, suggest that most homicides are impulsive. They are neither psychotic acts nor premeditated. Indeed, estimates are that no more than 5 percent of all homicides are planned or intentional killings (Wolfgang and Ferracuti, 1967). Typically, a minor contretemps between friends, lovers or spouses accelerates into a major disagreement and one of the disputants seeks a weapon. If this is a book, a brick or a table knife, injury may be inflicted but no one may be killed in the confrontation. If a gun is chosen as the weapon for defense or destruction, the chances for mortality are greatly increased.

It is possible that the level of interpersonal hostility in the United States has not changed over time but that firearms are increasingly available to disputants. A technological change--the rise in the supply of guns--may help account for the recent increase in homicide. One of the major findings of the National Commission on the Causes and Prevention of Violence, established by President Johnson after the urban violence of the 1960s, was that firearms became increasingly available late in that decade. In the 1950s about 400,000 new handguns were added to the domestic supply each year, about 600,000 during the first half of the 1960s but over two million a year in the latter half of that decade and in the 1970s. A peak was reached in 1969 when more than three million new handguns were produced or imported for domestic consumption. In brief, the sale of handguns quadrupled and the sale of long guns doubled during the 1960s (U. S. National Commission on the Causes of Prevention of Violence, 1969, Table C; U. S. Bureau of the Census, 1977, table 6/16; Pinkney, 1972, p. 170). The Commission found that in many cities a sharp increase in gun sales and registrations followed a riot. In Detroit, for example, the number of handgun permits issued by the police increased by a factor of five between 1965 and 1968 (Newton and Zimring, 1969, Figure 11-5).

If the rise in homicide occurs because disputants are now more likely to use guns than in the past, we should find that the rise in gun-inflicted homicide accounts for a large fraction of the recent increase in murder. Demographic data are available to investigate this hypothesis.

We will consider changes in homicide between 1960 and 1975. The former year was not the year of the minimum murder rates but for all groups, except white women, homicide rates in 1960 were lower than they were on the eve of World War II (Grove and Hetzel, 1968, Table 62). Since 1960, there has been a progression of murder rates with the biggest jumps recorded during the 1966 to 1972 span.4 The vital statistics system currently classifies homicide into four types: those resulting from firearms and other explosives, from cuttings, from other assaults and from legal interventions. The final category includes deaths inflicted by peace officers in the line of duty, as well as executions. There were 56 legal executions in 1960 but none in 1975 (U. S. Bureau of the Census, 1975, p. 422; U. S. National Center for Health Statistics, 1979b, Table 1-26).

Table 3 presents the results of a decomposition which seeks to describe the recent rise in homicide. Using age-standardized rates, it allocates the change in homicide in the four types of homicide cited in the previous paragraph. It reveals that, within the nonwhite community, the increase in homicide results almost exclusively from more murders by guns. That is, the age-standardized homicide rates for nonwhite men went up from 419 deaths per million in 1960 to 716 in 1975, the entire change resulting from

TABLE 3. Decomposition of Change Over Time in Homicide, 1960 to 1975, and Racial Difference in Homicide, 1975[a]

A. ANALYSIS OF 1960 TO 1975 CHANGE IN HOMICIDE

	Age Standardized Homicide Rates (Deaths Per Million)			Components of Change 1960 to 1975				Proportion of Total Change Attributable to Each Cause			
	1960	1975	Change	Firearms	Cuttings	Other Assaults	Legal Interv.	Firearms	Cuttings	Other Assaults	Legal Interv.
NONWHITE: MEN	418.8	716.1	+297.3	+299.1	-4.1	+8.9	-6.6	+101%	-1%	+3%	-2%
WOMEN	111.8	147.0	+35.2	+31.8	-4.5	+8.0	-.1	+90%	-13%	+23%	0
WHITE: MEN	39.3	94.2	+54.9	+42.1	+7.6	+5.4	-.2	+77%	+14%	+10%	0
WOMEN	15.2	29.5	+14.3	+6.5	+2.7	+5.1	0.0	+45%	+19%	+36%	0

B. ANALYSIS OF RACIAL DIFFERENCE IN HOMICIDE, 1975

	Age Standardized Homicide Rates (Deaths Per Million)			Components of Change 1960 to 1975				Proportion of Total Change Attributable to Each Cause			
	White	Non-White	Diff.	Firearms	Cuttings	Other Assaults	Legal Interv.	Firearms	Cuttings	Other Assaults	Legal Interv.
MEN	94.2	716.1	+621.9	+458.3	+112.6	+40.6	+10.4	74%	18%	7%	2%
WOMEN	29.5	147.0	+117.5	+70.9	+21.2	+25.3	+.1	60%	18%	22%	0

SOURCE: Robert D. Grove and Alice M. Hetzel, Vital Statistics Rates in the United States: 1940-1960 (Washington: Government Printing Office, 1968), Tables F and 63; U.S. National Center for Health Statistics, Vital Statistics of the United States: 1975, Vol. II, Part A, Tables.

a. This analysis uses age standardized rates throughout. Thus there is no component of differences or change attributable to differences or changes in the age structure of these populations.

additional shooting deaths. The small rise in homicide deaths and other assaults was offset by decreasing death rates from cuttings and the decline in both capital punishment and other police intervention deaths. For nonwhite women, approximately 90 percent of the total rise in homicide came about because of the increasing frequency of gun murders.

Among whites, the pattern is slightly different. Increases in the homicide rate from firearms account for about three-quarters of the total rise in the homicide death rate of white men but for less than one-half of the increase among white women. Among whites, there have been rises in the frequency with which people are murdered by knives or by other weapons.

This demographic evidence supports the hypothesis that among nonwhites the rise in homicide results almost exclusively from the more frequent use of guns. Among whites, this factor is responsible for much, but not for all, of the increase in homicide.

Throughout this paper we have stressed the large racial difference in murder rates. The decomposition technique can also be used to ascertain if this results because of racial differences in the use of firearms. Perhaps guns are more readily available within the black community than in the white and this may account for some or all of the racial difference in homicide.

An analysis of the white-nonwhite difference in homicide in 1975 is presented in the lower panel of Table 3. We find that the racial difference in the use of guns is a very important component of the overall difference in murder. For instance, the age- standardized homicide rate among nonwhite men was 716 per million in 1975; among white men, only 94. Approximately three-quarters of that difference is accounted for by more frequent gun murders within the nonwhite community. Among women, about three-fifths of the total racial difference was the consequence of the greater use of firearms by nonwhites. Nevertheless, there are substantial racial differences in other types of homicide. Among men in 1975, the age-standardized death rate from firearm homicide was 700 percent higher for nonwhites than for whites, for cuttings it was 605 percent higher among nonwhites, for other assaults 297 percent greater and for deaths from legal interventions, 509 percent greater.

Demographic evidence leads to several conclusions about homicide. First, homicide is not rare and it currently accounts for more than 1 percent of all deaths in the United States. Because younger people tend to be murdered, its impact upon the life span is greater than that of all infectious diseases, tuberculosis, diabetes, or arteriosclerosis (U. S. National Center for Health Statistics, 1975, Table D).

Second, homicide is much more common in the black community than in the white. Age-standardized homicide rates are currently about six times as great for nonwhites as for whites (U. S. National Center for Health Statistics, 1979c, Table 10). Homicide has a greater impact upon the life expectation of nonwhite men than all but three ailments--heart diseases, malignant neoplasms and cerebrovascular diseases. The consequences of homicide are at least half as great as those of cancer for these men.

Third, homicide mortality is more common among men than among women. For both races, the age-standardized homicide rate for men is about four times that for women (U. S. National Center for Health statistics, 1979b, Table 1-9).

Fourth, homicide rates are highest at ages 25 to 35 and generally decline thereafter. At the young adult ages, homicide is the leading cause of death among nonwhites and is the second most frequent cause of mortality for white men (U. S. National Center for Health Statistics, 1979b, Table 1-9).

Fifth, for both races and among both men and women, homicide death rates were approximately constant or falling for an interval after 1940. They began to increase in the 1950s and have risen very rapidly since the mid-1960s (Langberg, 1967; Klebba, Maurer and Glass, 1974, Chapter XIII; U. S. Bureau of the Census, 1977, Table 5/7).

Sixth, much of the recent rise in homicide, particularly within the black community, results from more killings by guns. Indeed, the proportion of all homicides resulting from the use of guns increased from 55 percent in 1960 to 67 percent in 1975 (U. S. National Center for Health Statistics, 1963, Table 5- 9; 1979b, Table 1-26). If there had been no increases in firearm murders, the homicide rates for nonwhites in the mid-1970s would have been just about what they were in 1960.

Seventh, a major component of the current racial difference in murder rates involves the use of guns. Nonwhites in the United States are seven times as likely to be shot to death as whites. Nevertheless, there are substantial racial differences in other types of murder: nonwhites are much more likely than whites to die of knife wounds or from assaults with other objects or to be killed by a policeman.

DISCUSSION

Most efforts to reduce death rates in the United States appear directed toward the development of medical procedures which will prevent, diagnose or cure diseases, chiefly cancer and cardiovascular ailments. To be sure, there are some efforts to make environmental changes and to minimize occupational hazards. Undoubtedly, the litigation and legislation dealing with safer working conditions have played some role in the decline in the nonvehicle accidental death rate (Grove and Hetzel, 1968, Table 62; U. S. National Center for Health Statistics, 1979c, Table 10). However, there seem to have been few successful efforts to lengthen the life span by altering behavior. Consumption of cigarettes is just about as great now as in 1960--approximately 4,100 cigarettes per adult per year (U. S. Bureau of the Census, 1978, Table 1427). The decrease in highway speed certainly explains some of the drop in motor vehicle mortality, but this change was induced more by a shortage of oil than by a desire to lengthen the life span.

When we turn to homicide, we are dealing with a cause of mortality, which differs from other causes since it is increasing. Since most murders are impulsive, it is unlikely that strategies which mitigate the contagious or degenerative ailments will affect murder rates. It is possible, although difficult to imagine, that campaigns against violence would modify the behavior of disputants and thereby de-escalate life-threatening situations. Perhaps a technological change--a reduction in the availability of guns--would have an even greater impact upon the homicide rate. Of course, we do not know the frequency with which other weapons would be substituted for guns. The ethnographic accounts, however, suggest that if firearms were not at hand, combatants would often use less efficacious weapons such as their hands, and that the murder rate would drop sharply (Lundsgaarde, 1977).

It seems improbable that gun ownership will decrease in this society. If the National Commission on the Causes and Prevention of Violence was correct, the urban riots of the 1960s led to a very rapid increase in the domestic supply of firearms. Since that time, crime itself has risen sharply. In 1977, there were 467 violent and 4,600 property crimes per 100,000 compared with figures of 253 violent and 2,700 property crimes per 100,000 a decade earlier (U. S. Bureau of the Census, 1978, Table 286). As Kleck (1979) demonstrates, increases in the crime rate lead to rises in gun ownership since individuals feel threatened and perceive a need for protection, but this increase in the supply of guns may result in higher homicide rates.

24

NOTES

1. The requisite data for the calculation of age-specific death rates for blacks and whites are available only for years after 1967.

2. Age-standardized rates were computed by the National Center for Health Statistics using the direct method. This procedure guarantees that the difference between any two rates does not result from differences between the age structures of the population. The standard population is the age distribution of the total population of the United States in 1940 (Grove and Hetzel, 1968, pp. 19-21 and Table F).

3. Although the Death Registration Area included all states as early as 1933, age-sex-color-cause specific death rates for the entire nation were not tabulated until 1940.

4. Between 1960 and 1975, the Eighth Revision of the International List of Causes of Death was adopted. This included a new category of violent deaths where it was uncertain whether the injuries were purposely or accidently inflicted. Relatively few deaths are classified into this category. Nevertheless, the rise in homicide between 1960 and 1975 might have been greater had not there been a change in the classification of deaths by cause. (For discussion, see U. S. National Center for Health Statistics, 1968).

REFERENCES

Bechdolt, B. V., Jr. 1977. Capital Punishment and Homicide and Rape Rates in the United States: Time Series and Cross Sectional Regression Analyses. The Journal of Behavioral Economics VI, Nos. 1 and 2:33-66.

Dennis, R. E. 1979. The Role of Homicide in Decreasing Life Expectancy. In Harold M. Rose (ed.), Lethal Aspects of Urban Violence. Lexington, Mass.: D. C. Heath.

Ehrlich, I. 1975. The Deterrant Effect of Capital Punishment: A Question of Life and Death. American Economic Review LXV:397-417.

Grove, Robert D., and Alice M. Hetzel. 1968. Vital Statistics Rates in the United States: 1940-1960. Washington, D. C.: U. S. National Center for Health Statistics, Public Health Service Publication No. 1677.

Henry, Andrew F., and James F. Short, Jr. 1954. Suicide and Homicide. Glencoe, Ill.: The Free Press.

Klebba, A. Joan, Jeffrey D. Maurer, and Evelyn J. Glass. 1974. Mortality Trends for Leading Causes of Death: United States: 1950-69. Washington, D. C.: U. S. National Center for Health Statistics, Vital and Health Statistics, Series 20, No. 16.

Kleck, G. 1979. Capital Punishment, Gun Ownership, and Homicide. American Journal of Sociology 84:882-910.

Langberg, Robert. 1967. Homicide in the United States: 1950- 1964. Washington, D. C.: U. S. National Center for Health Statistics, Vital and Health Statistics, Series 20, No. 6.

Lilienfield, Abraham M., Morton L. Levine, and Irving Kessler. 1972. Cancer in the United States. Cambridge: Harvard University Press.

Loftin, C., and R. H. Hill. 1974. Regional Subculture and Homicide: An Examination of the Gastil-Hackney Thesis. American Sociological Review 39:714-724.

Lowell, Anthony M., Lydia B. Edwards, and Carroll E. Palmer. 1969. Tuberculosis. Cambridge: Harvard University Press.

Lundsgaarde, Henry P. 1977. Murder in Space City: A Cultural Analysis of Houston Homicide Patterns. New York: Oxford University Press.

Moriyama, Iwao M., Dean E. Krueger, and Jeremiah Stamler. 1971. Cardiovascular Diseases in the United States. Cambridge: Harvard University Press.

Newton, George D., and Franklin E. Zimring. 1969. Firearms and Violence in American Life. Staff Report Submitted to the National Commission on the Causes and Prevention of Violence. Washington, D. C.: U. S. Government Printing Office.

26

Parker, R. M., and M. D. Smith. 1979. Deterrence, Poverty, and Type of Homicide. American Journal of Sociology 85:614-624.

Pinkney, Alphonso. 1972. The American Way of Violence. New York: Random House.

Shin, Yongsock, Davor Jedlicka, and Everett S. Lee. 1977. Homicide Among Blacks. Phylon 38:398-407.

U. S. Bureau of the Census. 1975. Historical Statistics of the United States: Colonial Times to 1970.

. 1977. Social Indicators, 1976.

. 1978. Statistical Abstract of the United States: 1978.

U. S. National Center for Health Statistics. 1963. Vital Statistics of the United States: 1960. Vol. II.

. 1968. Monthly Vital Statistics Report. Vol. 17, No. 8, Supplement (October 25).

. 1975. United States Decennial Life Tables for 1969-71, United States Life Tables by Causes of Death: 1969-71. Vol. 1, No. 5.

. 1977. Monthly Vital Statistics Report. Vol. 25, No. 11, Supplement (February 11).

. 1978. Vital Statistics of the United States, 1976. Vol. II, Section 5.

. 1979a. Monthly Vital Statistics Report. Vol. 27, No. 13 (August 13).

. 1979b. Vital Statistics of the United States, 1975. Vol. II, Part A.

. 1979c. Monthly Vital Statistics Report. Vol. 28, No. 1, Supplement (May 11).

U. S. National Commission on the Causes and Prevention of Violence. 1969. Firearms and Violence in American Life.

Yunker, J. A. 1977. Is the Death Penalty a Deterrent to Homicide? Some Time Series Evidence. The Journal of Behavioral Economics VI, Nos. 1 and 2:361-398.

Wolfgang, Marvin E., and Franco Ferracuti. 1967. The Subculture of Violence. London: Tavistock Publications.

PATTERNS AND RECENT TRENDS IN BLACK HOMICIDE

Patrick W. O'Carroll

and

James A. Mercy

Homicide among black Americans has emerged as one of the most important public health issues today. It has been known for some time that homicide victimization rates were much higher for blacks than whites (Wolfgang, 1958) but homicide has only recently begun to receive the attention it deserves as a public health problem. Homicide is the fifth leading cause of death among blacks overall and is actually the leading cause of death among blacks age 15 to 34 (Centers for Disease Control, 1985). The U. S. Department of Health and Human Services Secretary's Task force on Black and Minority Health notes that a large proportion of the disparity in health status between blacks and whites is due to high levels of homicide victimization in the black population. Indeed, for black males under age 45, homicide accounted for a greater proportion of this disparity than any other cause of death (Department of Health and Human Services, 1985).

Homicide has traditionally been considered a criminal justice problem, and the term "homicide" in that context connotes the commission of a criminal act. In this essay, however, homicide is considered as a cause of death, in the same sense that heart disease or cancer are causes of death. The term "homicide" in this context refers to victimization, rather than perpetration, and a "homicide rate" refers to the rate at which persons die from homicide, rather than the rate at which homicides are committed.

Patterns of homicide victimization among blacks are here described in terms of age, sex, the relationship of victim to assailant, weapon use, and the circumstances under which homicide occurred. Recent trends in black homicide rates are also described. Comparisons with patterns and trends noted for the majority white population are made where appropriate.

METHODS

A. Homicide Mortality Data.

Homicide is defined in this report as death resulting from the killing of one person by another, excluding death caused by law enforcement officers or legal execution. The information on homicide presented here is drawn primarily from the Federal Bureau of Investigation's Supplementary Homicide Reports (FBI-SHR). These reports are compiled by the Federal Bureau of Investigation's Uniform Crime Reporting Program, and are based on reports voluntarily submitted by over 15,000 city, county and state law enforcement agencies in the United States. Approximately 98% of the U. S. population falls within the jurisdiction of the participating agencies. The reports of the FBI-SHR program provide data on the age, race and sex of homicide victims and also on the weapons used, the circumstances of the homicides and the relationships between victims and assailants.

Homicide deaths classified as murder, non- negligent manslaughter (the willful killing of one human being by another) or citizen-justifiable homicide (e.g. homicide committed in self-defense) were extracted from the SHR computer files for each year from 1976 to 1984, (Department of Justice, 1983). Homicides due to police intervention and legal execution were not included. The racial status of homicide victims is recorded in SHR as reported by the investigating law enforcement official. In this report, homicide victims are classified into two race categories, black and white. The white racial category includes homicide victims reported as white, Mexican, Puerto Rican and all other caucasians. Not included in either the black or white category are Native Americans, Asians and Pacific Islanders.

Age-and region-specific homicide data were drawn from computer tapes of the Vital Statistics Program of the National Center for Health Statistics (NCHS). The NCHS compiles mortality statistics from death certificate information provided by the 50 states and the District of Columbia. These statistics are coded according to the International Classification of Disease (ICD) and include sex, race and geographic data. The ICD classification "Homicide and Injury Purposely Inflicted by Other Persons" (Ninth Revision, codes E960-E969) was used in this report to identify homicide deaths occurring in each age-group in 1983, and to identify homicides occurring in each State in 1980 (World Health Organization, 1977). These ICD codes do not include deaths resulting from interventions by law enforcement officers (ICD-9 codes E970-E977) or deaths caused by legal execution (ICD-9 code E978). As with FBI-SHR data, NCHS mortality statistics are classified into two race categories, white and black.

B. Population Data.

The modified 1980 census enumeration consistent with 1970 race data was used to calculate rates for 1980. Population data for the intercensal years 1976- 1979 and 1981-1984 were drawn from the P-25 series of the Current Population Reports compiled by the U. S. Bureau of the Census. These intercensal estimates incorporate data from both the 1970 and the modified 1980 censuses. Population data used to calculate homicide rates for specific regions in the United States were from the modified 1980 census enumeration.

FINDINGS

A. Patterns of Black Homicide: Rates by Age, Sex, and Region

During the period 1976 to 1984, over 75,000 black Americans lost their lives to homicide. Blacks experienced by far the highest homicide victimization rates of any racial group, with a combined nine-year rate of 31.7 homicide deaths per 100,000 persons per year. The risk of dying from homicide was six times greater for blacks than whites during this period.

Homicide is often considered primarily a "male" problem, because rates for males are consistently much higher than they are for females. Indeed, the risk of homicide was much higher for black males than black females

30

during the period studied (53.6 vs. 11.9). However, the rate for black females was higher than the rate for white males (Figure 1). Thus, although homicide rates are higher by far for black males than for any other race-sex group, black females also represent a group at high risk of homicide.

For both males and females in 1983, black homicide rates were highest among young adults age 20 to 39 (Table 1). Homicide rates for black males peaked at 99.8 for those age 25 to 29; for black females, rates also peaked in the 25 to 29 year age group, at 20.5. Black male rates were four to five times greater than black female rates in almost all age groups. A similar pattern is seen among whites in terms of the high risk among young adults and the consistently greater male than female rates in each age group. However, the ratio of male to female rates is not quite so great for whites, with white male rates generally ranging between two to three times white female rates.

The risk of homicide victimization varies among the different regions of the country (Table 2). In 1980, 43% of all homicides occurred in the South and, when all races were considered together, the South had the highest overall homicide rate. However, when blacks and whites were considered separately, the West had the highest homicide rate for each race group. The reason for this apparent inconsistency is that blacks (who have the highest homicide rates) make up a much greater proportion of the population in the South than in the other regions of the country. This affects the rate for all races considered together, such that even though the actual risk of homicide in 1980 was higher in the West than in the South for both blacks and whites, the crude rate for all races considered together was highest in the South.

B. Patterns of Black Homicide: Weapon Use,
   Victim-Assailant Relationship, and Crime Circumstance.

Two-thirds of all homicides of blacks during the period 1976 to 1984 were committed with firearms (Figure 2), 77% of which were handguns. Indeed, homicides committed with handguns accounted for over half of all homicides of blacks. A similar but less pronounced pattern is seen for whites: 60% of homicides of whites were committed with firearms, most of which were handguns. For blacks, knives or other cutting and piercing instruments were the weapons most frequently used after handguns, followed by long guns such as rifles and shotguns.

There is a common misconception that most homicides are committed by strangers in the act of perpetrating some other felony crime, such as rape or robbery. In fact, most homicide victims know their assailants (Table 3). During the period studied, 60% of homicides of blacks were committed by acquaintances or family members, and only 12% were committed by strangers. This pattern varies by sex. Of black male homicide victims, 44.9% were killed by acqaintances, while 13.2% were killed by family members. Of black female homicide victims, 37.2% were killed by acqaintances and 28.4% were killed by family members. Thus, homicides committed by family members are proportionately two times more important for black females than for black males. On the other hand, acquaintance homicide and stranger homicide are proportionately more important for black males. A similar pattern is seen for whites, although stranger homicide is somewhat more pronounced.

31

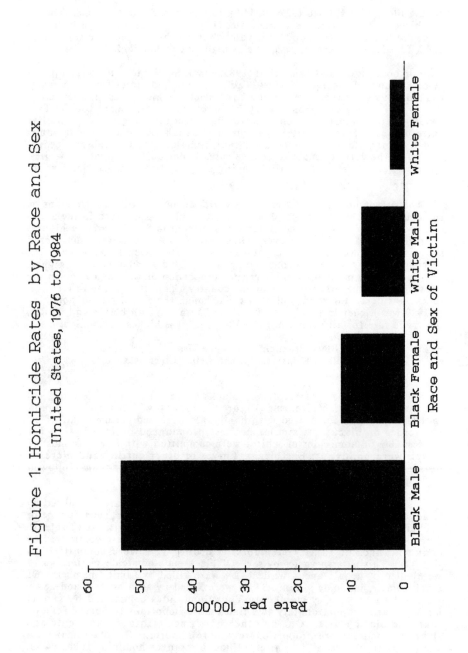

Figure 1. Homicide Rates by Race and Sex
United States, 1976 to 1984

Table 1. Homicide Rates* by Race and Age of Victim
United States, 1983

	Black			White		
Age Group	Male	Female	Both	Male	Female	Both
Under 1	12.8	14.2	13.5	3.3	3.8	3.6
1-4	6.9	5.9	6.4	1.7	1.2	1.5
5-9	2.2	1.4	1.8	0.8	0.7	0.7
10-14	4.1	1.5	2.8	1.1	0.7	0.9
15-19	42.6	10.6	26.7	7.5	2.9	5.2
20-24	85.2	20.2	52.0	14.6	4.4	9.5
25-29	99.8	20.5	58.1	15.3	4.6	10.0
30-34	98.5	19.1	56.0	13.7	3.5	8.6
35-39	84.0	16.2	47.2	12.3	3.4	7.8
40-44	76.0	12.9	41.4	11.9	3.5	7.7
45-49	61.7	11.6	34.1	9.6	3.3	6.4
50-54	54.7	7.5	28.4	8.4	2.5	5.4
55-59	50.0	8.1	26.5	6.8	2.4	4.5
60-64	45.6	4.4	22.5	5.9	2.0	3.8
65-69	30.6	8.8	18.0	4.8	2.1	3.3
70-74	27.3	5.3	14.2	4.5	1.8	2.9
75-79	29.9	11.9	18.9	4.3	3.0	3.5
80-84	31.9	8.7	17.1	4.6	3.2	3.7
85+	50.5	9.4	16.1	5.7	3.9	4.4
Total	50.6	11.3	29.9	8.4	2.8	5.6

*Rates per 100,000 population

33

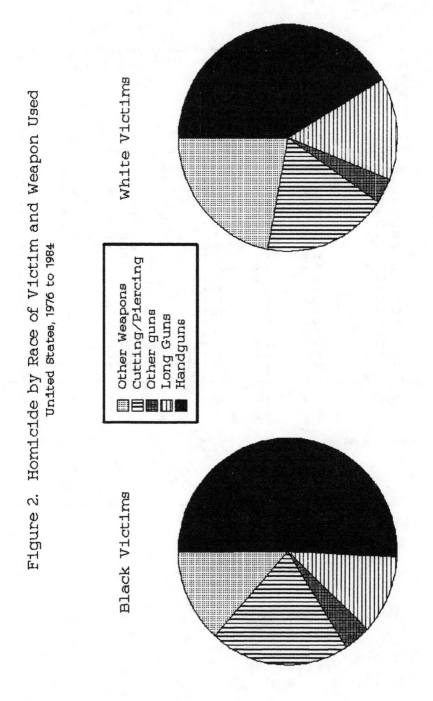

Figure 2. Homicide by Race of Victim and Weapon Used
United States, 1976 to 1984

White Victims

Black Victims

Other Weapons
Cutting/Piercing
Other guns
Long Guns
Handguns

34

Table 2. Homicide Rates by Geographic Region of Occurrence and Race of Victim, United States, 1980

	Total	White	Black
United States	10.6	6.8	38.4
Northeast	8.2	5.1	36.0
North Central	8.1	4.3	46.6
South	13.5	8.9	33.7
West	11.4	9.2	50.3

35

An examination of the circumstances surrounding homicide also belies the misperception of homicide noted above. Almost two-thirds of all homicides of blacks occurred in the context of arguments or some other non-felony circumstance (Figure 3). Only 13% to 17% of black victims were killed by assailants committing some other felony crime, such as robbery. The majority of homicides of whites also occurs under non-felony-associated circumstances, but felony- associated homicides account for a greater proportion of homicides among whites.

C. Temporal Trends in Black Homicide.

Overall blacks experienced a 20.4% decrease in homicide rates during the period under study (Figure 4). Rates for black males declined by 20.4%, from 53.4 in 1976 to 42.5 in 1984. Rates for black females declined by 19.4%, from 12.4 in 1976 to 10.0 in 1984. Almost all age groups experienced some decline in homicide rates. During the same period, white homicide rates increased by 6.5%. Declining black rates and increasing white rates narrowed the gap in homicide risk between blacks and whites, but in 1984 blacks were still 5.2 times more likely to die from homicide than whites.

DISCUSSION

The purpose of this analysis has been to describe the patterns and recent temporal trends of black homicide from a public health perspective. The danger in this sort of descriptive analysis is that the findings will be misinterpreted. This essay, for example, clearly documents that blacks are at high risk of homicide victimization relative to whites. However, it does not tell us why. Rather, it serves to identify blacks (and in particular, young black males) as a group at high risk of a particular cause of death, which helps to focus public health attention and direct limited resources for research and prevention to a population which is in greatest need.

A. Black Homicide: Directions for Research and Prevention.

In every year of the 9 year period studied, in every region of the country, for both sexes and for every age group, blacks were many times more likely to die from homicide than whites. Black males consistently experienced the highest homicide rates of any race/sex group, and young black males were at especially high risk of homicide victimization. These dramatic differences in the risk of homicide victimization must be explained, and factors which place blacks at such high risk of homicide must be identified.

There have been various explanations put forward in this regard. Poverty has been suggested as an underlying economic source of homicide (Wolfgang and Zahn, 1979; Flango and Sherbinou, 1976). and, indeed, poverty is more prevalent among blacks in this country than whites, (U.S. Bureau of the Census, 1984). The suggestion that poverty increases the risk of homicide is supported by research that shows that when socioeconomic status is taken into consideration, racial differences in homicide rates all but disappear, (Loftin and Hill, 1974; Williams, 1984). It has also been proposed that the high rate of homicide among blacks and other minority groups might be due to a subculture of violence, (Williams, 1984; Wolfgang and Ferracuti, 1964;

36

Table 3. Homicide by Relationship of Victim to Assilant,
Race and Sex of Victim, United Staes, 1976-1984

| | Black | | | | White | | | |
| | Male | | Female | | Male | | Female | |
	No.	%	No.	%	No.	%	No.	%
Known to Victim	35501	58.0	9944	65.6	31759	46.1	13899	56.2
--Family	8052	13.2	4309	28.4	8299	12.0	7891	31.9
--Acquaintance	27449	44.9	5635	37.2	23460	34.0	6008	24.3
Not Known	8512	13.9	932	6.1	13102	19.0	2628	10.6
Undetermined	17162	28.1	4288	28.3	24051	34.9	8184	33.1
TOTAL	61175	100.0	15164	100.0	68912	100.0	24711	100.0

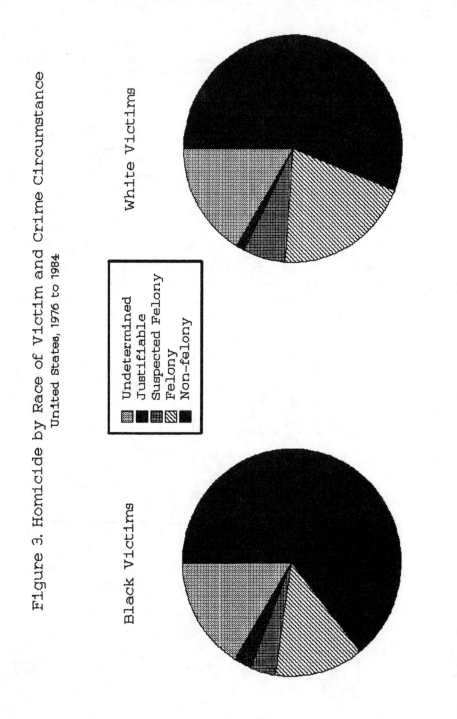

Figure 3. Homicide by Race of Victim and Crime Circumstance
United States, 1976 to 1984

White Victims

Black Victims

Undetermined
Justifiable
Suspected Felony
Felony
Non-felony

38

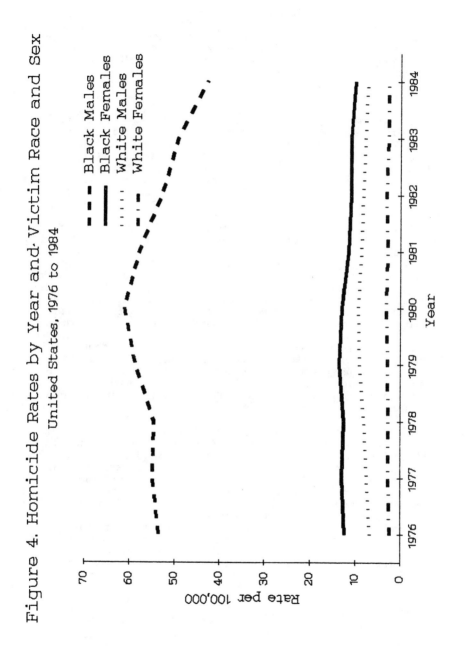

Figure 4. Homicide Rates by Year and Victim Race and Sex
United States, 1976 to 1984

Black Males
Black Females
White Males
White Females

Rate per 100,000
Year

39

Erlanger, 1974). According to this theory, high homicide rates can be attributed to cultural norms and traditions shared by a sub-group of society (a "sub-culture") that prescribe or reinforce violence as an acceptable behavior pattern under certain circumstances. Finally, minority group status itself might increase the risk of homicide: intense feelings of frustration arising from the experience of prejudice and discrimination might well increase the likelihood of violent interactions, (UCLA-Centers for Disease Control, 1985).

Unfortunately, neither the FBI-SHR nor the NCHS have information on the critically important variable of socioeconomic status. If the high homicide victimization among blacks is simply a reflection of higher average poverty rates, then preventive interventions should be targeted not toward blacks per se but toward the poor. Even if poverty unequivocally increased the risk of homicide, it would still remain to us to discover the mechanism by which poverty increased that risk. Such questions lie at the heart of the problem of homicide prevention.

As noted above, a large proportion of all black homicide victimization occurs among young black males, who are (typically) killed by friends or acquaintances using firearms (usually handguns) during the course of the argument. Further research is needed in order to understand the socioeconomic and cultural context in which friend/acquaintance violence occurs. In the meantime, educational efforts must be made to inform those at high risk that common arguments with friends and acquaintances may escalate to violent interactions with lethal consequences. Although much research remains to be done on the relationship between weapon availability and homicide risk, this lethality might be reduced if, on the occasion of violent quarrels, there were no lethal weapons (such as handguns) available within easy reach. Legislative or community action in this regard might go far toward decreasing the toll of homicide. Another approach might be the teaching of conflict resolution skills in school as part of the regular curriculum, in order that arguments might not escalate to homicidal violence.

With a significant proportion of homicide victims being killed by family members and intimate acquaintances, efforts to prevent homicide must also address domestic violence. Further research is needed to identify which strategies are most effective in decreasing domestic violence. Programs such as shelters for battered women, mandatory arrest policies, and treatment programs for abusive husbands already exists in some areas, and might be expanded if they are found to be effective. It may be that effective strategies are already in place, but that warning signs (e.g. of escalating spouse abuse) are not recognized until it is too late. If this is the case, physicians, social workers, and criminal justice personnel might be taught how to recognize these warning signs and make the appropriate referrals. Again, the ready availability of firearms in the home may be the final ingredient which turns a violent quarrel into a homicide.

This analysis has focused on homicides of blacks from a public health perspective. Yet an obviously important factor in the risk of victimization is exposure to persons who are themselves "at risk" of committing homicide. The issue of what factors lead a person to commit homicide has long been examined by the criminal justice system, sociologists, and criminologists. Thus, the most fruitful approach to homicide prevention would involve close collaboration among a variety of different disciplines.

B. Common patterns of homicide.

Considered in light of the dramatic differences noted here in the risk of homicide victimization for blacks and whites, it is perhaps remarkable that in a number of ways the patterns of homicide in the two race groups are very similar. Specifically, for both blacks and whites:

* males were many times more likely to die of homicide than females;
* for both males and females, homicide rates were highest among young adults, peaking among those age 20 to 39;

* homicide rates were highest in the West;

* at least half of all homicide victims were killed with firearms, most of which were handguns;

* the majority of homicides occurred during the course of an argument or some other non-felony circumstance; only a small proportion of homicides occurred during the perpetration of another crime (e.g. robbery);

* at least half of all homicide victims were killed by persons whom they knew;

* a greater proportion of female homicide victims were killed by family members than male homicide victims; conversely, a greater proportion of male than female homicide victims were killed by acquaintances or strangers.

This commonality in homicide patterns among blacks and whites suggests that, despite dramatic differences in risk of victimization, the fundamental causes of homicide may be much the same regardless of race. Differences in homicide rates presumably arise because those factors which increase the risk of homicide victimization are experienced more frequently or more intensely by blacks than they are by whites. Patterns of homicide that are common to all race groups also suggest that preventive interventions developed for high risk groups may ultimately be applicable to the general population.

The fundamental causes of homicide may indeed be related to such pervasive societal influences as poverty and prejudice. To the extent that this is true, this is yet another reason to work toward the elimination of these evils. But there is much that can be done on a more immediate scale as well that may be effective in the prevention of homicide. Since most homicides are not associated with the commission of some other felony crime (e.g. robbery) and since most homicide victims are killed by acquaintances or family members, preventive strategies must include, but also go beyond, the purview of the criminal justice system. Community leaders and health and social service professionals must work together with law enforcement agencies if we are to reduce the tremendous, tragic toll exacted by homicide.

References

Centers for Disease Control. Homicide Among Young Black Males - United States, 1970-1982. Morbidity Mortality Weekly Rep 1985; 34; 629-33.

Erlanger, H. 1974. The empirical status of the subculture of violence thesis. Social Problems 22: 280-91.

Flango, V. E. and E. L. Sherbinou. 1976. Poverty, Urbanization, and Crime. Criminology 14: 331-46.

Loftin, C. and R. H. Hill. 1974. Regional Subculture and Homicide. American Sociological Review 39: 714-24.

U. S. Bureau of the Census. 1985. Statistical Abstract of the United States (105th edition). Washington, D. C., 1984.

U. S. Department of Health and Human Services. 1985. Report of the Secretary's Task Force on Black and Minority Health. Washington, D. C.: Department of Health and Human Services, August.

U. S. Department of Justice, Federal Bureau of Investigation. 1983. Crime in the United States. Uniform Crime Reports, 1982, release date September 11, 1983.

University of California at Los Angeles, Centers for Disease Control. 1985. The Epidemiology of Homicide in the City of Los Angeles, 1970-79. U. S. Department of Health and Human Services, August.

Williams, K. R. 1984. Economic Sources of Homicide: Reestimating the Effects of Poverty and Inequality. American Sociological Review 49: 283-9.

Wolfgang M. 1958. Patterns in Criminal Homicide. New York: John Wiley and Sons, Inc.

Wolfgang, M. E. and F. Ferracuti. 1967. The subculture of violence: toward an integrated theory in criminology. London: Tavistock.

Wolfgang, M. E. and M. A. Zahn. 1979. Criminal Homicide, in S. H. Kadish, ed., Encyclopedia of Crime and Justice. New York: Free Press.

World Health Organization. 1977. Manual of the International Statistical Classification of Diseases, Injuries, and Cause of Death (based on the recommendations of the Revision Conference, 1975), Geneva.

CRIMINAL HOMICIDE OFFENDERS IN THE U.S.:
BLACK VS. WHITE

William Wilbanks

Though it is well known that blacks are far more likely than whites to be victims and offenders in homicides, the literature has given more attention to the racial disproportionality in homicide victimization rates (e.g., Wolfgang, 1958; Curtis, 1974; Klebba, 1975; Goldcamp, 1976; Shin, 1977; Rose, 1978; Letcher, 1979; Lane, 1979; Riedel, 1984; Rose, 1984). Literature on racial differences in homicide offender rates have historically been less frequent though a survey of more recent literature indicates that scholars are becoming more interested in explaining this black versus white gap in homicide offending (e.g., Wolfgang, 1958; Reasons, 1972; Wolfgang and Cohen, 1972; Block, 1977; Wilbanks, 1979; Lane, 1979; Riedel, 1984; Rose, 1984; Lane, 1985).

One reason for this lack of attention is that it is more difficult to find data on offenders than victims. Data and rates on homicide victims can be obtained from death certificates and are published in the **Vital Statistics of the United States**. Data on race of offenders in cases of criminal homicide can be found in the **Uniform Crime Reports** though rates are not presented. It may also be that many researchers believe as Geis (1972: 68) that racial classifications for arrest statistics should be eliminated since such statistics tend to polarize the white and black community. Thus one who writes about racial differences in offending may be accused of feeding racial fears and bigotry. I believe that the gap in homicide offense rates between blacks and whites should be presented and discussed so that a number of misconceptions and myths might be dispelled.

Most of the earlier treatises on blacks and crime do not address the issue of racial disproportionality in offender rates for criminal homicide or seek to explain that difference (see Gary and Brown, 1975; Woodson, 1977; Owens, 1980). However, the number of published works that do attempt to explain racial differences in homicide offender rates has increased in recent years (Wolfgang, 1958; Lalli and Turner, 1968; Wolfgang and Cohen, 1972; Perdue and Lester, 1974; Staples, 1974; Curtis, 1975; Swigert and Farrell, 1976; Heilbrun and Heilbrun, 1977; Rose, 1978; Pope, 1979; Lane, 1979; Rose, 1984; Riedel, 1984; Wilbanks, 1984; Comer, 1985; Lane, 1986). Unfortunately, many of the explanations presented in the literature do not have the benefit of a good description of the "facts" of criminal homicide with respect to black versus white offenders. This study presents some basic data on black versus white criminal homicide offenders so that explanations for that racial gap in offending may be enriched (and perhaps challenged).

DATA BASE AND METHODOLOGY

The Federal Bureau of Investigation (FBI) collects several items of information on every criminal homicide reported to the agency by the local police and this data serves as the basis of the figures reported in the annual **Uniform Crime Reports**. However, there is much more data collected that bears on race of offender than is published in the annual FBI report. For each homicide incident the local police complete and send to the FBI (via the Supplementary Homicide Report--The SHR) data on the month of the

43

incident; whether the incident involved one or more victims and one or more offenders; the age, sex, race and ethnicity (whether Hispanic or not) of victim(s) and offender(s); weapon used; the victim/offender relationship; the circumstance/motive; and the state, region, population group, county, Standard Metropolitan Statistical Area (SMSA), and city of occurrence.

The SHR data tape containing all criminal homicide events (N=21,002) reported to the FBI for 1980 was obtained so that breakdowns not reported by the FBI (such as age, sex and race of offenders by motive) could be produced. Before analyzing this data base it should be noted that one might question the validity of these figures in describing racial disproportionality in criminal homicide. First, one might question whether all homicides are reported to the FBI by the local police. However, research (Hindelang, 1974) has demonstrated that the homicide figures reported by the FBI closely parallel those found in the death certificate data reported in the Vital Statistics of the United States. Thus confidence in both data bases is increased.

Second, one might question the exclusion of certain types of homicides in the FBI figures. The data tape includes only murder and non-negligent manslaughter and thus excludes some types of manslaughter which whites (and women, the wealthy, etc.) are more likely to commit. For example, deaths that many might consider to be "murder" (such as deaths resulting from mine or industrial "accidents," deaths resulting from defective automobiles, unnecessary surgery, abortion, etc.) are ignored in the legal and traditional definitions of murder. Several writers (e.g., Reiman, 1979; Swartz, 1975) have criticized this narrow definition of murder and claim that it protects the rich, the powerful, and whites from being defined as "murderers."

Third, offender data on the SHR may be faulty since such data are turned in monthly and many offenders are not arrested until months after the event. Police departments are supposed to update the SHR with each arrest but it is questionable whether this is always (often?) done. No research has been published which tests the accuracy of SHR offender data. Thus any data on homicide offenders from the SHR should be viewed with caution since the offenders described on the tape probably exclude many persons arrested after the initial report is sent to the FBI by the local police.

Since many of the 21,002 criminal homicide incidents for 1980 included multiple victims and/or multiple offenders, I decided to count only the first three offenders in each incident. This did not result in the loss of many offenders and greatly simplified the analysis. The total number of offenders utilized for the study was less than the 21,002 incidents since many cases go unsolved. The tape did list 14,480 first offenders; 1,572 second offenders, and 481 third offenders where the race of the offender was known. Thus a total of 16,533 offenders was used for the total number of offenders in the U. S. for 1980.

Rates were calculated for whites versus blacks based upon population figures from the 1980 census. Each rate was calculated by dividing the number of offenders by the population and multiplying that figure by 100,000. Race of offender was crosstabulated with the victim/offender relationship, the circumstance/motive, the state of occurrence and the race of the victim.

RESULTS

Table I presents a comparison of white versus black criminal homicide offenders in terms of the victim/offender relationship. First, the 8,153 white offenders represent a rate per 100,000 of 4.3 while the 8,380 black offenders represent a rate of 31.6 (the calculation of these rates is shown in the footnote). The ratio of the black to the white rate is 7.3:1 (31.6/4.3=7.3) or, in other terms, blacks were seven times as likely as whites to be charged as criminal homicide offenders.

In data not reported in Table 1 (see Wilbanks and Murphy, 1984) the rate for subgroups of blacks were: non-elderly (under 60) black males, 50.05; elderly black males, 19.25; non-elderly black females, 10.18; and elderly black females, 2.61. White subgroup rates were: non-elderly white males, 7.46; elderly white males, 1.95; non-elderly white females, 0.99; and elderly white females, 0.11.

Table I indicates a similar victim/offender pattern for white and black offenders. For example, black and white offenders were about equally likely to kill an acquaintance (44.2% to 39.5%), other family members (7.5% to 11.9%), a lover or spouse (15.1% to 15.7%), and a stranger (19.4% to 17.7%). However, the differences in rates for each category do differ markedly. Note that blacks were 8.2 times as likely as whites to kill an acquaintance (13.99/1.71=8.2), 4.6 times as likely to kill another family member (2.37/0.52=4.6), 7.0 times as likely to kill a lover or spouse (4.78/0.68=7.0), and 8.0 times as likely to kill a stranger (6.14/0.77=8.0).

Table II presents a breakdown of circumstance/motive for black versus white criminal homicide offenders in the U. S. This table is designed to indicate the extent to which the 7.3:1 black versus white gap in offense rates varies by type of circumstance/motive. The largest black versus white gap occurred for gambling (19.0:1), robbery (12.9:1), and arguments over money or property (10.9:1). The smallest racial gap in offending occurred for gangland killings (1.0:1) and juvenile gang killings (2.4:1). Thus it would appear that blacks were far more likely than whites to kill in gambling, robbery and arguments over money, equally likely to kill in a gangland incident, and about twice as likely to kill in juvenile gang incidents.

Table III presents a breakdown of weapon choice by race of offender. In terms of the percent of weapon choice by each race, it appears that black offenders more often than white offenders chose handguns (52.5% to 40.3%) and knives (20.2% to 19.8%) while whites more often chose long guns (18.7% to 11.8%), blunt objects (5.6% to 4.1%), hands or feet (7.7% to 5.4%) and other weapons (5.7% to 3.6%). It is also interesting to note that Asians and Indians were more likely than blacks or whites to use a knife and less likely to use a handgun.

It has often been stated that criminal homicide is intraracial (e.g., white offenders against white victims and black offenders against black victims) and the 1980 SHR homicide data confirms this view. It is important to make this point in view of the common misconception by many, especially whites, that blacks are more likely to kill whites. There is some recent evidence that black offenders are more likely to choose whites than blacks as victims in

45

Table 1

Relationship of Victim to Offender
By Race of Offender for United States
Criminal Homicides, 1980

	Black Offender	White Offender
Relationship of Victim To Offender		
Acquaintance		
acquaintance	2,952	2,530
employee	3	6
employer	3	10
friend	390	362
neighbor	156	152
other known to Victim	201	163
	3,705 44.2% Rate=13.99	3,223 39.5% Rate=1.71
Other Family		
stepson	18	28
brother	117	106
daughter	67	115
father	50	113
in-law	67	156
mother	23	82
other family	124	151
step-daughter	7	9
step-father	22	46
sister	26	20
step-mother	1	6
son	105	142
	627 7.5% Rate=2.37	974 11.9% Rate=0.52
Lover/Spouse		
boyfriend	205	70
common-law husband	132	25
common-law wife	93	26
girlfriend	195	173
homosexual	20	21
husband	306	314
wife	280	577
ex-husband	14	24
ex-wife	20	47
	1,265 15.1% Rate=4.78	1,277 15.7% Rate=0.68
Stranger		
stranger	1,626 19.4% Rate=6.14	1,441 17.7% Rate=0.77
Unknown		
unknown	1,157 13.8% Rate=4.37	1,238 15.2% Rate=0.66
Total		
total	8,380 100% Rate=31.64	8,153 100% Rate=4.33

*The 8,380 black offenders represent a United States rate of 31.6 (8,380/26,488,218 X 100,000=31.6). The 8,153 white offenders represent a U.S. rate of 4.3 (8,153/188,340,790 x 100,000=4.3). The ratio of the black rate to the white rate is thus 7.3:1 (31.6/4.3).

**The 16,533 cases in this table represent the relationship of the victim to the first offender (N=14,480), the second offender (N=1,572), and the third offender (N=481) listed on the 21,002 criminal homicide incidents for 1980 by the FBI. Obviously the victim/offender relationship was unknown in many cases. In other incidents as many as nine offenders were listed. This analysis examined the victim/offender relationship of all first, second, or third offenders to their victim(s).

Table II

Circumstance/Motive of Incident
By Race of Offender for All U.S.
Criminal Homicides, 1980

Felony Type	No. of Blacks	Black Rate	No. of Whites	White Rate	Ratio of Black Rate to White Rate
rape................	66	0.25	99	0.05	5.0:1
robbery.............	1,261	4.76	695	0.37	12.9:1
burglary............	82	0.31	117	0.06	5.2:1
larceny.............	7	0.03	9	0.005	5.2:1
motor vehicle theft	13	0.05	17	0.01	5.0:1
arson...............	43	0.16	53	0.03	5.3:1
prostitution.......	9	0.03	9	0.005	6.0:1
other sex offenses.	22	0.08	37	0.02	4.0:1
narcotic drug laws.	146	0.55	131	0.07	7.9:1
gambling...........	50	0.19	18	0.01	19.0:1
other, not specified	44	0.17	92	0.05	3.4:1
Total	1,743 20.8%	6.58	1,277 15.7%	0.67	9.8:1

Other Than
Felony Type

	No. of Blacks	Black Rate	No. of Whites	White Rate	Ratio of Black Rate to White Rate
lover's triangle...	212	0.80	241	0.13	6.2:1
child by babysitter	11	0.04	17	0.01	4.0:1
brawl, alcohol.....	318	1.20	578	0.31	3.9:1
brawl, narcotics...	35	0.13	41	0.02	6.5:1
argument over money or property......	348	1.31	223	0.12	10.9:1
other arguments....	3,991	15.07	3,292	1.75	8.6:1
gangland killings..	2	0.01	20	0.01	1.0:1
juv. gang killings.	44	0.17	140	0.07	2.4:1
institutional killings	16	0.06	23	0.01	6.0:1
sniper attack......	1	0.00	7	0.00	1.0:1
other..............	1,040	3.93	1,560	0.83	4.7:1
Total	6,018 71.8%	22.72	6,142 75.3%	3.26	7.0:1

Suspected Felony Type.............	140 1.7%	0.53	307 3.8%	0.16	3.3:1
Unknown........	479 5.7%	1.81	427 5.2%	0.23	7.9:1
Total.........	8,380 100%	31.64	8,153 100%	4.33	7.3:1

*Table is based on 16,533 incidents of criminal homicide in 1980 where the race of the offender was known.

47

robberies, assaults and rapes (Wilbanks, 1985) but there is no evidence that black homicide offenders are more likely to choose white than black victims. The misconception (that black homicide offenders are more likely to choose white victims) is likely due to the tendency of the media to give greater publicity to the types of homicides (e.g., those involving robberies) that more often involve black offenders and white victims. Thus the public, "informed" by media coverage, appears to believe that robbery and other felony-type homicides (which disproportionately involve black offenders) are more frequent than domestic or acquaintance homicides.

The examination of intraracial vs. interracial criminal homicides for 1980 utilized only the first offender and the first victim listed for the 13,921 incidents of criminal homicide where the race of both offender and victim was known. Races other than black or white were excluded. Only 9% of these criminal homicides were interracial as 7% (N=940) involved a black offender against a white victim and 2% (N=344) involved a white offender against a black victim. Thus 91% of the homicides involved a white offender against a white victim or a black offender against a black victim.

A recent article (Wilbanks, 1985) has suggested that an overall figure (e.g., 9%) to measure the extent of interracial crime may mask a predominantly interracial pattern from the perspective of the offender. For example, it was pointed out that the National Crime Survey for 1981 found that only 17.7% of robberies, assaults, and rapes were interracial. However, this single figure masked the fact that black offenders chose white victims in 55.2% of these crimes while white offenders chose black victims in only 3.1% of such crimes. It was suggested that the intraracial versus interracial issues be examined from four perspectives: (1) the extent to which whites are victimized by whites versus blacks, (2) the extent to which blacks are victimized by blacks versus whites, (3) the extent to which white offenders choose white versus black victims, and (4) the extent to which black offenders choose black versus white victims. The violent crimes of robbery, assault, and rape were found to be interracial only from the viewpoint of the fourth perspective--black offenders were more likely to choose white than black victims.

However, criminal homicide is intraracial from all four of these perspectives and thus does not fit the pattern found for robbery, assault and rape. The data indicate that 87% of white victims were killed by other whites (Perspective 1); 95% of black victims were killed by other blacks (Perspective 2); white offenders chose white victims in 95% of the incidents (Perspective 3); and black offenders chose black victims in 87% of the incidents.

It should be noted that the 940 incidents of black-on-white and the 344 incidents of white-on-black criminal homicides do not include killings of the police that are ruled justifiable. Approximately 60% of police killings involve black victims though it is unknown how many of these involve black police officers. There are on the average about 150 blacks killed each year by the police with approximately 20% of police killings being by black officers (Matulia, 1982: 64, 72). Thus the number of interracial killings involving white against blacks would not greatly increase if justifiable homicides by the police were included. Also in most jurisdictions (e.g., Fyfe, 1981; Wilbanks, 1984) justifiable homicides by citizens greatly outnumber those by the police and these tend to be intraracial.

Table III

Weapon Choice of Offender by Race of Offender
For U.S. Criminal Homicides, 1980

| | Race of Offender | | | | |
	Black	White	Asian	Indian	All
Handgun...............	4,400	3,288	33	27	7,748
	52.5%	40.3%	32.0%	21.8%	46.2%
Firearm type unknown..	201	180	1	3	385
	2.4%	2.2%	1.0%	2.4%	2.3%
Other gun					
rifle............	338	697	4	13	1,052
shotgun..........	633	811	3	11	1,458
other gun........	15	13	0	0	28
	11.8%	18.7%	6.8%	19.4%	15.1%
Knife................	1,693	1,612	37	35	3,377
	20.2%	19.8%	35.9%	28.2%	20.1%
Blunt instrument......	344	456	7	9	816
	4.1%	5.6%	6.8%	7.3%	4.9%
Hands, feet, body.....	455	630	12	17	1,114
	5.4%	7.7%	11.7%	13.7%	6.6%
Other................	301	466	6	9	782
	3.6%	5.7%	5.8%	7.3%	4.7%
Total................	8,380	8,153	103	124	16,760
	100%	100%	100%	100%	100%

*The 16,760 cases in this table represent the weapon used by the first
offender (N=14,677), the second offender (N-1,596) and the third
offender (N=487) listed on the 21,002 criminal homicide incidents for
1980 by the FBI. These cases exclude those in which the weapon or race
of the offender was unknown.

49

A separate analysis was conducted of all homicides involving offenders who killed a victim of the opposite race. There were 344 incidents involving white offenders against black victims and 940 incidents involving black offenders against white victims. The most common circumstance/motive in the white-on-black homicides was "other arguments" (37%) while the most common circumstance/motive in the black-on-white homicides was robbery (41%). And yet when only robbery murders were considered, the black offender was more likely to choose a black than white (404 to 387) victim. Likewise, whites who killed in a robbery were more likely to kill whites than blacks (449 to 21). Thus from the offender perspectives it appears that robbery/murder is intraracial from the perspective of both the white offender (Perspective 3) and the black offender (Perspective 4).

The literature sometimes speaks of "the" black or white homicide offender rate as if it did not vary across the nation (figures already presented demonstrate that it varies within subgroups of the black population for the nation as a whole). Table IV suggests that the black offender rate also varies by state. The SHR data tape did not include figures for Alaska but did include figures for Washington, D. C. and thus 50 jurisdictions were utilized in comparing black versus white offender rates across jurisdictions. The states are ranked in Table IV by the rates for all offenders (includes first, second and third offenders in a given incident) for which the weapon was known. In many cases the weapon but not the race of the offender was known and thus the black and white rates do not approach the total offender rate.

Table IV indicates that the white rate for the 50 jurisdictions is positively related (r=.+65) to the total (weapon) offender rate. In other words, the states with the highest white offender rates are the same states that have a high overall rate. On the other hand, there was not a significant correlation between the black offender rates and the overall offender rates in the 50 jurisdictions (e.g., the states with the highest black rates do not cluster at the top of the ranked (by the overall rate) list. Thus, one could not predict a state's black offender rate by knowing the total offender rate for the state (as one could for the white offender rate).

Surprisingly, the states with the highest black offender rates are states not known for high crime rates (or large numbers of blacks). Note that Maine had the highest black offender rate (63.94), followed by Montana (55.99), Utah (54.20), Nevada (53.16), California (50.73) and New Hampshire (50.13). Also, the states with the largest ratios of black to white offender rates are clustered at the bottom of the lists of states ranked by overall homicide rates. Note that Iowa had the highest black to white rate ratio of 39:61:1 and New Hampshire followed with a rate ratio of 34:06:1. This means that in Iowa, on a per capita basis, blacks were 39.61 times as likely to be arrested for murder as were whites. By contrast, in Washington, D. C., blacks were only 3.28 times as likely to be arrested for criminal homicide.

The tendency of the low crime rate states to have higher black offender rates may in part explain the surprising finding by Christianson and Dehais (1980) that similar states had the highest black incarceration rates in the U. S. and the greatest black to white incarceration rate ratios. For example, Iowa had the highest black incarceration rate and the third highest black to white incarceration rate ratio.

Table IV

Criminal Homicide Offender Rates for Fifty States
For Blacks and Whites and Black to White Rate Ratio
And Total Offender Rate for 21,002 Incidents in 1980

Rank	State	Total Rate	Black Rate	White Rate	Black to White Rate Ratio
1	Washington, D.C.	42.66	20.97	6.40	3.28:1
2	Nevada	23.77	53.16	10.01	5.31:1
3	California	17.20	50.73	8.47	5.99:1
4	Texas	17.14	40.58	10.83	3.75:1
5	Florida	15.80	36.57	5.37	6.81:1
6	Alabama	15.27	30.94	6.06	5.11:1
7	Louisiana	14.08	26.43	3.88	6.81:1
8	New York	13.31	33.68	2.41	13.96:1
9	Missouri	13.20	35.58	3.24	10.98:1
10	Michigan	12.12	43.89	2.67	16.44:1
11	Kentucky	11.77	32.37	7.99	4.05:1
12	South Carolina	11.54	23.10	5.45	4.24:1
13	Maryland	11.48	20.98	3.29	6.38:1
14	New Mexico	11.08	24.96	7.48	3.34:1
15	North Carolina	11.05	24.70	5.52	4.47:1
16	Hawaii	10.98	5.76	6.59	0.87:1
17	Illinois	10.91	34.26	3.43	9.99:1
18	Arizona	10.71	42.65	7.90	5.40:1
19	Tennessee	10.41	31.27	4.56	6.86:1
20	Arkansas	10.33	30.01	4.02	7.47:1
21	Oklahoma	10.02	31.27	6.70	4.67:1
22	Georgia	9.68	18.01	2.68	6.72:1
23	Virginia	9.58	21.42	4.19	5.11:1
24	Mississippi	8.73	16.57	2.85	5.81:1
25	Delaware	8.57	16.67	3.48	4.79:1
26	Indiana	8.43	38.58	2.72	14.18:1
27	West Virginia	7.90	24.60	5.55	4.43:1
28	Ohio	7.88	34.36	2.87	11.97:1
29	Colorado	7.58	32.45	3.58	9.06:1
30	New Jersey	7.54	24.22	2.64	9.17:1
31	Pennsylvania	7.47	37.61	2.43	15.48:1
32	Wyoming	7.01	29.73	6.03	4.93:1
33	Kansas	6.69	37.26	3.64	10.24:1
34	Connecticut	5.89	24.38	1.82	13.40:1
35	Washington	5.76	30.32	2.97	10.21:1
36	Rhode Island	5.28	29.00	3.46	8.38:1
37	Oregon	5.24	35.08	3.41	10.29:1
38	Massachusetts	4.90	20.79	2.11	9.85:1
39	Utah	4.38	54.20	2.31	23.46:1
40	Montana	3.69	55.99	2.97	18.85:1
41	Nebraska	3.44	35.13	2.01	17.45:1
42	Idaho	3.16	0.00	2.11	-------
43	Wisconsin	2.89	23.55	1.31	17.98:1
44	Minnesota	2.85	46.87	1.40	33.45:1
45	Maine	2.40	63.94	1.98	32.29:1
46	Iowa	2.23	43.17	1.09	39.61:1
47	New Hampshire	2.17	50.13	1.43	35.06:1
48	North Dakota	1.38	0.00	0.98	-------
49	Vermont	1.37	0.00	1.38	-------
50	South Dakota	0.72	0.00	0.31	-------

Thus it appears that the states with the lowest proportion of blacks and the lowest crime rates tend to have the highest black criminal homicide offender rates. There is no obvious explanation for this finding though it should challenge theoreticians interested in crime by blacks. The most common explanation for high rates of violence by blacks is the subcultural view (see Wolfgang, 1958; Curtis, 1975) which suggests that blacks maintain values that allow or encourage the use of force and violence to settle conflicts. However, those who advocate the subculture of violence thesis seem to speak as if there is "a" subculture of violence among blacks and do not attempt to explain the variation in black offender rates across jurisdictions.

However, if one infers a subculture of violence from high violence rates, one would also have to infer a higher degree of that subculture in jurisdictions that have higher offender rates. And yet that logic would lead to the suggestion that states such as Maine, Iowa, and New Hampshire have a greater degree of the black subculture of violence than states which one usually associates with high crime rates (e.g., southern states). Or perhaps the whites in such states as Maine, Iowa and New Hampshire do not endorse the subculture of violence of the blacks who live in the state while whites in the southern states do endorse the subculture of violence.

It would appear that a higher degree of the subculture of violence develops in states where the black population is small, the crime rate low, and the environment is more rural than urban. There appears to be no obvious reason why these characteristics should produce a higher black offender rate (and thus by the logic of the theory) and a higher black subculture of violence. On the other hand, one might argue that where the black population is small and the overall crime rate low, there is more attention paid to black offenders than in the more populous and urban states. Theoreticians need to explore the variation in black offender rates to determine what explanations would be most consistent with the facts presented in Table IV.

REFERENCES

Block, R. 1977. **Violent Crime.** Lexington, MA: D. C. Heath.

Christianson, S. and R. Dehais. 1980. "The Black Incarceration Rate in the United States: A Nationwide Problem." Albany, NY: School of Criminal Justice.

Comer, J. P. 1985. "Black Violence and Public Policy," in L. A. Curtis (ed.), **American Violence and Public Policy: An Update of the National Commission on the Causes and Prevention of Violence.** New Haven, CT: Yale University Press, pp. 63-86.

Curtis, L. A. 1980. **Criminal Violence.** Lexington, MA: D. C. Heath.

. 1975. **Violence, Race and Culture.** Lexington, MA: D. C. Heath.

Fyfe, J. J. 1981. "Race and Extreme Police-Citizen Violence," in R. L. McNeely and C. Pope (eds.), **Race, Crime and Criminal Justice.** Beverly Hills, CA: Sage, pp. 89-108.

Gary, L. E. and L. P. Brown (eds.). 1975. **Crime and Its Impact on the Black Community.** Washington, D. C.: Howard University.

Geis, G. 1972. "Statistics Concerning Race and Crime," in C. E. Reasons and J. L. Kuykendall (eds.), **Race, Crime and Justice.** Pacific Palisades, CA: Goodyear Publishing Co., pp. 61-69.

Goldcamp, J. J. 1976. "Minorities as Victims of Police Shooting: Interpretation of Racial Disproportionality and Police Use of Deadly Force." **The Justice System Journal,** 2, 2, pp. 169-183.

Hindelang, M. J. 1974. "The Uniform Crime Reports Revisited." **Journal of Criminal Justice,** 2, pp. 1-17.

Heilbrun, A. B. and K. S. Heilbrun. 1977. "The Black Minority Criminal and Violent Crime: The Role of Self-Control." **British Journal of Criminology** 17, pp. 370-377.

Klebba, A. J. 1975. "Homicide Trends in the U. S., 1900-1974." **Public Health Reports** 90, pp. 195-204. paLalli, M. and S. Turner. 1968. "Suicide and Homicide: A Comparative Analysis by Race and Occupational Levels." **Journal of Criminal Law, Criminology and Police Science** 59, 2, pp. 9- 100.

Lane, R. 1979. **Violent Death in the City: Suicide, Accident, and Murder in Nineteenth-Century Philadelphia.** Cambridge, MA: Harvard University Press.

. 1986. **Roots of Violence in Black Philadelphia, 1860- 1900.** Cambridge, MA: Harvard University Press.

Letcher, M. 1979. "Black Women and Homicide," in H. M. Rose (ed.), **Lethal Aspects of Urban Violence.** Lexington, MA: D. C. Heath, pp. 83-90.

Matulia, K. J. 1982. **A Balance of Forces.** Gaithersburg, MD: International

Association of Chiefs of Police.

Owens, C. 1980. **Mental Health and Black Offenders.** Lexington, MA: D. C. Heath.

Perdue, W. C. and D. Lester. 1974. "Racial Differences in the Personality of Murderers." **Perceptual and Motor Skills 38,** p. 726.

Pope, C. E. 1979. "Race and Crime Revisited." **Crime and Delinquency 25,** 3, pp. 347-357.

Reiman, J. H. 1979. **The Rich Get Richer and the Poor Get Prison.** New York: John Wiley and Sons.

Riedel, M. 1984. "Blacks and Homicide," in D. Georges-Abeyie (ed.), **The Criminal Justice System and Blacks.** New York: Clark Boardman, pp. 51-60.

Rose, H. M. 1978. "The Geography of Despair." **Annals of the Association of American Geographers 68,** 4, pp. 453-464.

. 1984. "Black-on-Black Homicides: Overview and Recommendations," in D. Georges-Abeyie (ed.), **The Criminal Justice System and Blacks.** New York: Clark Boardman, pp. 61- 74.

Shin Y. et al. 1977. "Homicide Among Blacks." **Phylon 38,** pp. 398-407.

Staples, R. 1974. "Violence and Black America." **Black World,** May, pp. 17-34.

Swigert, V. L. and R. A. Farrell. 1976. **Murder, Inequality and the Law.** Lexington, MA: D. C. Heath.

Swartz, J. 1975. "Silent Killers at Work." **Crime and Social Justice,** pp. 15-20.

Uniform Crime Reports for the United States. 1980. Washington, D. C.: U. S. Government Printing Office.

Wilbanks, W. 1979. "Homicide and the Criminal Justice System in Dade County, Florida." **Journal of Crime and Justice 2,** pp. 58- 74.

and D. Murphy. 1984. "The Elderly Homicide Offender," in E. S. Newman, D. J. Newman, M. L. Gewirtz and Associates (eds.), **Elderly Criminals.** Cambridge, MA: Oelgeschlager, Gunn and Hain, pp. 79-92.

. 1984. **Murder in Miami: Homicide Patterns and Trends in Dade County (Miami) Florida, 1917-1983.** Washington, D. C.: University Press of America.

. 1985. "Is Violent Crime Intraracial?" **Crime and Delinquency 31** (1), pp. 117-128.

Wolfgang, M. 1958. **Patterns in Criminal Homicide.** Philadelphia, PA: University of Pennsylvania Press.

54

and B. Cohen. 1972. "Seeking an Explanation," in C. E. Reasons and J. L. Kuykendall (eds.), **Race, Crime and Justice.** Pacific Palisades, CA: Goodyear Publishing Co., pp. 124-131.

Woodson, R. L. (ed.). 1977. **Black Perspectives on Crime and the Criminal Justice System.** Boston, MA: G. K. Hall & Co.

RACE, SEX, AND CRIMINAL HOMICIDE
OFFENDER-VICTIM RELATIONSHIPS

John A. Humphrey
Stuart Palmer

To understand violence it is necessary to focus on the chain of interactions between aggressor and victim, on the sequence that begins when two people encounter each other and which ends when one harms, or even destroys, the other.

Hans Toch (1969:6)

INTRODUCTION

Violence characterizes much of social interaction. Human aggression often extends beyond psychological torment or minor physical abuse to serious assault or fatal attack. Yet our understanding of interpersonal violence and the dynamics of the relationship between offenders and their victims is disturbingly limited.

Violence among blacks is particularly little understood. Recently, national attention has focused on the disproportionate involvement of blacks in homicidal death. The black homicide rate, on the average, exceeds that for whites by five to ten times (Jeff, 1981: 26). Rice (1980: 551) reports that the risk of homicide victimization ". . . for blacks at all ages--measured in terms of the age-adjusted death rate--was more than six times that of the white population." Black males between the ages of 15 and 44 are particularly vulnerable to homicide victimization (Jeff, 1981: 26). Murder is the leading cause of death for black males 25-44; and the second leading cause of death for those 15-24 (Rice, 1980: 549). However, blacks between 20-24 are the single most likely group to become either a victim of murder or an offender (Jeff, 1981: 26). The National Center for Health Statistics reports that in 1977 the homicide victimization rate for black males 25-44 was 125.5 per 100,000 compared to 14.2 for white males in the same age range (Rice, 1980: 549). Jeff (1981: 31) considers poor black males between the ages of 18 and 35 to be an endangered species. Consider, for example, that the risk of becoming a victim of homicide is one in 10,000 for a white upper class suburbanite; one in 5,000 for a member of the white middle class; one in 500 for a black middle class individual; and one in 77 or less for a poor black resident of the inner-city (Jeff 1981: 31). It is startling to note that in 1977 more blacks were murdered by other blacks in the United States than died in the nine years of the Vietnam War (Rice, 1980: 549).

Homicide is a decidedly intra-racial crime. Block (1976: 498) observed that in Chicago over the nine year period, 1965-1973, intra-racial killings varied between 86 and 90 percent. Similarly, Curtis (1974: 21) found that in a 17 city survey of victim- offender relationships in only 6.5 percent of the cases a black killed a white; and 3.8 percent a white killed a black. Wolfgang (1958: 222) has reported that 94 percent of the 550 offender-victim relationships he studied in Philadelphia involved assailants and victims of the same race. And in Houston, Pokorny (1965) found that 97 percent of black homicide was intra-racial compared to 91 percent for whites and 86 percent for Mexican-Americans.

57

While homicidal death among blacks is exceedingly high, the dynamics of this violence remains a relatively neglected area of research. Black homicide must be considered in its historical context (Kirk, 1982; and Silberman, 1978). Black violence is not now nor has it ever been an inherent part of African culture; rather, it is a consequence of the long- standing experiences of racial discrimination (Silberman, 1978: 167). To Kirk, (1982) the rage of blacks is directly related to the persistence of racial oppression. This racial oppression has, in part, taken the form of the dominant society's disparagement of Afro-American culture. Blacks tend to be accepted to the extent that they reject their cultural heritage and adopt the prevailing customs and values of white America. Many blacks are unable or unwilling to accommodate themselves to such rigidly prescribed status-role behavior. Malintegration with the dominant culture, evidenced mainly by lack of economic success, often results in markedly diminished self-esteem (Davis, in Newman, 1976: 89-98). But why does this rage result in violent attacks on other blacks?

Homicide typically results from the passions of the moment and the vestiges of deep-seated wrongs of the past. The experience of slavery is no more distant to poor blacks now than are the consequences of racial oppression. For poor blacks social, economic, and political parity is available only on a sporadic basis. The barriers of racism effectively deny disadvantaged blacks the possibility of self- determination. The experience of the remnants of slavery, the sense of exploitation, and personal denigration often result in consuming frustration and outbreaks of interpersonal violence.

Coser (1956) notes that the closer the relationship, the more intense the conflict between the members. Interpersonal violence usually involves individuals who stand in a primary relationship to one another. An analysis of offender-victim relationships, therefore, uncovers the patterns of particularly important, emotionally strong relationships in a given culture (see von Hentig, 1948: 349). The more individuals rely on certain relationships for their self-worth, and social support, the greater the potential for devastating emotional harm. It is against those persons who significantly affect an individual's self-esteem that deadly violence is typically directed.

Violent behavior can only occur within a socio- cultural context. The web of social relationships and the meanings that individuals attach to those relationships must be understood before advances in theorizing about interpersonal aggression can be made.

To understand violent human interaction, it is necessary to analyze the structure of the basic dyadic relationship between the victim and his offender (von Hentig, 1948; Schafer, 1968; and Toch, 1969).

Hans von Hentig's (1948) conception of the "duet frame of crime" focuses attention on the importance of the offender-victim relationship. To von Hentig the victim often draws criminal activity to himself. Schafer (1968: 79) holds that, "(I)n a way, the victim is always the cause of a crime, even if the crime is motivated for abstract reasons ...." The victim to Schafer (1968: 79) "not only creates the possibility of a crime but precipitates it."

58

Sparks (1982: 26-33) outlines six situations in which persons increase the probability of their victimization. A brief discussion of each will be followed by its particular applicability to black homicide offender-victim relationships. **Precipitation** occurs when the victim is the first to use physical force against his offender (Wolfgang, 1958) or otherwise induces the offender to commit a crime. **Facilitation** refers to the failure of persons to take due precaution to prevent themselves from becoming victimized. Unnecessary risk-taking behavior or negligence with regard to the protection of property are common examples of **facilitation**. **Vulnerability** may be the result of: (1) personal attributes that make one physically unable to defend one's self; (2) socio-cultural conditions--inner city residence, being black, male, and unemployed increase the odds of victimization; (3) status-role determinants--being unmarried or incarcerated also places individuals at greater risk. **Opportunity** refers broadly to the availability of attractive targets, either person or property for criminal victimization. **Attractiveness** is the estimated benefit (usually, but not always monetary) to be gained from the victimization of a given target. **Impunity** refers to the odds of avoiding apprehension after the commission of a crime. Some individuals make "safer" victims than others.

Sparks' (1982: 26-33) typology of victimization "proneness" is particularly useful for the analysis of black homicide offender-victim relationships. Much of black-on-black violence is **precipitated** by the actions of the victims. Wolfgang (1958) reports that victim- precipitated homicide is more common among blacks than whites. The intensity of interaction within the black community tends to preclude overly cautious behavior, thereby **facilitating** interpersonal conflict and increasing the **opportunities** for victimization.

Further, black-on-black assault typically is of less concern to law enforcement agencies. The relative **impunity** of black offenders when assaulting other blacks makes these victims far more **attractive** and; therefore, more **vulnerable** to interpersonal violence.

This research, albeit exploratory, focuses on black homicide offender-victim relationships. The structure of the relationship between assailants and victims is analyzed in terms of its demographic characteristics: race, sex, and the nature of the basic role relationships that exists between the murderer and victim.

DATA

Data on all homicide offenders incarcerated during 1972, 1976, and 1977, and identifying information on their victims were obtained from the North Carolina Department of Corrections. Demographic data on the homicide victims were provided by the Office of the Chief Medical Examiner in North Carolina. North Carolina is one of the few states with a state-wide medical examiner system.

Data were gathered on 985 homicide offenders and 943 homicide victims. Of the homicide offenders, 605 (61.4%) were black; 350 (35.5%) were white; and 30 (3%) were American Indian. Among black offenders, the sex ratio (males to females) was 6 to 1; among white offenders, 8.7 to 1.0. The victims included 499 Blacks; and 415 Whites. The sex ratio for black victims

59

was 3.1 to 1.0; and for white victims, 2.32 to 1.0.

North Carolina's homicide rate historically has exceeded that for the nation. The criminal homicide rate for the United States in recent years has been about 9.0 (United States Federal Bureau of Investigation, annual). Although the homicide rate in North Carolina declined 17 percent from 12.8 in 1972 to 10.6 in 1977, it has nonetheless remained above the national average.

Table 1 shows that overall blacks (26%) are more prone than are whites (18.8%) to murder friends. Whites, however, are more given to the victimization of members of their own families (25.9%) than are blacks (20.9%). The proportion of killings that involves acquaintances and strangers varies little between the two races.

Table 1 also provides data on homicide offender- victim relationships by race and sex. Because males constitute 87.2 percent of the homicide offenders, overall patterns of offender-victim relationships are expected to be typical of male assailants. Black males are less likely to victimize members of their own families (16.7%) than are white males (22.3%). But black males fatally assault their friends (23.6%) more so than do white males (18.8%). Again no differences were noted in stranger or acquaintance killings between black and white men.

While intra-familial murder is the predominant form of homicide for both black and white females, black females are less likely to kill a family member (45.9%), than are white females (58.3%). One-third of black murderesses kill their husbands compared to about 39 percent of white murderesses. Black females are more than twice as likely to kill their friends (40.2%) than are white females (19.4%). However, white women (8.3%) are 3.6 time more apt to victimize a person unknown to them than are black women (2.3%).

Primary relationships tend to exist between black homicide victims and their offenders. Blacks are murdered by family members slightly more so than are whites but fall victim to strangers less often. One in four black victims are killed by a family member compared to about 22 percent for whites. Blacks are considerably more likely to be killed by a friend (30.5%) than are whites (16.1%). However, whites (32.5%) are over three times more prone to being victimized by a stranger than are blacks (10.8%).

Similar patterns hold when considering the race and sex of the victim together. Both black males and females are more likely to be murdered by a family member, or by a friend, than are their white counterparts. However, black men are 2.7 times less vulnerable to being murdered by a stranger and black females are ten times less vulnerable than are same sex whites.

In North Carolina, 63.5 percent of criminal homicide involves both male offenders and victims; 23.8 percent male offenders and female victims; 10.1 percent female offenders and male victims; and 2.6 percent both female offender and victims. The data in Table 2 suggest that when either a black or white male kills another male the victim usually stands in a non- primary relationship to the offender. Acquaintances and strangers rank as the first and second most likely targets of male-male murder, friends are third, and male family members are the least likely to die at the hands of another

- TABLE 1

HOMICIDE OFFENDER-VICTIM RELATIONSHIPS,
BY SEX AND RACE OF OFFENDER AND VICTIMS,
1972, 1976, 1977, IN PERCENTS

All Three Years

Relation of Offender to Victim	Offenders						Victims					
	Total Black	Black Male	Black Female	Total White	White Male	White Female	Total Black	Black Male	Black Female	Total White	White Male	White Female
Family Member	20.9	16.7	45.9	25.9	22.3	58.3	25.2	18.2	46.3	22.2	14.1	40.8
Spouse	12.0	8.4	33.3	14.2	11.5	38.9	14.4	7.9	34.1	12.3	4.8	29.6
Other	8.9	8.3	12.6	11.7	10.8	19.4	10.8	10.3	12.2	9.9	9.3	11.2
Friends	26.0	23.6	40.2	18.8	18.8	19.4	30.5	28.8	35.8	16.1	15.9	16.8
Acquaintances	31.4	34.7	11.5	31.3	33.4	13.9	33.3	39.2	15.4	29.2	34.1	17.6
Strangers	21.4	24.8	2.3	23.6	25.2	8.3	10.8	13.5	2.4	32.5	35.9	24.8
TOTAL	605	521	84	350	314	36	501	378	123	415	290	125

TABLE 2

SEX OF OFFENDER IN RELATION TO SEX OF VICTIM,
BY RACE AND HOMICIDE OFFENDER-VICTIM RELATIONSHIP,
NORTH CAROLINA, 1972, 1976, 1977, IN PERCENTS

Homicide Offender
Victim
Relationship   All Three Years

	BLACK				WHITE			
	M-M	M-F	F-M	F-F	M-M	M-F	F-M	F-F
Family Member	8.5	40.8	47.3	41.7	11.7	47.4	72.7	38.5
Spouse	--	33.1	39.2	--	--	37.9	63.6	--
Other	8.5	7.7	8.1	41.7	11.7	9.5	9.1	38.5
Friends	20.9	32.3	43.2	16.7	17.8	20.0	18.2	15.4
Acquaintances	41.2	15.4	6.8	41.7	41.8	14.7	9.1	23.1
Strangers	28.9	11.5	2.7	--	28.6	17.9	--	23.1
TOTAL	388	157	47	12	213	95	22	13

62

family member.

When a male kills a female, more pronounced disparities between the races are evident. Black males are more apt to fatally assault their female friends, while white males are more given to killing females within the family, usually wives, or women who are totally unknown to them.

Black murderesses choose men as their targets 6 to 1 over women. White women, however, kill 1.7 men for every woman victim. A primary role relationship invariably exists between a male and his female killer. When a female kills a male, nine out of ten times the victim is a family member or close friend. Black females (43.2%) are considerably more prone to murder a male friend than are white females (18.2%). White females, however, murder their husbands and other male relatives (72.7%) more than do black females (47.3%).

Intra-racial murder accounts for 87.2 percent of the homicide offender-victim pairs analyzed; 53.2 percent involved black offenders and black victims; and 34 percent involved white offenders and white victims. Of the inter-racial murders, 10.6 percent included black offenders and white victims; and 2.2 percent white offenders and black victims.

Table 3 shows that black-on-black homicide (57%) more often involves a primary relationship between the offender and victim than does white-on-white murder (47.9%). Intra-racial homicide among blacks results in the death of a friend considerably more so than does white-on-white homicide. White-on-white murder, however, involves stranger killings 2.2 times more frequently than does black-on-black murder.

Inter-racial homicide is marked by the non- primary relations between offenders and victims. When blacks murder whites, 90 percent of the offenders and victims are strangers or merely acquainted. Seven out of ten black offenders kill whites who are totally unknown to them. Similarly when whites kill blacks, the victims and offenders are for the most part strangers or mere acquaintances.

DISCUSSION

Patterns of black homicide offender-victim relationships were compared to those for whites. The central findings are these: (1) both black male and female offenders tend to victimize less members of their families and more their friends than do whites; (2) black males and females are murdered more so by friends, while whites are far more likely to be killed by a stranger; (3) when either a black or white male kills another male, there tends to be a non-primary relationship between the offender and victim; (4) when either a black or white male kills a female, the victim is most apt to be his wife; (5) black males who kill females are more apt to murder a friend, while white males are more likely to victimize a female unknown to him; (6) black murderesses are considerably more likely to kill a male than are white murderesses; (7) black murderesses are only slightly less likely to kill a male friend than they are their husbands, while white murderesses overwhelmingly murder their husbands; (8) intra-racial homicide predominates for both whites and blacks. However, black-on-black murder more often involves a primary relationship between the offender-victim. Stranger killings are more

63

TABLE 3

RACE OF HOMICIDE OFFENDERS IN RELATION TO RACE OF VICTIMS,
BY HOMICIDE OFFENDER-VICTIM RELATIONSHIPS,
NORTH CAROLINA, 1972, 1976, 1977, IN PERCENTS

Relation of Offender to Victim	All Three Years			
	W-W	B-W	B-B	W-B
Family Member	29.3	1.1	26.1	0
Spouse	16.1	1.1	14.9	0
Other	13.2	0	11.2	0
Friends	18.6	8.3	30.9	23.2
Acquaintances	30.5	20.8	33.0	46.4
Strangers	21.2	69.8	9.8	30.4
TOTAL	311	95	482	17

NOTE: Data for 49 offender-victim pairs were unavailable.

common in white-on-white homicide; and (9) inter- racial murder tends to involve non-primary relations between the offender and victims.

An inordinately high risk of homicidal death exists within the black community. Fatal confrontations among blacks typically result in the murder of a young black male by another young black male. This recurring pattern of black interpersonal violence seems inextricably tied to the persistent difficulty black males have in obtaining a viable masculine identity. Cazenave (in McAdoo, 1981: 176- 184) refers to this struggle as the black males' "quest for manhood." It remains that American men are judged in terms of their ability to enact traditional occupational and familial roles. Above all, they are expected to provide substantially to the financial well being of the family. Social structural restraints, however, continue to mitigate against the likelihood that black underclass men will be able to meet even the minimal normative expectations of them as "men."

Masculine identity is often sought outside the home and away from the job. Cazenave (in McAdoo, 1981: 180) writes that ". . . even before an underclass black male inherits the economic problems that have contributed to a low level of involvement for his father in family affairs, he is socialized to expect that men demonstrate their manhood in the streets, not the home."

Violence becomes a means to attain a sense of "manhood", a sense that an individual in not powerless to influence what happens to him (Cazenave, in McAdoo, 1981: 181). Subcultures of black men emerge to counteract their collective alienation from society at large. Ironically, attempts to assume control over their lives, to visibly demonstrate that they are "real men" may result in spontaneous, impassioned acts of violence directed towards each other. The consequences are often fatal.

REFERENCES

Block, R. 1976. "Homicide in Chicago: A Nine-Year Study (1965- 1973)." The Journal of Criminal Law and Criminology 496-510, 66.

. 1981. "Victim-Offender Dynamics in Violent Crime." The Journal of Criminal Law and Criminology, 743-761, 72.

Cazenave, N. A. 1981. "Black Men in America - The Quest for 'Manhood'." In Harriette P. McAdoo (ed.), Black Families, Beverly Hills, CA: Sage, 176-184.

Coser, L. 1956 The Functions of Social Conflict. New York: Free Press.

Curtis, L. A. 1974. Criminal Violence. Lexington, MA: Lexington Books.

Davis, J. A. 1976. "Blacks, Crime and American Culture." In Graeme R. Newman, (ed.), Crime and Justice in America: 1776- 1976. Annals of The American Academy of Political and Social Science, 89-98, 423.

Gary, L. E. (ed.). 1981. Black Men. Beverly Hills: Sage.

Jeff, M. F. X. 1981. "Why Black-On-Black Homicide." Urban League Review, 25-34, 6.

Kirk, A. 1982. "Black Homicide." In Bruce L. Danto, John Bruhns, and Austin H. Kutscher, (eds.), The Human Side of Homicide. New York: Columbia University Press.

Letcher, M. 1979. "Black Women and Homicide." In H. M. Rose (ed.), Lethal Aspects of Urban Violence, Lexington, MA: Lexington Books.

McAdoo, H. P. (ed.). 1981. Black Families. Beverly Hills: Sage.

Pokorny, A. D. 1965. "A Comparison of Homicide in Two Cities." Journal of Criminal Law, Criminology and Police Science, 479- 487, 56.

Rice, D. 1980. "Homicide from the Perspective of NCHS Statistics on Blacks-Meeting." Public Health Reports, 550-552, 95.

Robins, L. 1968. "Negro Homicide Victims--Who Will They Be?" Transaction, 15-19, 5 (7).

Schafer, S. 1968. The Victim and His Criminal: A Study in Functional Responsibility. New York: Random House.

Shin, D., D. Jedlicka and E. S. Lee. 1977. "Homicide Among Blacks." Phylon, 398-407, 38.

Silberman, C. E. 1980. Criminal Violence, Criminal Justice. New York: Vintage Press.

Sparks, R. F. 1982. Research on Victims of Crime: Accomplishments, Issues, and New Directions, U. S. Department of Health and Human Services,

Rockville, MD: National Institute of Mental Health.

Toch, H. 1969. Violent Men: An Inquiry to the Psychology of Violence. Chicago: Aldine.

U. S. Federal Bureau of Investigation, Crime in the United States. Washington, D. C.: U. S. Government Printing Office: (Annual).

Von Hentig. H. 1948. The Criminal and His Victim. New Haven: Yale University Press.

Wolfgang, M. E. 1958. Patterns of Criminal Homicide. Philadelphia: University of Pennsylvania Press.

HANDGUNS AND HOMICIDE IN URBAN BLACK COMMUNITIES:
A Spatial-Temporal Assessment of Environmental Scale Differances

Harold M. Rose and Donald R. Deskins, Jr.

By the mid-1960s, levels of interpersonal violence began to increase in the nation's larger black communities. This followed a series of years in which previously high levels of risk were in abatement. Explanations for the more recent rise in levels of risk vary greatly although several analysts have assigned a substantial role in that growth to increased availability of handguns (Block and Zimring, 1973; Farley, 1980). The prevalence of handgun use in committing homicide in urban settings is frequently cited, but attention has seldom been directed toward the role of handguns on escalating violence in a specific urban niche: the urban black community. In this paper, the primary focus will be to examine the role and availability of handguns in a sample of urban black communities that experienced varying levels of risk between 1970 and 1975.

The association between growing availability of handguns and the increase in the incidence of lethal violence has not been overlooked by researchers interested in issues relating to environmental safety (Cook, 1979; Farley, 1980; Fisher, 1976; Phillips, Votey and Howell, 1976; Zimring, 1979). But several researchers expressing an interest in this topic are unconvinced that a simple relationship exists between ownership of a gun and changes in risk of homicide victimization. Rather, they imply that risk has increased because more people are attracted to criminal lifestyles and that the tool of the trade just happens to be the handgun (Danto, 1982).

Kleck (1979) takes the position that "The mere possession of a gun does not necessarily make deadly violence more likely, and thus the connection between levels of gun ownership and violence is one which must be evaluated empirically." Yet Turner and others (1977) contend that the mere possession of a gun stimulates the probability of its use. These two positions no doubt represent polar positions that evolve out of different philosophical and disciplinary orientations.

Even though there is no general consensus on the issue, it is important that we begin to direct some attention to issues associated with owership and availability of handguns in settings where homicide is a principal cause of death. Therefore, selected urban black neighborhoods are a logical target of this type of investigation. Microscale investigations of homicide risk in such neighborhoods are seldom undertaken, and thus our perspective regarding the role of handguns on risk is most often based on macroanalytic investigations.

Although we acknowledge the general absence of microanalytic investigations of the type suggested above, we are fully aware of the assumed linkages between macroscale and microscale outcomes associated with various types of interpersonal violence. It is frequently suggested that the social and economic situation of large segments of the black population leads parts of that group to direct feelings of aggression against one another (Poussaint, 1983). These aggressive acts have been attributed to high levels of impulsivity (Brearley, 1932) and to membership in a subculture of violence (Wolfgang and Ferracuti, 1967).

Whatever the explanation for the higher frequency of involvement in overt expressions of violence, it is the outcome of these interactions that constitutes our central concern. Nevertheless, those outcomes are more often lethal when the weapon the combatants have is a handgun. Logically, then, each episode of aggression should be expected to increase the risk of death based on the availability of weapons of greater lethality.

Given the increase in accessibility to these more lethal weapons, it is difficult to ascertain if the frequency of black participation in violent episodes has increased, leading to higher homicide risk, or if current levels of risk are occurring under declining frequency of violent outbursts, but with a higher proportion ending in death. If the latter situation is nearer to reality, then the recent increase in homicide risk could indeed be attributed to a weapons effect.

We suspect, however, that the changing relationship between victim and offender is likely to provide stronger clues to the association between risk and handgun availability than does information on the frequency of violent outbursts. Moreover, there is an expectation here that the modal victim-offender relationship will vary as a function of the regional location of our sample communities.

If culture represents a critical intervening variable as some researchers suggest (Gastil, 1971; Wolfgang and Ferracuti, 1967), then differences in patterns of victimization should be observed. Therefore, we decided to accord the role of region a central position in our assessment of the role of handguns on risk elevation in our sample communities.

Regional Variations in Weapon of Choice in Violent Confrontations

The modal weapon employed in lethal altercations involving black victims and offenders is the handgun. Brearley (1932) indicated during the 1920s that the popular image of the black homicide offender as a razor-toting villian was a myth. Even then, guns were used more often as the death weapon; but long guns, not handguns, were most often the weapon of choice. So, even prior to the most recent upsurge in homicide victimization, blacks were more likely to be killed with a gun than with any other single weapon.

During the more recent period, the handgun has more often been the weapon of choice. A good illustration of this turn of events is the pattern of weapon use associated with deaths of black males in Cleveland from 1958 to 1974. In the base period (1958-1963), firearms accounted for 55.6 percent of such deaths, whereas in the final five-year period firearms were employed in 85.9 percent of black male victimizations (Rushforth et al., 1977).

A similar pattern has been noted in Chicago and Detroit (Block, 1976; Zimring, 1979). This increase in the use of handguns is thought to be associated with changing patterns of victimization. Moreover, this growth is strongly associated with an increase in felony-related deaths. Block (1976) has shown that 100 percent of the excess increase in homicides in Chicago during a recent nine-year period could be attributed to gun violence. Furthermore, fully one- third of the increase was associated with robbery homicide. The previous illustrations of the changing circumstances of handgun use imply a difference in probable markets for handguns as a function of intended use.

The Role of Regional Differences in Patterns of Victimization

During an earlier era when the vast majority of all homicides were an outgrowth of angry confrontations, the gap between guns and knives as weapons of choice was much smaller. But the changing character of patterns of interaction between victims and offenders has resulted in an altered pattern in the weapon mix involving homicide transactions. Thus an increase in the frequency of felony-related conflict as opposed to conflict based anger has increased the demand for handguns by both those with criminal intentions and those who simply wish to defend themselves and their property.

All crime rates increased between 1960 and 1970, especially in urban areas. The involvement of blacks in escalating crime rates is well known, but from a regional perspective it is critical to distinguish between the South and the non-South with regard to elevation of risk.

It is thought that blacks became increasingly associated with robbery during the 1960s and early 1970s because they becme more involved with drugs (Hoch, 1974). During this same interval, however, Jacobson (1975) demonstrated evidence of a regional convergence of crime patterns. Nevertheless, regional differences in personal crime rates, i.e., homicide and assault, continued to reveal exaggerated levels in the South.

Clearly, the issue of use and availability of weapons in terms of their consequences for increased levels of lethality are tied to an understanding of a set of very complex configurations. For instance, one important feature relates to the changes in national character and to the subsequent adjustment to those changes (Harris, 1981). The adjustment favored a change in pattern of gun use during the 1960s.

Block (1976) presented evidence which suggests that the increased use of guns in situations resulting in death was related to an increase in robbery homicide. Other researchers suggest that drug-related victimizations are especially likely to involve handguns. Yet homicide has historically been more strongly associated with aggravated assault than with any other type of crime.

Prior to the most recent period, the same conditions that led to aggravated assault also led to homicide. In support of this position, Pittman and Hardy (1964) indicate that the primary distinguishing feature of these two acts is one of weapon used. They state as follows: "The weapon most often used differed between homicide and aggravated assault; a pistol or revolver was most common in homicide, while a knife was most common in assaults" (Pittman and Hardy, 1964). On the other hand, robbery homicide represents a break with the past and does not reflect the modal pattern of violence associated with southern culture.

Assault, like homicide, has generally distinguished the South from the non-South in terms of prevalance, and both behaviors continue to reach higher peaks in the South. But robbery tends to occur more often in the non-South, especially in selected Manufacturing Belt states. In the latter area, both robbery and assault rates are high, whereas in most southern states the assault rate is likely to exceed the robbery rate by a ratio of at least 2:1 (Kowalski et al., 1980). Most southern states, with the exception of those with large urban populations, are still likely to have robbery rates that were characteristic of the U. S. circa 1967.

Of course, the observed regional differences in patterns of criminal behavior should be expected to have an impact on the demand for handguns. Changes in the structure of criminal behavior have led to an alteration in homicide risk, especially in the nation's larger black communities.

How have these changes influenced the market for lethal weapons? Has the demand for handguns increased simply because of the need for greater protection? Or, is the increase basically related to the rise in the market for weapons that can be used to commit crimes, especially robbery? We will try to address these issues at the conclusion of our discussion of selected aspects of environmental attributes on homicide risk in a sample of black urban communities.

Are blacks in the urban South more likely to actively participate in the market for lethal weapons than are blacks from the urban North? More precisely, which of these groups is most likely to own guns? And do people's basic motives for seeking weapons differ on the basis of regional location? Very little research addresses itself to these kinds of issues within the context of urban black communities. But if we are to fashion a rational policy on guns, the foregoing questions must be addressed.

Southern blacks who were socialized in small towns and rural areas are more likely to have grown up in a home where guns were present. Recent survey results (Stinchcombe et al., 1980) show that ownership of guns among rural blacks averaged 69.4 percent, whereas in large cities it averaged only 26.7 percent. Stinchcombe and others (1980) state "that exposure to a big city environment decreased probability of gun ownership among both blacks and whites."

The differential propensity for persons to own weapons based on size of place no doubt reflects various cultural and structural differences that have an impact on the primary motive for ownership. For example, people who live in rural areas or small towns are more likely to purchase guns for recreational use, whereas people in large inner city areas may be motivated to acquire guns because they perceive a need for protection.

It should be expected that more blacks in the urban South will own guns than will blacks in the urban North. Furthermore, the larger number of blacks who previously lived in rural areas and their continuous contact with such areas is thought to promote stronger values about gun ownership. Thus recreation and protection are the primary motives for legal ownership of guns in the urban South.

In the urban North, on the other hand, the size of the black population of southern origin is likely to influence the ownership of weapons. Moreover, protection probably represents an important motive for onwership. In a recent investigation by McClain (1982-1983), more than two-thirds of a sample of black householders in Detroit who owned guns had them for protection.

The size of the criminal market for handguns is unknown, but the higher incidence of robbery in the urban North would lead one to conclude that this market is more substantial in the North than in the South. Not only is demand for handguns in the North likely to be stimulated by more people participating in criminal lifestyles, but the market for guns should be greater because of the perceived need for protection.

WEAPON USE AND WEAPON MIX IN A SIX-CITY SAMPLE

In order to more carefully examine some of the previously identified issues, we evaluated data collected from a six-city sample. Among the six cities, two are in the urban South (Atlanta and Houston); the remainder are nonsouthern cities. Both Detroit and Los Angeles, however, were targets of large scale migration of southern blacks during the 1960s. The influence of southern culture, at least in terms of its impact on youth, should be less evident in St. Louis and Pittsburgh because black migration to these cities had slowed to very low levels by the end of the 1950s. The central question becomes the following: In this six-city sample, are primary differences in the pattern of weapons use in the commission of homicide based on regional location?

The Growing Reliance on Handguns

We used 1975 data on victimization extracted from the FBI's monthly homicide reports for the six cities. This information described the weapon mix associated with the death of a 25 percent sample of black victims. In each instance, guns represented the modal homicide weapon, ranging from a high of 88 percent in Atlanta to 76 percent in Detroit and Pittsburgh.

When type of gun employed is assessed--instead of all guns versus other weapons--another view emerges. Although handguns are the most frequently used type of gun, major differences exist among places in the frequency with which handguns represent the weapon of choice. For example, handguns were employed in 69 percent of the killings in Houston, but were used in only 33 percent of the homicides in Pittsburgh. In all other places, handguns accounted for 60 percent or more of all deaths.

The mean percent of handgun use was 65.3 percent. But handguns were used more often when the relationship between victim and offender was unknown (76.9 percent) and when the victim and offender were strangers (70.9 percent). Relationships classified as "stranger" and "unknown" are most likely to represent felony-related deaths. Therefore, one would expect use of handguns to be greater in cities where felony- related deaths accounted for a higher proportion of total deaths. Nevertheless, this effect could be offset in cities where primary homicides turned out to be mostly caused by guns. Almost one-third of the deaths caused by handguns in the six-city sample were thought to be related to felonies.

Still, the extent to which handguns are most likely to constitute the preferred weapon is a function of the victim-offender relationship and the

73

ages of the dyad. Gender is also a discriminator in choice of weapon, with guns becoming less significant when the victim or offender is female. Thus a decline in violent family confrontations in which the victim or offender happens to be female is likely to increase the share of handgun deaths among aggregate deaths.

Patterns of Weapon Use at the Neighborhood Scale

In 1973, Detroit was recognized as one of the most dangerous cities in the nation based on the continued escalation of its annual homicide rate. Nevertheless, wide differences exist in the extent to which risk varies by neighborhood in that city. This can partially be explained by differences in lifestyle and environment and the ensuing levels of stress accompanying each. These forces will probably have an impact upon choice of weapon. Thus neighborhoods where violent victimization is more often a product of a felony are likely to be targets of more effective demand for handguns than are neighborhoods where violent acts are not related to felonies.

To highlight differences in weapon mix, we have selected two Detroit neighborhoods where victimizations of residents reached a maximum in 1973. Each of the foregoing neighborhoods had 12 homicide victims during that year. But the modal weapon in these neighborhoods was different. We contend that the relationship between victim and offender and the age and sex of participants, as well as motivation, greatly influenced the choice of weapon.

These two neighborhoods differed in socioeconomic status as well as in age structure. In the west side neighborhood, which had a slightly higher status and a younger population, two-thirds of the victims were killed with a gun. These victims were all males, were more often involved in a felony transaction and were less emotionally involved with the offender. Among west side dyads, felonies and suspected felonies motivated the majority of contacts. Moreover, robberies and drug-motivated actions appear most commonplace. In the majority of incidents, guns were the weapon of choice.

In the east side neighborhood, there was evidence of greater personal involvement between the victim and the offender. In fact, most victims had previously been involved with the offender in a social setting where drinking, gambling and sex-related activity had taken place. Acts motivated by felonies constituted only a minimum number of deaths among this series of lethal situations. Furthermore, knives and other physical objects were used more frequently than were guns.

Because traditional lifestyles of lower status populations manifested themselves in the east side neighborhood, it often led to a quickness to anger and the subsequent escalation of discord. That resulted in people using whatever weapon was available. Also, conflict between members of opposite genders was widespread: one-third of the victims were females who were killed by males, and one female killed a male companion.

From the foregoing two examples, it appears that a series of external influences heighten the probability of violent confrontations. But when confrontations are associated with young black males who are motivated by felony considerations, then guns (and especially handguns) will represent the favored weapon. Confrontations between an individual and a felon, either in

74

the street or in a residential setting, heighten the likelihood of violence with a gun. At the same time, these confrontations stimulate a dual demand for handguns, from the perspective of the prospective felon and the prospective victim. Often, the actual victim is the person who is most vulnerable to attack among those involved in the transaction.

Among the six cities in the sample, there are differences in the frequency of weapon use. But these differences were not large enough to be statistically significant.

When an analysis is done of male victims, only Atlanta differs on the handgun dimension. There, more than four-fifths of all male victims were killed with a handgun. This contrasts with the close to 66.7 percent that characterized the other cities, with the exception of Pittsburgh where only about three-fifths of the males were killed with handguns.

Handguns are less likely to be employed in confrontations between older black males than in confrontations between younger black males. The younger the victims and offenders in the homicide transaction, however, the greater likelihood that a handgun will be used. Whether this reflects generational changes in weapon preference based on differences in patterns of socialization or simply indicates better access to more lethal weapons is at this point open to conjecture.

The Homicide Setting and Choice of Weapon

Since regional patterns of victimization are characterized by numerous distinguishing features, some of which have an impact on what weapon is used, it is quite possible that regional differences will also manifest themselves in other aspects of the lethal transaction. Therefore, we choose to examine an additional facet of the fatal interaction keeping these differences in mind.

One aspect of the lethal transaction that lends itself to a weapons choice effect is place of death occurrence. In this instance we refer to the character of the immediate setting, e.g. vacant lot, alley and so forth. Likewise, a weapons effect may also manifest itself in the temporal dimension of the place of death occurrence.

In earlier efforts, Wolfgang (1958) and Block (1977) describe the importance of the setting on the transaction. Wolfgang noted the limited treatment that had been given to the role of the overall setting in which the homicide transaction occurs. Furthermore, Block has continued to advance the importance of the setting by distinguishing between role of the setting in a macroenvironmental and a microenvironmental context. Although analysts differ in the importance they assign one or the other of the foregoing labels, there is less difference regarding the general importance of environmental context on the transaction. In the present investigation, the neighborhood is defined as the microenvironment; the site where the transaction occurs is labeled the setting, e.g., place of residence, tavern and so forth.

From a weapons use perspective, the setting where the transaction takes place can indirectly provide information about the motive for owning a weapon. Yet it is clear that the amount of information that can be acquired

75

via this process is limited. At least, however, it provides a point of departure in terms of assessing the possibility of whether the weapon should be viewed as defensive or offensive.

Guns are usually kept in the home for protection or for recreational use. Nevertheless, situations (e.g., domestic conflict) arise within the home that lead to people using guns during violent altercations. One would assume that long guns in the house would indicate a primary interest in the recreational aspects of gun ownership, whereas owning a handgun would indicate an interest in protecting one's home from intruders. Both the foregoing instances are perceived as legitimate reasons for owning weapons. It is expected that the handgun-long gun onwership ratio will differ between southern and nonsouthern cities, but that the ratio will be influenced by the percent households of southern origin in nonsouthern locations.

Killings that occur outside of a residential context imply, at least on the surface, that at least one member of the dyad was armed prior to the encounter. This raises the issue of why the person was carrying a weapon. There are numerous possibilites such as anticipating recurrence of a previous angry confrontation, anticipating engaging in predatory crime and wishing to intimidate the prospective target, warding off a potential attacker or simply engaging in a symbolic display that connotes membership in a specific subculture.

We contend, however, that some qualitative differences distinguish those who carry weapons on their person from those who keep them in their homes. Yet these are not mutually exclusive concepts; and without an intensive investigation of the situation, the relationship between weapon and site could be misread. Nevertheless, some initial insight might be gained by simply viewing the environmental context in which a given weapon was employed in a fatal transaction.

The Structure of Victimization and the Homicide

Setting

It was previously noted that the structure of victimization differed among cities on the basis of location. Consequently, we would also expect the modal homicide setting to differ among places. For instance, most family-related homicides happen in the home. Lethal transactions among acquaintances also occur frequently in the home, but are highly likely to take place in the street. Variations in the residence-street dichotomy, however, should be expected to show a differential pattern of weapon choice.

In our six city sample, an obvious difference exists in the extent to which handguns dominate as the weapon of choice. The observed differences are related to place-specific differences corresponding to the homicide setting. This being the case, we should logically expect a stronger correlation in pattern of weapons use among those cities that have a very similar structure of victimization.

Still, it appears that as handguns become increasingly important as the death weapon, the setting where the lethal transaction occurred becomes

76

somewhat less important. Therefore, the growing dominance of handguns and the complex motives promoting the fatal act might be expected to reduce the strength of association between setting and weapon mix.

A review of Table 1 provides a picture of the dichotomous setting of handgun use in lethal transactions in our six-city sample. Only in Atlanta and Houston do handgun deaths occur most often in places of residence. This may suggest that handguns were most often kept in the home for protection. Since most homicides that take place in a residence involve a primary relationship in which emotional arousal is temporarily heightened, we assume handguns were used during the altercation simply because they were available.

Table 1

Variations in Use of Handguns for the Commission of Homicides in Residential and Non-Residental Settings

	Residential	Non-Residential
Atlanta	65.8	34.2
Detroit	46.8	55.2
St. Louis	37.8	66.2
Houston	54.1	45.9
Los Angeles	45.7	54.3
Pittsburgh	31.6	69.4

Source: FBI Monthly Supplemental Homicide Reports, 1975.

In the remaining cities, a handgun can be assumed to have been carried by at least one of the members of the interacting dyad. In such instances, the person who had the weapon anticipated needing protection while away from his or her residence or anticipated using the weapon to induce compliance with a request, e.g., armed robbery. The latter practice is more likely to be associated with a felony-related act; the former is viewed as somewhat likely to fall into this category. Thus in Pittsburgh, St. Louis, Detroit and Los Angeles, the offender and possibly the victim were inclined--for whatever reason--to arm themselves prior to leaving home.

The above findings perhaps connote differences in lifestyle orientations among persons residing in southern and nonsouthern environments. A sharper impression of differences in lifestyle may be deduced by directing our attention to the time the death occurred, i.e., time of day, day of week.

Weekends and late evenings have traditionally represented periods of heightened risk in settings characterized by the potential for intense interpersonal discord. Where this temporal rhythm is absent or is only weakly developed, one would expect nonresidential homicides to assume greater importance for this implies a breach with the traditional pattern of confining one's leisure activities to a limited and fixed temporal niche.

77

Likewise, this would imply that people who were at greatest risk of victimization (e.g., young adult males not in the labor force) had more discretionary time.

Diurnal Variations

Among our sample cities, diurnal variations in frequency of occurrence of death do not vary significantly on the basis of death setting. In most settings, deaths occur more often between 8:00 p.m. and 2:00 a.m. than during any other quarter of the day. The single deviation from this pattern is the predominance of deaths occurring in commercial establishments between 2:00 p.m. and 8:00 p.m. Although the setting and diurnal periodicity of death were not found to be associated statistically, the inverse of the previous pattern was observed between the diurnal pattern and the structure of victimization.

The victim-offender relationship shows a strong association with timing of victimization. Family- related deaths and stranger-related deaths are more uniformly distributed throughout the 24-hour period although both elevate somewhat during the early evening and late evening, with a slight peak in the latter period. Deaths in relationships classified as "unknown" are concentrated more in the late evening, with other time periods having limited importance in their association with the lethal transactions. These findings show that family members and strangers are at risk throughout the day, but acquaintances and unknowns encounter higher risk during a more restricted period within the diurnal cycle.

Once again, differences in association among the six-city sample in the aggregated and the disaggregated units show conflicting results. A strong statistical association exists between diurnal periodicity and the city where death occurred. The differences among cities no doubt relate to both the age structure of victimization and the victim-offender relationship.

Although most cities had a late evening peak, this was not the case in Los Angeles. Secondary early evening peaks were observed in St. Louis and Houston. The early evening was the peak period of death in Los Angeles. In Atlanta and Pittsburgh, diurnal differences were less pronounced than elsewhere.

Handguns tend to represent the preferred weapon in the lethal transaction regardless of time of day, but handguns were used even more often by those who committed homicides during the late evening (72.9 percent) and early morning (71.9 percent). Other guns, which were involved in approximately 15 percent of these transactions, were used most often in the late and early evening, a pattern paralleling that of acquaintance victimizations.

Knifings manifested a pattern similar to that of other guns, with a slight peak occurring in the late evenings. All other modes of death were more nearly randomly distributed within the diurnal cycle. There is a strong likelihood that handguns will be employed during hours of darkness; other guns are less often associated with that diurnal period. Just why this is so is not entirely clear. But it probably reflects conflict occurring during periods of relaxation where a handgun just happens to be available, and it indicates that greater comfort associated with carrying a gun on one's person under cover of darkness.

78

Weekly Periodicity

Another important element in the temporal sequence of violence is that of the day in the weekly cycle of occurrence. Traditionally, victimization has been highest on the weekend. Saturday night has been distinguished both in fact and in lore as the single time in which social conflict can be expected to peak.

During periods when blacks had a high rate of participation in the labor force, the weekend provided the largest block of discretionary time available to that group. Therefore, the weekend was to be viewed with anticipation, especially by those who engaged in an exciting life. So, too much alcohol, arguments over money, and acts of sexual indiscretion occurring during this period of maximum relaxation subjected some blacks to heightened risk of assault. Thus the likelihood of that assault leading to death was a function of the intensity of the stimulus to action and the type of weapon available.

Both the amount of discretionary time and the availability of weapons of greater lethality have changed over two decades. During the 1930s, 1940s and 1950s, the average American had less discretionary time than he or she has today. Likewise, the ratio of knives to guns used in interpersonal assaults has also changed.

So, even without a change in the number of assaults, we would expect more fatalities to occur simply as a function of the alteration in the weapon mix. According to Zimring (1972), the gun is four times more lethal than the knife. Thus the combination of weapons of greater lethality and more discretionary time is thought to have had an impact on risk levels in our sample communities.

Changes in the amount of discretionary time in the black community are associated with people moving from rural areas to cities and with changes in skills required for entry level jobs. The latter change has seriously affected the extent to which black youths are likely to be employed.

In reviewing the changing labor force experience of black and white youths (16-19 years old) between 1960 and 1970, Calvin (1981) showed their rate of participation in the labor force was 45.8 percent in 1960 and 41.4 percent in 1970. Likewise, he found that the unemployment rate for that population had increased from 24.4 percent to 29.1 percent during the same period of time.

The increase in discretionary time among that segment of the population with the weakest attachment to traditional values is thought to add to the risk of victimization. Under these circumstances, the traditional patterns of homicides peaking on the weekend can be expected to weaken, and a more even distribution of risk over the seven-day cycle should emerge. Likewise, as the change in the weekly cycle is altered, we expect that the primary-nonprimary ratio between victim and offender will also change. The traditional pattern of weekend peaks in risk of victimization is heavily weighted toward primary relationships.

The pattern of the weekly cycle of victimization prevailing among our

79

sample cities is characterized by some notable differences (see Figure 1 for data on three cities). Weekend peaks are most pronounced in Houston (61.1 percent) and Atlanta (56.3 percent). The traditional peaking pattern manifests itself in our two southern cities but is less evident in other sample locations. Because primary homicides account for such a large percentage of the victimizations in southern cities, it is assumed that the combination of traditional lifestyles and higher rates of participation in the labor force reduces the time available for heightened emotional discord to the weekend period.

Nonweekend peaks, however, distinguish St. Louis (54.2 percent), Los Angeles (51.9 percent) and Pittsburgh (51.6 percent) from the rest. The implication of these peak nonweekend victimizations is that young black males have encountered greater difficulty entering the work force and have more discretionary time, leading them to engage in behaviors that heighten risk of victimization. Nonweekend peaking patterns are more often associated with confrontations between people with nonprimary relationships, e.g., vague acqauintances and strangers.

Although differences exist among our sample cities, the two-day weekend is clearly the riskiest period of victimization in all places. Yet the tradition is being altered, but less so in southern cities than in nonsouthern cities.

Handgun Caliber and the Increase in Risk of Victimization

Handguns as the principal weapon of violence have grown in importance in a very short period of time. Because of the greater lethality associated with these weapons, numerous efforts have been initiated to curtail supply or to deny access. But much of the effort to restrict the supply has centered on small caliber handguns, which are cheap and are thought to be used extensively by segments of the criminal population. These weapons have often been labeled "Saturday night specials." The contention is that criminals from minority groups use this weapon extensively because it is cheap and easily concealed (Bruce-Briggs, 1976), and thus a national policy on gun control should place heavy emphasis on restricting its availability.

To date in the literature, there has been only a limited discussion of weapons caliber in relationship to homicide patterns and risk. Zimring (1972), however, has provided an exhaustive treatment of this topic, and this work serves as the basis for a further examination of the weapons effect operating in our six-city sample. More specifically, we wish to examine the role of handgun caliber on several dimensions of the lethal transaction. Thus handguns were disaggregated on the basis of caliber.

Small caliber weapons were defined as .25 caliber or less; large caliber weapons were identified as handguns with a caliber exceeding .25. The former category is thought generally to represent those guns previously referred to as "Saturday night specials" although not totally so. It has been said, however, that such guns cannot be precisely defined (Bruce- Briggs, 1976). Nevertheless, we have established an operational definition for facilitating and examining patterns of use of large and small caliber weapons.

Figure 1

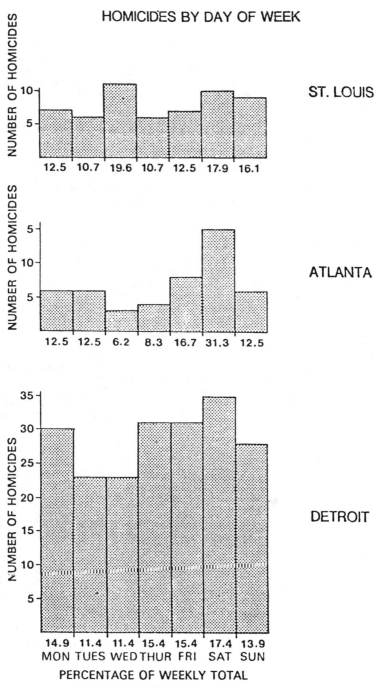

HOMICIDES BY DAY OF WEEK

81

Caliber Preferences

Offenders in our six-city sample seldom chose small caliber weapons. Yet, there were differences among cities in terms of the share of victimizations associated with them. Only in Houston was there evidence of substantial reliance and use of small caliber weapons in lethal altercations. In 1975, more than 25 percent of all black victims in Houston were killed with small caliber weapons.

In the sample cities, the mean share of victim deaths resulting from small caliber guns was approximately 13 percent. Los Angeles, St. Louis and Atlanta were within three percentage points of the mean. Pittsburgh and Detroit represented the deviant cases in that deaths caused by small caliber handguns occurred infrequently. Thus in this investigation the Saturday night special is not the primary weapon associated with the death of black victims. Its level of importance generally approaches that of knives as the preferred weapon.

In situations where small caliber weapons were used, the victim was most often a member of the family; the victim was more frequently between 30-39 years old; death occurred in the early morning hours; and the setting was more likely to be residential. Only is Los Angeles does there appear to exist a significant deviation from this pattern. In that city, there was evidence of small caliber handguns being used more often in stranger victimizations, which most often occurred in street settings. The latter situation would seem to imply that the most substantial market for smaller caliber weapons is associated with the demand stimulated by youthful offenders who frequently engage in efforts to rob.

Although one cannot put great faith in data that describe conditions during a single year, our results coincide with those expected in terms of the target market for producers of small inexpensive handguns. These handguns are generally viewed as defensive weapons for home protection, and the ghetto is thought to represent a logical threat. One producer of these weapons described the guns as "night-stand models" (Brill, 1977).

So, small caliber handguns are used more extensively by protagonists who know each other and espeically by individuals who are emotionally linked to the victim. Therefore, a weapon that is ostensibly sold for home protection in low income communities is used most often, at least in terms of its lethality, in conflicts between family members or close friends.

Earlier we indicated that our dependence upon data from a single year lessened the reliability of our assessment. It is possible to overcome some of the weakness based on single year data as it relates to caliber of weapons. Our multiyear data on caliber of weapons, however, are confined to a single city in the sample. Data from St. Louis describing the universe of homicide victims at four different time intervals (1970, 1973, 1975 and 1977) permit us to evaluate the stability of the ratio of small caliber- large caliber weapons in lethal transactions. Furthermore, it allows us to disaggregate caliber into its individual components, e.g., .22 caliber revolver, .38 caliber revolver, rather than to simply describe it in terms of a dichotomous classification. Thus greater precision in terms of preference of caliber can be specified, but for a single place.

In each of the selected years, more people used large caliber handguns in St. Louis. In each year, offenders showed a decided preference for the .38 caliber handgun. In fact, about one-fifth of all deaths were associated with this weapon. In 1970, the rate of black homicides caused by the .38 caliber handgun was 13.2 per 100,000, which is higher than the national average for all homicides regardless of method of commission. The total black homicide rate in 1970 in St. Louis was 66 per 100,000.

The second most frequently used handgun during this period was the .32 caliber. But prior to 1977 it never seriously threatened the dominance of the .38. In most years, the ratio of the former to the latter was 3:1. Therefore, it is apparent from an analysis of longitudinal data that the Saturday night special was seldom the preferred weapon among persons involved in homicides in St. Louis.

The .38 caliber and the .22 caliber were employed as the death weapons in primary and nonprimary homicides. Acquaintance and stranger deaths were almost equally associated with either a large gun or a small gun. Yet the .38 was much more important as a nonprimary homicide weapon than was the .22 during the early 1970s. By 1977, however, the smaller caliber weapon was observed to have gained in popularity, a finding that might represent a bias that grows out of the changing structure of victimization as well as the age of the offender. The increasing percentage of offenders described as "unknown" and its association with unknown gun caliber might well distort the .38 caliber and .22 caliber frequencies. Likewise, the choice of weapon might well reflect what is available in the local market, the purpose of which the weapon is intended, and the cost of the weapon.

Nevertheless, in St. Louis during the early 1970s, the small caliber handgun while frequently employed in lethal confrontations was the weapon of secondary choice rather than primary choice. Beyond 1975, however, evidence describing weapons preference had become more obscure as an outgrowth of the increasing number of victimizations involving an unknown relationship between victim and offender.

Deaths of Black Males Caused by Hanguns: Changing Urban Patterns

Our previous discussion focused more sharply on the microenvironmental context of the homicide transaction in order to highlight its role on weapons preference. That discussion was generally limited to a cross-sectional assessment of gun risk in a set of black communities.

It was demonstrated that handguns are used more often than other weapons against black victims simply because the guns are easy to acquire, can be concealed, and are generally the weapon of choice of most black offenders. Yet it is important that we single out for additional discussion the changing pattern of handgun use among the primary market for handguns in the black community: black males. The rate of gun victimizations among that group undergirds the homicide epidemic that swept through a number of the nation's larger black communities during the early 1970s. This position is supported by Farley's (1980) analysis, which shows that the total increase in homicide rates of black males between 1960 and 1975 could be attributed to shooting deaths.

Although Farley's position suggests cause and effect, the actual situation is no doubt much more complex than his statement implies. Therefore, we have chosen to review the pattern of gun victimizations of males over an extended period in our sample communities. It is hoped that the outcome of this brief review will provide additional insight in understanding levels of risk as well as the lifestyles that influence levels of risk. More importantly, it should aid us in addressing the question of the type of gun policy that might best assist in the amelioration of risk.

In reviewing patterns of handgun use, we chose a five-year interval (1970-1975). As previously indicated, only male victims were chosen since they make up the vast majority of all victims (see Table II); and the instrument most often employed in their demise is the handgun. Yet, in an effort to demonstrate variations in the pattern of deaths caused by guns in individual urban places, we must better understand how guns find their way into the possession of those who eventually use them in taking the life of another. Table II illustrates the prevalence of handgun use in the victimization of black males in 1975.

Table II

Handgun Deaths Among Black Males as a Percent
of Total Black Homicides--1975

City	Males as Percent of Total	Percent Handgun Victims (of Total)
Atlanta	74	81
Detroit	86	68
St. Louis	87	68
Houston	89	67
Los Angeles	85	68
Pittsburgh	91	61

Source: FBI Supplementary Monthly Homicide Reports, 1975.

Only in Atlanta did black males account for fewer than four-fifths of all black homicides. Handguns were the dominant weapon used in killings of black males in all cities but Pittsburgh, where other guns (43 percent) assumed the dominant role. Since males constitute the preponderant population at risk and since that risk is partially related to greater availability of handguns, there seems to be sufficient justification for limiting this discussion to black males. (Females are more often killed with weapons other than handguns.)

The Market for Handguns

The market for handguns is known to vary among places. Ownership of handguns has been shown to be higher in the South and lower in the Northeast than elsewhere. Cook (1980) reports that 50 percent of urban householders in Texas own guns, whereas only 10 percent of householders in the Northeast and Midwest own guns. He attributes this discrepancy to differences in cultural traditions. Thus as a function of a value system that encourages ownership of guns, we should expect southern cities to have high gun density and many legitimate commercial outlets for guns, with few constraints on access.

Ownership of guns is not soley dictated by cultural values that give rise to substantial markets for such weapons. It is also prompted by the fear of householders that their homes are no longer safe and by the demand generated by persons recruited into a life of crime. Recent estimates indicate that guns are used in 45 percent of all robberies. Thus a variety of markets for handguns exists, and demand is satisfied through a diverse set of outlets. Nevertheless, we are primarily concerned with how handguns find their way into urban black communities and eventually form a critical link between life and death.

The question of the importance of specific sources of weapon supply becomes very significant in trying to evaluate accessibility of guns. Most of the current proposals intended to restrict access are aimed at legitimate local gun dealers. Because of an increase in the demand for handguns, local operators of gunshops represent a single source of supply--and possibly one of declining importance. Black-market operators and gun thieves also add to the gun supply as well as to the distribution of guns within local markets. Kaplan (1984) suggests, however, that our efforts to forge a sensible handgun policy might benefit by focusing attention on curbing the activity of illegal distributors of guns.

Zimring (1975) documented the role of illicit interstate trafficking in handguns for street distribution. As a market for weapons intended for use in criminal transactions, street sales are thought to assume growing importance. In New York City, Zimring found that many of the guns confiscated in association with crimes were new and were basically related to recent increases in production of handguns. According to Cook (1982), new guns used by criminals are thought to represent illegal imports and are thereby available from illegal suppliers.

The source of the gun supply in our sample cities is likely to be dictated by intended use. Illicit suppliers serve as the major providers in markets dominated by criminal demand, whereas legal suppliers will attempt to satisfy legitimate demand in high gun- density cities like Atlanta and Houston. In southern cities with a high gun density, legitimate outlets will tend to be major providers of handguns. On the other hand, one would expect a more diverse source of suppliers to be operating in Detroit, St. Louis and Los Angeles. Since the latter cities have a higher frequency of felony homicides, an increased outlet for black-market weapons is likely to exist.

A crude estimate of source can be deduced from a sample of responses from offenders in our primary sample cities. Because of small sample size, caution is advised. Nevertheless, we should be able to gain some insight into the source of supply of weapons used to commit fatal assaults.

Forty percent of the responding offenders from Atlanta, Detroit and St. Louis reported they did not own a gun at the time of the offense, which indicates handguns were used somewhat less often by the sample than by the universe. But of those who employed handguns in the fatal transaction, the sources of supply cited were street (37 percent), followed by gun store (23 percent), friend (21 percent) and other (19 percent).

Based on the response of the foregoing group, it appears that informal sources of supply are substantially more important than are sources that most proposed gun legislation is designed to influence. On the other hand, one might contend that all of the sources--with the exception of store sales--are so amorphous that the original source of supply cannot be determined.

Even if that is the case, however, it is safe to assume that a minimum of two-fifths of all handguns used by this population were secured illicitly and/or through nontraditional sources. In fact, almost three-fifths of our sample of offenders who identified themselves as hustlers obtained weapons through street sales. The latter group no doubt view the handgun as a standard tool of the trade. As hustling becomes more important in declining inner city communities, the role of the illicit gun trader can be expected to increase.

Among the individual cities, street sales accounted for a larger share of all handgun purchases in St. Louis than elsewhere. On the contrary, street sales were of limited importance in Atlanta, where most offenders bought weapons through legitimate outlets. Friends and other sources were relatively more important in Detroit than elsewhere, but even so the primary source of supply was street sales.

The network of handgun supply appears to differ among places and is thought to be related to the intended use of the weapon. Where home protection is paramount, purchases from gun stores are likely to represent the dominant source of weapons. But when other uses prevail, i.e., criminal intent, then sources other than standard commercial outlets take on additional importance. Moreover, the disaggregated pattern of sources of supply conforms to our intuitive notion of what should be expected in terms of modal victim-offender relationships, age structure of victimization and regional differences in attitudes about owning guns.

The pattern of handgun homicide over a period of six years should allow us to indirectly assess the nature of the market for the handgun and the extent to which the market fluctuates from year to year. Since the authorities permanently confiscate weapons used in homicides, providing the individual is found guilty of committing the crime, this either reduces the number of handguns available to individuals or increases the demand for replacement or substitute weapons. Moreover, the lack of any significant decline in deaths caused by handguns from year to year would seem to imply that the supply of handguns is adequate to at least ensure that the target of the previous year will be satisfied. The extent to which the intended use of the weapon changes, however, should influence demand and thus have an impact on the annual number of homicides caused by handguns.

As was previously noted, among the individual cities, deaths caused by handguns varied substantially by choice of target and circumstances of death. In cities with a traditionally high density of guns, however, it is conjectured that choice of target is less likely to be related to choice of weapon. But in cities that have a somewhat weak tradition of gun ownership, the association between weapon used and target would be expected to be higher. And, this difference should be expected to show itself in the age structure of victimization. In cities with high gun density or in cities with a strong tradition of gun ownership, one would not expect great discrepancies between the number of young victims (below 30) killed with handguns and the number of older(over 30) people killed with handguns. We explore this presumption and others below.

Longitudinal Variations Among Cities in the Pattern of Gun Deaths

During a period of rising violence, black males experienced a variety of patterns of death in the sample cities. The six-year period under investigation shows that in some places the incidence of lethal violence was highest in the base year and lowest in the terminal year. In other cities, the inverse of this pattern was observed. In one city, no appreciable change occurred between the base year and the terminal year, but in other cities the peak incidence of lethal violence occurred between the base year and the terminal year. This would suggest that whatever the external forces are that abet confrontations, they operate on a different set of temporal rhythms as it relates to place.

The foregoing is somewhat consonant with Fischer's (1980) position on the diffusion of violence down the size-of-place continuum. In this instance, however, the diffusion appears to be characterized by a directional bias in which peaks of violence are initially observed in the larger black communities in the East and eventually spread to the West. Some weak evidence to support that contention is revealed in the increase in homicide deaths in Houston and Los Angeles since 1975; Atlanta and Detroit experienced a decline over the same interval.

In St. Louis, 1970 was the peak year of deaths for black males, after which a decline set in that was not reversed until 1975. During this six-year period, constrasting trends were observed in St. Louis. Throughout the interval, the number of victimizations of young adult males increased steadily. At the same time, the incidence of death among mature black males constantly declined. The foregoing pattern is associated with a slight increase in the proportion of mature victims killed by guns. A 52 percent increase in handgun deaths occurred among young adult males, while handgun deaths among mature black males decreased by 47 percent.

Although the basis for this observed change is not entirely clear, it is apparently associated with differences in lifestyle that are related to age. Nevertheless, substantial evidence points to the increasing importance of drug-related disputes in placing young black males in St. Louis at risk.

Standing in contrast to St. Louis in terms of age structure of victimization is Los Angeles, where the pattern of deaths among young adults differs less than that of mature adults. In fact, the young adult

87

populations of St. Louis and Los Angeles are somewhat similar in the pattern of changing incidence. In Los Angeles it is among mature adults, however, that an upward trend in incidence was observed in all but a single year. In fact, an 80 percent increase in handgun deaths occurred among all black males, but that increase amounted to 115 percent for mature adults. In the base year among the cities currently under review, Los Angeles had the lowest rate of deaths caused by guns. By 1975, however, it had the highest gun death rate.

The reasons for the higher incidence among older adults during this interval can only be conjectured. A reasonable assumption is to attribute the observed pattern to a continuation of young adult lifestyles into the thirties or to the greater vulnerability of mature blacks to the risk of felony death. A more detailed assessment of these possibilities will be necessary before a definitive position can be assumed.

Although much has been written about the violent tradition in Houston, that city was seemingly least affected by the epidemic of violence that characterized other large cities from 1970 to 1975. Yet, according to Lundsgaarde (1977), "Over the years, Houston has had one of the highest per capita homicide rates in the nation." No appreciable change was noted among either young or mature adults during this time.

In Houston only during a single year was there significant variation in the year-to-year incidence. In that year, which occurred almost midway in the interval, there was an appreciable drop in victimizations of young adults and an appreciable increase in mature adult homicides. Yet there was no significant variation in the alteration of the pattern of weapons use.

Houston was a high gun-density city at both the beginning and end of the period, with handgun deaths hovering around 70 percent of all deaths in each year. Furthermore, the incidence and instrument of death remained stable over the interval.

Atlanta, unlike Houston, experienced an unstable pattern of incidence during this period. In fact, Atlanta had a series of ups and downs, with lows being reached in the early years and in the final year of the period. The increase from the base year to the year in which the incidence maxima occurred was only 27 percent. But for the entire period there was a 27 percent decline based on the precipitous drop in incidence in the final year.

In some ways the pattern in Atlanta is more reminiscent of that in Los Angeles than elsewhere. In both cities, mature adults dominated the homicide totals, and similarities existed in the pattern of temporal fluctuations. Nevertheless, in Atlanta there was a much greater reliance on handguns to terminate angry confrontations. Yet during this period, there was a decrease in handgun deaths among young adult blacks in Atlanta; however, the decrease among mature adults was much more modest.

Outside of New York and Chicago, no city approached Detroit in the number of homicides from 1970 to 1975. In neither of these places, however, was the risk of homicide as great as in Detroit since Detroit's black population is smaller than that found in New York and Chicago.

Since 1975, however, homicides have begun to decline in Detroit; and in

1979, Los Angeles and Houston recorded a larger total of homicides. Los Angeles, the city with the lowest homicide risk among our original sample at the beginning of the period, began to assume the risk characteristics prevalent in Detroit at the initial date, lending support to our diffusion hypothesis. Nevertheless, some analysts attribute the downturn in Detroit to effective work by the police in the area of reducing the number of preventable deaths, e.g., those committed within public view.

Control of Handguns as a Measure of Environmental Safety

The post-1965 escalation of homicide risk in the nation's larger black communities is a topic that has received inadequate attention. This lack of attention is partially an outgrowth of a general individual orientation to the study of homicide and secondarily to ecologically oriented investigations that restrict the scale of analysis to the city or to the metropolitan area.

By confining the scale of analysis to larger territorial aggregates, investigators frequently overlook the seriousness of risk at the neighborhood scale. But it is not risk per se that this essay has addressed. Instead, we have chosen to direct our attention to the modal instrument of risk in a selected set of urban black communities.

By approaching the problem in this way, we were able to establish the differential prevalence and dependence upon handguns as instruments of death at different locations in an urban ethnic network. The prime motivation for that review was to attempt to ascertain if an effective gun policy could be forged that would substantially lower the risk levels in the nation's higher risk environments: selected urban black communities.

In order to shed light on the possibility of attaining the above goal, we explicitly focused on the role of culture on attitudes about gun ownership and implicitly on the structure of victimization as an indicator of both weapon demand and choice. Southerners are more prone to own guns than are nonsoutherners, and persons who live in rural areas are more likely to own guns than are their urban counterparts. Likewise, it was suggested that higher gun densities were likely to prevail in southern than in nonsouthern cities. But Cook (1979) indicates that gun density is also high in Detroit, St. Louis, Cleveland and Cincinnati. These cities have sizeable black populations, and all but Cincinnati have been cited as places that experienced high levels of homicide risk during the 1970s.

The question of what causes a high rate of gun ownership by blacks outside of the South is thought in part to revolve around the traditional attitudes about gun ownership held by southern blacks who migrate to the North, and a response to neighborhood crime rates in the new environment (Bordua and Lizotte, 1975). Therefore, adherence to aspects of traditional culture and a propensity to defend oneself against criminal attach have helped to promote higher rates of handgun ownership in selected black communities.

Structure of Victimization and Handgun Policy

Changes in the structure of black homicide victimization during the previous two decades likewise suggests changes in intended weapon use as well as a strong preference for the handgun as a weapon of choice. The question of how one might more effectively define structure of victimization must be addressed.

Generally, in defining the structure of victimization, a dichotomous categorization scheme is employed based on the intensity of bonding between victim and offender and/or the underlying motivation for the attack. In some instances, these two taxonomic approaches to structure produce incongruent results. For instance, the primary/secondary dichotomy, based on intensity of bonding, implicitly suggests a stable relationship between relatives, friends and others over time.

So, by identifying the relationship between the victim and the offender, we should be able to generally deduce motivation. But there is growing evidence that this assumption is no longer valid (Dietz, 1983).

Researchers who advocate only limited restriction on access to handguns seem unaware of the weaknesses in the traditional taxonomic approaches. They comfortably assert that the vast majority of all homicides in the United States are an outgrowth of interpersonal conflict, i.e., primary homicides, which .pawould be highly likely to occur even if a handgun were not available.

But growing evidence suggests that an increasing number of what on the surface would appear to represent primary homicides may in fact be felony related, e.g., drug disputes, contract killings and so forth. That is, in both of the previous examples the victim-offender relationship could be described as acquaintance, while the motivation for the confrontation is felony related.

Tardiff, Gross and Messner (1986), demonstrating a sensitivity to the weakness of the traditional taxonomic schema, recently suggested an alternative. The alternative was prompted by the need to define more precisely the circumstances surrounding victimization in New York City. They found that drug- related activity had emerged as the primary circumstance bringing the victim and offender together. More often than not, the victim and offender were acquaintances, a situation that would normally lead to classifying the relationship as primary and therefore thought to be not easily preventable.

The Issue of Access to Handguns

The arguments for and against attempts to establish an effective policy on guns usually pit against one another persons with polar ideological biases. These biases also appear to manifest themselves in the positions that some academic researchers assume.

In attempting to address the issue of an optimal policy on guns, or at minimum a policy that would have a positive impact on high-risk black communities, we will briefly examine some of the issues that emerge in most general discussions of attempts to regulate access to handguns. Among the most frequently raised issues are those associated with limited access versus freedom of access.

Since people who own guns vary widely in their basic motivation for ownership, they may negatively perceive any policy that limits access. In particular, sportsmen and recreational owners often oppose efforts to restrict access to handguns even though such guns find limited use among this population. Moreover, limiting access is generally viewed as a curtailment of liberty that must be defended at all cost. Nevertheless, at least one-half of the states have laws governing access (Cook, 1982). In fact, several states have passed additional legislation that imposes a mandatory minimum penalty for use of a weapon in the commission of a crime.

Laws of the latter type reflect a growing interest in efforts to deter individuals from using handguns for criminal activity. The evidence of the extent to which these laws have succeeded in lowering rates of violent crime is ambiguous. Still, Loftin and McDowall (1984) suggest that the Michigan law has led to a reduction in handgun deaths in Detroit since the law was introduced in 1977. Although opposition to efforts to curb access abounds, there is growing support for curbing the access of proscribed individuals (e.g., convicted felons, juveniles, mental defectives and so forth) to handguns. This is based on the likelihood that such individuals are not legitimate users.

The effort of this type that has received the greatest support is an attempt at interdiction. Specifically, this effort restricts the flow of small inexpensive handguns often described as "Saturday night specials." A general belief exists that handguns are the preferred weapons of street criminals, and therefore an attempt should be made to limit the availability of handguns. Policies of this type are thought to be discriminatory because they attempt to deny access to a specific class of user. Further, evidence was previously offered that the so- called Saturday night special was not the weapon of choice of people engaged in criminal lifestyles. The absence of unambiguous evidence demonstrating a positive association between gun laws and the level of violent crime does much to diminish support for the adoption of potentially effective laws.

Can an Effective Handgun Policy be Developed?

The prevailing high levels of homicide risk in the nation's larger black communities should be viewed as unacceptable and no doubt would be if such risk levels were to spill over into the broader urban arena. Instead, Barnett (1982) suggests that we have learned to live with homicide and thus are not sufficiently motivated to take action to prevent what the general public is likely to view as routine killings.

Even though the United States Public Health Service recently acknowledged the epidemiclike quality of homicide risk in the nation's inner cities and has vowed to intervene, that organization is resistant to suggesting a gun policy as an appropriate intervention technique (Meredith, 1985). Therefore, it appears that a gun policy option is unlikely to be assigned a high priority as a recommended tool for curbing risk. Nevertheless, this option should not be simply ignored because of its lack of support by recreational and other urbane gun users.

Investigations that incorporate an environmental as well as an individual orientation should enable us to more effectively evaluate the potential impact of a specific gun policy on reduction of risk. The environmental orientation of this essay represents a crude first attempt to delineate the nature of the problem. Subsequently, we will suggest what gun policy options seem to be most promising under a variety of circumstances that motivate violence. Moreover, an effective gun policy should address the issue of source of supply; identify proscribed groups; and develop an appropriate set of penalties to deter illicit use (Moore, 1983).

After doing a cross-sectional review of both the structure and the microspatial pattern of victimization in our sample cities, we then expanded that review to include a longitudinal analysis of the changing pattern of handgun use involving black male victims. It is now possible to suggest a series of gun policy options that would hopefully have a positive impact on levels of risk.

Throughout this essay we have attempted to establish a link between risk and structure of victimization as well as between structure of victimization and regional culture. To be potentially effective, any policy on guns would need to at least pay attention to the role of these factors on demand for handguns and subsequently on intended use of the gun. The implication of this position is that in order to effectively intervene in the risk process, a unique gun policy based on the structural and cultural characteristics of places should be developed. Therefore, the kind of gun policy that is shaped by the dictates of the sociocultural environment in Atlanta may be totally inappropriate for St. Louis. Needless to say, however, we support efforts to design gun policies that would have the greatest potential of having an impact on the leading contributors to elevation of risk in a specific risk situation, e.g., domestic quarrels, drug-related disputes, street robbery and so forth.

Demand for Handguns and Policy Recommendations

Some of the existing opposition to attempts to restrict access to the handgun supply seems to stem from a lack of clarification of how the intended regulation would impact individual user groups. But by no means is this suggested to imply that this represents the core of the opposition. Nevertheless, some evidence exists that a rural/urban-oriented perspective undergirds the polar viewpoints held by supporters and opponents on the issue of access. It seems possible to address some of the legitimate concerns arising out of user intent relative to the question of access.

Residents of large cities who are concerned about individual safety are likely to take a different stand on the issue than are people whose primary concern comes out of very different circumstances. Although these groups may be motivated by a different set of perceived needs and intended use, there appears to exist growing evidence of convergence on the issue of aggregate access or opposition to restrictions generally.

Loftin and McDowall (1983) contend that as the perception of declining security heightens, based on the assumption that policy will be unable to

92

provide adequate protection in big cities experiencing economic decline, the market for handguns for home protection increases. Thus home defense seems to have emerged as a potentially important intended use for handguns. Context, then, is likely to play an important role in gaining support for restricting access to handguns as fear of inadequate collective security becomes more pervasive.

State laws that address the issue of access vary greatly and no doubt represent cultural sanctions that are an outgrowth of the state's developmental history. It is at the municipal level, however, that the most promising policy on guns is likely to emerge, for at this level one is in a stronger position to address the question of proscribed use and to stipulate appropriate penalties for criminal use. Likewise, the issue of illicit transfers can also be addressed more sensibly. Therefore, we will essentially confine to the scale of the municipality our recommendations for the development of an effective policy on handguns.

The recent rise in levels of homicide risk in the nation's larger black communities has incorporated victim-offender pairs representing the complete range of structures of victimization. Historically, however, primary homicides have accounted for the vast majority of all victimizations leading many to conclude that the possibility of risk intervention was minimal.

Among our sample cities there is strong evidence of a weakening of the contribution of primary victimization to total victimization. The intensity of that weakening was strongest in Detroit and St. Louis and weakest in Atlanta and Houston. By the mid- 1970s, the pattern in Los Angeles had begun to move away from the level of primary dominance akin to that which had prevailed earlier in Atlanta. At the latter date, it had begun to take on structural characteristics akin to those that prevailed in Detroit. Thus a knowledge of structural shifts should enable us to deduce something about changes in demand in handguns as well as to determine how demand is likely to be satisfied, i.e., commercial sales or sales on the black market.

Apparently as secondary homicides become more important--as is evident in each of our sample locations--illicit transfers of guns also become a more important source of supply. Thus in recommending a policy on guns, one must be aware of the changing circumstances that could lead the suggested policy to have only a minimal impact.

In cities that have a high density of guns, such as Atlanta and Houston where access is easy and strong values about gun ownership are widespread, the catalyst for an elevation in risk was made probable simply by a change in weapon preference, i.e., the choice of handgun over the long gun or knife. No doubt the actual situation was more complex than this. In this instance or under similar circumstances, a policy that would stiffen the penalty for committing a homicide with a gun, when a self-defense plea was not sustainable, should be expected to act as a deterrent. In locations where such policies have been introduced, they seem to have been more effective in reducing risk associated with interpersonal conflict rather than with crime-related confrontations (Rossman et al., 1980).

Discouraging the Ownership of Guns

In southern cities, characterized by a slowness to adopt new lifestyles favoring interpersonal violence, the greater problem may be that of attempting to deter lethal violence through imposing more severe sentences when guns are used in violent confrontations. This position may become invalid as values that originate in one setting rapidly diffuse to another. Most mature adults, however, are likely to continue to practice the modal lifestyles into which they were socialized as youths. Thus an appropriate gun policy under these circumstances would discourage the carrying of concealed weapons.

A measure similar to Massachusetts' Bartley-Fox amendment is suggested as an appropriate one. Likewise, we would advocate that steps be taken to weaken enthusiasm for ownership of handguns in general, provided that one did not live in a high crime district.

A decline in the propensity for individuals to arm themselves should be expected to lower the risk of homicide by diminishing the possibility of personal confrontations. The simple fact is that being armed may create a false sense of security and thereby escalate a minor conflict into one of major proportions leading to death. Likewise, domestic conflicts leading to lethal confrontations might be reduced if a handgun were not in the home. Nevertheless, in the 1980s, these simple prescriptions may be inadequate even in those parts of the country where the traditional structure of victimization was thought to be firmly anchored.

It seems the more difficult problem is to design a policy on guns that will be effective in more complex urban environments outside the South. In nonsouthern environments the traditional circumstances leading to death, as well as the circumstances associated with emerging lifestyles, do much to catalyze risk. Thus simple recommendations will be unlikely to suffice in the nonsouthern sociocultural context.

Yet it should be noted that there is growing evidence of a decline in risk in gender-based conflict (Zimring and Zvehl, 1983) such that family violence is much less likely to represent a substantial contributor to aggregate risk in nonsouthern urban settings than in southern ones. But the problems associated with single young black males (15-24 years old), who join together to form street gangs and/or other roving bands, are thought to do much to heighten risk. Among this group, risk elevation reaches its peak both in terms of victim and offender behavior.

Illicit Transfer of Guns

Although legal access to guns is often made more difficult in nonsouthern environments, as more states stiffen registration policies, a large and easily available illicit supply makes it difficult to deny access to proscribed individuals. Kaplan (1979) suggests that the suppression of this traffic will not be easy, but in support of efforts in that direction states as follows:

One would expect it to be able to shrink the illegal market sufficiently so that at least some would-be purchasers would have a good deal of difficulty finding illegal sellers or convincing them that they could be trusted enough to be able to purchase illegal weapons. (p. 25)

One may try to shrink this market by enacting a series of local ordinances that would impose stiff fines on anyone who engages in the following behaviors or who fails to abide by the provisions of the ordiance: sells a handgun to a person who subsequently uses it to commit a felony; requires all noncommercial sellers to register the sale in order to be immune from the prior provision; and imposes a mandatory minimum sentence on a seller convicted of being the source of an illicit sale that led to the commission of two or more felony-related acts. Unless stringent penalties are imposed, the traffic in illicit weapons is unlikely to be suppressed.

A Radical Policy Proposal

The growing contribution of secondary homicides to risk in general and to risk elevation in nonsouthern urban environments leads us to consider the little discussed merits of a policy on guns that would favor legitimate sale and distribution of handguns for self-defense in the home. In general, conventional wisdom has been to attempt to restrict access rather than to openly encourage it. Yet as robbery homicide and armed invasions of the home become more commonplace, more people are buying weapons for protection.

It was recently demonstrated that in Chicago there was a higher than average dependence on handguns that led to death in residential and commercial robberies (Zimring, 1986). The growing tendency for individuals known to the victim to engage in residential robbery has sent shock waves through the community and has resulted in people wanting to protect themselves and their family from crime.

Under the circumstances, should we entertain the possibility of encouraging households in high-risk, violent crime neighborhoods to provide their own secondary level of residential defense? If the answer is affirmative, we would be encouraging people to buy handguns for protection rather than to leave law enforcement to the police.

To take the above possibility seriously would represent a new direction in the area of gun policy and one that should not be taken lightly. But if some of the estimates describing the volume of handguns currently present in American homes are accurate (Wright, Rossi, and Daly, 1983), some urban neighborhoods may have already attained the de facto status of an armed camp.

To guard against people who lack knowledge of good gun safety practices making improvident purchases, scme municipalities may wish to foster a gun policy that would encourage households in certifiable high crime neighborhoods to purchase guns specifically for household defense. If it were found useful to puruse such a policy, a series of very strict guidelines would need to be developed. Some suggested guidelines are shown below.

Persons purchasing handguns under the provisions of such a proposed policy should be required to register the weapons; to undergo special training in the defensive use of weapons and in the care and handling of weapons; and to learn to secure the weapon properly so as to minimize the possibility of its theft and to keep it out of the hands of unauthorized users. Similarly, persons operating under the provisions of such a proposed policy should be subjected to penalties for any infraction of the rules relative to the official designated use of the weapon.

The major problem might be how to deny access to proscribed individuals. But the more important philosophical consideration is whether the American public will fail to take the necessary earlier steps to ameliorate risk in high risk environments so as to negate the conditions that foster the need for a radical policy on guns.

Summary and Conclusion

During the mid-1970s, black homicide risk reached its highest level, surpassing a previous high during the Depression of the early 1930s (Holinger and Klemen, 1982). There is some evidence that homicide risk is now on the decline and that blacks as a group are somewhat less vulnerable to homicide than they were only a few years earlier. But it is also true that gratuitous and/or random acts of violence have become more widespread causing us to question the association between aggregate level risk and perceptions of environmental safety.

Even though one dimension of the problem-- aggregate national risk levels--seems to have abated, local risk levels continue to vary substantially from one black community to another. But the risk is always higher for blacks than for other races or ethnic groups in the same locality.

This paper emphasized regional variations in the structure of risk and subsequently highlighted aspects of the setting in which lethal confrontations occurred. We chose this approach in order to set the stage for demonstrating the association between observed levels of risk and availability and type of handgun.

Handgun density was high in four of our six sample communities. Only in the two cities (Los Angeles and Pittsburgh) with low handgun density in the base year (1970) was risk substantially lower than that usually observed in large central cities with sizeable black populations. Handgun density, however, appears to be increasing rather than declining, a situation that could lead to a bleak future for those who have limited options to move to a different or better home.

There is little question that the easy availability of handguns has facilitated a sharp increase in the homicide rate in the nation's larger black communities. Likewise, it is clear that effective intervention strategies will be necessary if this epidemic is to be effectively brought under control.

But the problem is complex, impinging on both values and economic opportunity in ways not fully and easily comprehended. Nevertheless, in a crude first effort, we have suggested some steps that should be considered in attempting to keep guns out of the hands of proscribed individuals, to discourage access in general, and to weaken the role of illicit gun traders as principal suppliers in selected black communities.

Ultimately, we considered the unthinkable--the promotion of a gun policy that favored distribution of weapons for home defense. One would hope such a policy would never need to be adopted. But if the factors that promote risk are not brought under control, a de facto gun policy will evolve that could have serious negative consequences.

Homicide has become a leading cause of death in the nation's larger black communities, striking with greater frequency among young adult males. Recently, the U. S. Public Health Service said that homicide had reached epidemic status and agreed to intensify their effort to bring the epidemic under control. Yet unless people are willing to address the issue of the contribution of handguns to risk, it is feared that risk will not be successfully abated. In this essay we have simply set the stage for establishing whether a feasible gun policy might be developed. If successful, such a policy would relieve the extraordinarily high levels of risk that permeate a broad range of urban black neighborhoods across the breadth of the nation.

References

Barnett, Arnold. 1982. "Learning to Live with Homicide: A Research Note," Journal of Criminal Justice, Vol. 10, pp. 69- 72.

Block, Richard. 1976. "Homicide in Chicago: A Nine Year Study (1975-1973)," The Journal of Criminal Law & Criminology, Vol. 66, No. 4, pp. 496-510.

. 1977. Violent Crime. Lexington, Mass.: Lexington Books.

Bordau, David J. and Alan J. Lizotte. 1979. "Patterns of Legal Firearms Ownership," Law and Policy Quarterly, Vol. 1, No. 2, April, pp. 147-175.

Brearley, H. C. 1932. Homicide in the United States. Chapel Hill, NC: University of North Carolina Press.

Briggs-Bruce, B. 1976. "The Great American Gun War," Public Interest, Vol. 45, pp. 38-62.

Brill, Stephen. 1977. "The Traffic (Legal and Illegal) in Guns," Harpers, September, pp. 37-44.

Calvin, Allen D. 1981. "Unemployment Among Black Youths, Demographics and Crime," Crime and Delinquency, April, pp. 234- 244.

Cohen, Lawrence E., Marcus Felson, and Kenneth Land. 1980. "Property Crime Rates in the United States: A Macrodynamic Analysis, 1947-1977, with Ex Ante Forecasts for the Mid-1980s," American Journal of Sociology, Vol. 86, No. 1, pp. 90-118.

Cook, Philip J. 1979. "The Effect of Gun Availability on Robbery and Robbery-Murder," Policy Studies Review Annual, Vol. 3. Sage Publishers, pp. 743-788.

. 1982. "The Role of Firearms in Violent Crime," Criminal Violence, Marvin E. Wolfgang and Neil A. Weiner, eds. Sage Publications, pp. 236-291.

Danto, Bruce L. 1982. "A Psychiatric View of Those Who Kill, The Human Side of Homicide, eds., Bruce L. Danto, John Bruhns and Austin K. Kutscher. Columbia University Press, pp. 3-19.

Dennis, Ruth E. 1977. "Social Stress and Mortality Among Non-white males," Phylon, Vol. 38, pp. 177-188.

Dietz, Mary L. 1983. Killing for Profit. Chicago: Nelson- Hall.

Farley, Reynolds. 1980. "Homicide Trends in the United States," Demography, Vol. 17, No. 2, pp. 177-188.

Fischer, Claude S. 1980. "The Spread of Violent Crime from City to Countryside, 1955 to 1975," Rural Sociology, Vol. 45, No. 3, pp. 416-434.

Fisher, Joseph C. 1976. "Homicide in Detroit," Criminology, Vol. 14, No. 3, pp. 387-400.

Harris, Marvin. 1981. **America Now:** The Anthropology of a Changing **Culture.** New York: Simon and Schuster.

Hoch, Irving. 1974. "Factors in Urban Crime," **Journal of Urban Economics,** Vol. 1, pp. 184-229.

Holinger, Paul C. and Elaine H. Klemen. 1982. "Violent Deaths in the United States, 1900-1975," **Social Science and Medicine,** Vol. 16, pp. 1929-1938.

Jacobson, Alvin L. 1975. "Crime Trends in Southern and Non- Southern Cities: A Twenty Year Perspective," **Social Forces,** Vol. 54, pp. 226-242.

Kaplan, John. 1979. "Controlling Firearms," **Cleveland State Law Review,** Vol. 28, No. 1, pp. 1-28.

Klebba, A. Joan. 1975. "Homicide Trends in the United States, 1900-1974," **Public Health Report,** Vol. 90, pp. 195-204.

Kleck, Gary. 1979. "Capital Punishment, Gun Ownership and Homicide," **American Journal of Sociology,** Vol. 84, pp. 882-910.

Kowalski, Gregory S., Robert L. Dittman, Jr., and Wayne L. Burg. 1980. "Spatial Distribution of Criminal Offenses by States, 1970-1976," **Journal of Research in Crime and Delinquency,** Vol. 17, No. 1, January, pp. 4-25.

Loftin, Colin and David McDowall. 1984. "The Deterrent Effects of the Florida Felony Firearm Law," **The Journal of Criminal Law and Criminology,** Vol. 75, pp. 250-259.

Lundsgaarde, Henry P. 1977. **Murder in Space City.** New York City: Oxford University Press.

McClain, Paula. 1982-83. "Environment of Risk and Determinants of Racial Attitudes Toward Gun Regulation: A Test of Social Reality Thesis," **Journal of Environmental Systems,** Vol. 12, No. 3, pp. 229-248.

McDowall, David and Colin Loftin. "Collective Security and the Demand for Handguns," **American Journal of Sociology,** Vol. 88, No. 6, pp. 1146-1161.

Moore, Mark H. 1983. "The Bird in Hand: A Feasible Strategy for Gun Control," **Journal of Policy Analysis and Management,** Vol. 2, No. 2, pp. 1825-195.

Phillips, L., H. Votey, and J. Howell. 1976. "Handguns and Homicide: Minimizing Losses and the Costs of Control," **Journal of Legal Studies,** Vol. 5, June, pp. 463-478.

Pittman, David J. and William Hardy. 1964. "Patterns of Criminal Aggravated Assault," **The Journal of Criminal Law and Criminology and Police Science,** Vol. 55, pp. 462-470.

Poussaint, Alvin F. 1983. "Black on Black Homicide: A

Psychological-Political Perspective," **Victimology**, Nos. 3 and 4, pp. 161-169.

Rossman, David and others. 1980. "Massachusetts' Mandatory Minimum Sentence Gun Law," **Criminal Law Bulletin**, Vol. 16, No. 2, March-April, pp. 150-163.

Rushforth, Norman B. and others. 1977. "Violent Death in a Metropolitan County," **New England Journal of Medicine**, Vol. 297, No. 10, 1977, pp. 531-538.

Shin, Yongsock, Devor Jedlicka, and Everett S. Lee. "Homicide Among Blacks," **Phylon**, Vol. 38, pp. 398-407.

Stinchcombe, Arthur L. and others. 1980. **Crime and Punishment-- Changing Attitudes in America.** San Francisco: Jossey-Bass Publishers.

Tardiff, Kenneth, Elliot M. Gross, and Steven F. Messner. 1986. "A Study of Homicides in Manhattan, 1981," **American Journal of Public Health**, Vol. 76, No. 2, pp. 139-143.

Turner, Charles W. and others. 1977. "The Stimulating and Inhibiting Effects of Weapons," **Aggressive Behavior**, Vol. 3, pp. 355-378.

Wolfgang, Marvin. 1958. **Patterns in Criminal Homicide.** Philadelphia: University of Pennsylvania Press.

Wright, James D., Peter Rossi, and Kathleen Daly. 1983. **Under the Gun: Weapons, Crime and Violence in America.** New York: Aldine Publishing Co.

Zimring, Franklin E. 1968. "Is Gun Control Likely to Reduce Violent Killing?" **University of Chicago Law Review**, Vol. 35, pp. 721-724, 730-737.

. 1972. "The Medium is the Message: Firearm Caliber as a Determinant of Death from Assault," **The Journal of Legal Studies**, Vol. 1, January, pp. 97-123.

. 1975. "Firearms and Federal Law: the Gun Control Act of 1968," **The Journal of Legal Studies**, Vol. 4, January, pp. 133-198.

. 1979. "Determinants of the Death Rate from Robbery: A Detroit Time Study," H. M. Rose, editor, **Lethal Aspects of Urban Violence**, Lexington, Mass.: Lexington Books, pp. 31-50.

and others. 1983. "Intimate Violence: A Study of Intersex Homicide in Chicago," **The University of Chicago Law Review**, Vol. 50, pp. 910-930.

and James Zuehl. 1986. "Victim Injury and Death in Urban Robbery: A Chicago Study," **Journal of Legal Studies**, Vol. 15, January, pp. 1-41.

PART II
EXPLAINING BLACK HOMICIDE

PART II

EXPLAINING BLACK HOMICIDE

Introduction

This section includes articles that provide statistical data but also attempt to propose more elaborate explanations for rates and patterns of black homicide than those articles included in the first section. As noted earlier, even though it has been well documented that the overall rate of homicide among blacks is much greater than that of other racial and ethnic groups, no consistent theory has been proposed to explain this difference. As also previously noted, some early analysts argued that high rates of black crime, especially homicide, was a product of the general physical and social depravity of blacks. As today, many researchers attributed this depravity to genetic differences between blacks and whites. DuBois, Sanborn and other "liberals" of the immediate post-Emancipation era stressed the sociopathology of the black population but attributed this condition to the effects of slavery. Sanborn (1904: 65) argued that high rates of black crime during the 1880s and 1890s were due to the fact that the mass of the black population was in a transient stage between slavery and freedom. He believed that the higher rates of homicide and other crimes would decrease as racial oppression was lessened and blacks became more accustomed to conditions of freedom.

There may have been a slight diminution in the rate of black homicide during the early part of the twentieth century. But as Shin et al. note in Part I of this volume, the black homicide rate began to rise around the time of World War I. By the time that the first major social scientific investigations of homicide began to appear (1930s) researchers attempted to explain the continuing high rates of this crime and others among blacks. Some researchers such as Sellin (1928, 1935) Brearley (1932) and Johnson (1941) continued to stress the role of slavery and racial prejudice in the genesis of black crime and the treatment of black offenders. But for the most part, later researchers and many analysts writing during the same period as the researchers above offered few, if any, explanations for high rates of black homicide. It may be that researchers had concluded that even well-intentioned efforts at explanation would be interpreted as racist and thus avoided the question of reasons for black-white differences.

In particular, carto-demographic studies, such as those described by Harries (1974), seldom provided elaborate explanations for the race-related rates and patterns observed. In reviewing these studies Harries observed that when one considers regional geographies of crime in the United States during the 1930s, 1950s and 1960s, the most striking finding "...is the persistence of high homicide rates in the South." (p. 16) In keeping with the researchers he reviewed, little note is made of racial differences. In a brief attempt at explaining high rates of black homicide, he concludes that "Black violence seems to be but a special case of white southern violence, in the sense that white homicide rates in the South are higher than white rates elsewhere." (p. 34) This same explanation was earlier offered by Pettigrew and Spier (1962). This explanation is based, of course, on conclusions similar to those reached by advocates of the subculture of violence hypothesis that has been used to explain regional patterns of homicide in the United States during the last quarter-century. The emphasis on regional differences rather than racial differences likely reflects a bias of carto-demographic researchers, i.e., a tendency to highlight spatial rather than group differences and to attribute any observed group differences to the unexamined social conditions that characterize geographic regions. That bias seems to have carried over into subculture of violence research which has primarily been used to explain North-South rather than racial differences in rates of homicide.

Brearley (1932) in a chapter on "The Negro and Homicide" offered additional explanations. He noted that many attempts have been made to find a satisfactory explanation for the high rate of black homicide and that these range from more credible ones to those based upon prejudice or hasty generalization. Yet, Brearley himself concludes: "there is some evidence, however, that the Negro is lacking in the power to control himself in accordance with the requirements of others." (p. 112) He goes on to suggest that the higher rates of manslaughter as compared to premeditated murder among blacks is proof of their impulsiveness. Brearley also says:

His historical background may also help to explain the Negro's attitude toward the taking of human life. In central Africa, his ancestral home, both birth and death rates are high and violent death was frequent and often unpunished, especially if the victim was a slave. A lack of regard for the person and personality of others seems to have been almost characteristic of central African culture. When the Negro was brought to America as a slave, his owners did little to encourage high esteem for the sanctity of life. On the contrary, they often treated the Negro as if he were only a relatively valuable domestic animal, disciplining him by corporal punishment, using his wives and daughters as concubines, and increasing the instability of his family by the sale or exchange of its members. This background may influence the traditions and attitudes of the Negro today and decrease his regard for the sacredness of human life. (pp. 113-114)

Variations of this theme have been used to explain high rates of black homicide for many years. This is essentially the same argument made by Curtis (1975) in his recent discussion of criminal violence among blacks in the United States. Silberman (1978) offers a similar explanation, but disavows the idea that current levels of black violence can be traced to Africa.

Wolfgang (1958) devotes surprisingly little attention to explaining the extremely disproportionate rate of black homicide in Philadelphia. However, after cautioning researchers against making hasty judgments about the link between race and crime (Wolfgang and Cohen, 1964), he proposed an essentially subcultural explanation for the high rate of black and lower class white homicide (Wolfgang and Ferracuti, 1967). Although, subcultural theory emphasizes the economic and social deprivation of blacks, the history of racial oppression in the United States is only implicitly linked to high black homicide rates. In fact, the role of slavery and racial oppression has been underemphasized by most recent researchers as contributing factors for high rates of black homicide. This has caused critics to suggest that most recent analysts, especially those in the subcultural tradition, *underestimate* the impact of slavery and racism on the etiology of black crime today. Most subcultural explanations do acknowledge the historical role played by slavery in producing present day social conditions among blacks but fail to specify how racial oppression may produce violence among blacks during more recent years. That is, subcultural values are not explicitly situated within

104

the context of racial oppression.

Indeed, it is accurate to say that conflict, social control, and racial oppression models have seldom been used to explain the etiology of black American homicide during the last 30 years. Noticeably absent are Marxist explanations. During the last few years, some researchers have begun to propose models that incorporate non-subcultural concepts. For example, some investigators have sought to incorporate concepts derived from Fanon's (1967, 1968) studies of colonial oppression and Blauner's (1972) theory of internal colonialism into the study of black American crime, including homicide. Poussaint (1972) uses such a model in his essentially psychological-psychiatric study of black homicide; and Staples (1976) utilizes a similar model in his study of race and family violence. Yet, very seldom has the work of Fanon and Blauner been fully integrated into a cohesive social theory designed to explain the continuing high rate of black homicide.

Recent quantitative studies have led to another form of explanation for high rates of black homicide. These studies most often involve multivariate analyses in an attempt to identify factors assocaited with varying rates of homicide among cities or regions. For these researchers, the racial composition of the community under study is but one of many variables considered. That is, these studies are not designed to examine black homicide, per se, nor to explain black-nonblack differences. In fact, the aggregate data used do not allow the researcher to determine the race of the offender or victim in some instances. Nevertheless, given the association between race and aggregate homicide rates, investigators have had to provide possible explanations. Some recent studies in this tradition have shown significant correlations between rates of homicide and various structural measures of inequality. This has led to suggestions that race differences in homicide are primarily attributable to social class differences including intra-race class differences (Blau and Blau, 1982; Messner, 1982; Bailey, 1982).

A review of the literature on homicide suggests that few researchers have attempted to tie together these various potential forms of explanation into a theoretical model specifically designed to explain the gap between black and nonblack homicide rates in the United States. Most researchers continue to rely upon traditional notions of subcultural differences as the major form of explanation. Thus, many questions remain regarding the reasons for the disproportionately high rate of homicide among blacks which is well documented in the first section of this volume.

A plausible theory of black homicide etiology must not only account for overall black-white differences but also for the extremely disproportionate and increasing rates of homicide among young black males. Such rates have led some researchers to posit ideas similar to those of Paul Goodman (1960) who stressed the significance of adolescence-to-adult transitions among American youth. These researchers have suggested that for youth in America's black underclass, this transition is much more problematic than for youth in other social strata. It is precisely among these young, unemployed or underemployed blacks that homicide rates are currently the highest.

The "selective inattention" (Dexter, 1958) by social scientists to a thorough examination of both the patterning of black homicide and its

105

etiology must also be viewed from a sociology of knowledge perspective. To a large extent black homicide has been ignored by social scientists and the general public because it is primarily intraracial and often perceived as an inevitable or normal occurrence within the black community. This devaluing of black life is also evident in areas of social interaction apart from homicide and crime. Black-white differences in working conditions, health care, housing, nutrition, and so forth all illustrate a lesser regard for black than for white life in the United States. The greater likelihood of the imposition of the death penalty for acts of homicide against whites than for those against blacks (see Part III of this volume) also shows the devalued status of black Americans. Thus, along the lines of reasoning suggested by Silberman (1978) we must ask whether such inattention to black homicide would exist if a larger proportion of it were interracial.

Swigert and Farrell (1976, 1977) have also argued convincingly that perceptions of not only the homicide victim but also of the homicide offender have shaped the response to homicide among black Americans. They propose that subculture of violence theory with its emphasis on the inevitability of violence among blacks is quite similar to the conception of the normal primitive that has become institutionalized in judicial procedures. The depiction of much of black America as a pathological subculture has led to little interest among researchers in conducting research that might lead to alternative explanations. Such a depiction, for example, does not foster investigations of the patterning of homicide *within* the black community. It has also meant that researchers have largely ignored the need to *explain* differential rates of homicide across regions and across social class lines *within* the black population. Potential explanations for high rates of black homicide have been so inextricably linked to views of overall black sociopathology as to severely limit the range of alternatives. At other times the causes of black homicide are seen as so obvious (given black sociopathology) that no elaborate explanation is thought to be needed.

No single paper presented in this section claims to provide a model that fully integrates these various strands of research into an explanation for high rates of black homicide. However, in the aggregate they do begin the kind of scholarly dialogue that has been neglected in the past. In the first article, Hawkins provides a review of past theories designed to explain disproportionate rates of homicide among blacks. He goes further to suggest direction for subsequent research and provides a number of testable hypotheses. Many of these hypotheses are partly derived from the subculture of violence conceptualization while others offer alternative forms of explanation. His emphasis on the behavior of the law as an etiological factor contrasts with the approaches taken by earlier researchers who generally have tended to ignore legal considerations.

The essays of Staples and Harvey are significant for their focus on explaining the disproportionately high rate of homicide found among young black males. Both of these researchers stress the need to view the problem of black male homicide in proper socioeconomic perspective. Staples also argues that black male homicide must be considered within the context of violence and aggression that has characterized life in the United States for several centuries. In his view black homicide is "normative" not because of a subculture of violence but rather because it is part of a larger pattern of American violence. Staples also probes the dynamics of family relations among blacks as these affect the black homicide rate. Harvey proposes that

106

homicide among both black males and females is largely the result of economic marginality. Both of these essays depart from traditional subcultural views of the etiology of black homicide as a result of their emphasis on "situating" black homicide within the historical-structural and normative context of American society. That is, black violence is not seen as occurring within a sociopathological substrata of the larger society. On the other hand, both researchers argue for the need to consider certain unique features of the social position of blacks in the United States that contribute to the high rate of homicide among them. This theme is also developed by Hawkins.

References

Bailey, William C. 1984. "Poverty Inequality and City Homicide Rates: Some Not So Unexpected Findings." Criminology 22 (November): 531-550.

Blau, Judith R. and Peter M. 1982. "Metropolitan Structure and Violent Crime." American Sociological Review 44 (February):114-129.

Blauner, Robert. 1972. Racial Oppression in America. New York: Harper and Row.

Brearley, H. C. 1932. Homicide in the United States. Chapel Hill, NC: University of North Carolina Press.

Curtis, Lynn A. 1975. Violence, race and culture. Lexington, MA: D. C. Heath.

Dexter, Lewis Anthony. 1958. "A Note on Selective Inattention in Social Science." Social Problems 61 (Fall): 176-82.

Fanon, Frantz. 1967. Black Skin, White Masks. New York: Grove Press.

. 1968. The Wretched of the Earth. New York: Grove Press.

Goodman, Paul. 1960. Growing Up Absurd. New York: Random House.

Hackney, Sheldon. 1969. "Southern Violence," in H. D. Graham and T. R. Gurr (eds.), Violence in America. New York: Signet Books.

Harries, Keth D. 1974. The Geography of Crime and Justice. New York: McGraw-Hill.

Johnson, Guy B. 1941. "The Negro and Crime." Annals of the American Academy of Political Science 217: 93-104.

Messner, Steven F. 1982. "Poverty, Inequality and the Urban Homicide Rate." Criminology 20 (May): 103-114.

Loftin, Colin and Robert H. Hill. 1974. "Regional Subculture and Homicide: An Examination of the Gastil-Hackney Thesis." American Sociological Review 39 (October): 714-724.

Pettigrew, Thomas F. and Rosalind B. Spier. "The Ecological Structure of

Negro Homicide." American Journal of Sociology 67 (May): 621-629.

Poussaint, Alvin. 1972. Why Blacks Kill Blacks. New York: Emerson-Hall.

Sanborn, Frank M. 1904. "Negro Crime," in W. E. B. DuBois (ed.), Proceedings of the Ninth Atlanta Conference for the Study of Negro Problems. Number 9. Atlanta: Atlanta University Press. Proceedings reprinted as Some Notes on Negro Crime, Particularly in Georgia, 1968, New York: Octagon.

Sellin, Thorsten. 1928. "The Negro Criminal: A Statistical Note." The Annals of the American Academy of Political Science 140: 52-64.

. 1935. "Race Prejudice in the Administration of Justice." American Journal of Sociology 41: 212-217.

Silberman, Charles. 1978. Criminal Violence-Criminal Justice: Criminals, Police, Courts and Prisons in America. New York: Random House.

Staples, Robert. 1976. "Race and Family Violence: The Internal Colonialism Perspective." Unpublished manuscript.

Swigert, Victoria Lynn and Ronald A. Farrell. 1976. Murder, Inequality, and the Law. Lexington, MA: D. C. Heath.

. 1977. "Normal Homicides and the Law." American Sociological Review 42 (February): 16-32.

Wolfgang, Marvin E. 1958. Patterns in Criminal Homicide. New York: Wiley.

and Bernard Cohen. 1964. Crime and Race: Conceptions and Misconceptions. New York: Institute of Human Relations Press.

and Franco Ferracuti. 1967, 1982. The Subculture of Violence: Towards an Integrated Theory in Criminology. Beverly Hills, CA: Sage Publications.

BLACK AND WHITE HOMICIDE DIFFERENTIALS:
ALTERNATIVES TO AN INADEQUATE THEORY

Darnell F. Hawkins

Over the last 50 years or more, social science studies and official crime statistics have shown consistently higher rates of homicide among American blacks than among whites. Recent data suggest that the black homicide rate is also substantially higher than that of other disadvantaged minority groups such as Hispanics (Silberman, 1978).[1] Indeed, given the fact that white American rates of homicide are higher than those of many other countries, the black American rate of homicide may be among the highest in the world. Bohannon (1960) showed that they far exceed those found in African societies.

Somewhat surprisingly, social scientists have not done much about assessing and explaining black criminal violence (in comparison to other areas of actual or perceived sociopathology among blacks). There may be several reasons for the relative neglect of this question. First, during the last two decades criminologists have shown decreasing interest in the study of crime etiology. Labeling and conflict theory have shifted attention to the society's part in defining crime and deviance, and in the identification and processing of criminal offenders. Thus, social researchers have chosen to study such topics as patterns of racial discrimination in arrest and sentencing rather than the causes of pathological behavior. Second, black-white crime difference has been a socially and politically sensitive topic during the last twenty years. Some researchers have tended to underemphasize such differences. Finally, it appears that the preeminence of subcultural theory among criminologists has prevented the kind of critical discourse and analysis needed for the study of this topic and many others. Subculture of violence theory has remained the most widely used sociological explanation for the etiology of criminal homicide.

Today, there is renewed interest in the etiology of crime, especially crimes of violence. In this regard, Hindelang (1981) has suggested that sociological theorists of crime must begin to use clues provided by known correlates of criminal behavior as a basis for generating and modifying theory. However, it is also obvious that the traditional notions of crime causation must be reconceptualized to include a variety of concerns raised by labeling and conflict theorists and by current and historical studies of crime and criminal justice.[2]

In this paper I present a theoretical framework for the study of homicide among blacks in the United States. First, I assess the statistical evidence. Next, I discuss and criticize competing theories that are designed to explain disproportionately high rates of black homicide--particularly the concept of a subculture of violence. Finally, I offer three theoretical propositions, along with conclusions and hypotheses, as supplementary or alternative to subculture of violence theory for the disproportionately high rate of homicide offending and victimization among American blacks.

Incidence of Homicide, Blacks and Whites

Studies conducted by Brearley (1932), Wolfgang (1958), Pokorny (1965a), Voss and Hepburn (1968), Boudouris (1970), Block (1975), Lundsgaarde (1977), and Farley (1980) are among those which have provided data on the extent of black homicide in the United States. Shin, et al. (1977) provide one of the most comprehensive recent summaries of national trends in homicide victimization. They note that during the twentieth century homicide rate trends have been different for blacks and whites. From 1910 to 1930 the white rate was relatively stable at about 4 to 5 per 100,000 population. By 1940 the rate was around 2. The pre-World War II rates for blacks were more irregular. The rate was 22 in 1910, 43 during the middle 1920s and down to 26 in 1940. The downward trend continued for both blacks and whites until 1955 when rates began to increase considerably. However, it is shown that for blacks the proportional increases were less than for whites through 1974, when the researchers end their investigation.

Shin, et al. (1977) also provide sex- and age- specific data which show more clearly the patterns of black homicide victimization. From 1940 to 1974 the black male homicide rate had increased from 57 to 78 per 100,000. They report that in 1973, nonwhite males between the ages of 25 and 34 had a homicide rate of 153 compared to 15 for white males in this age range. Rates for black men in this age range have shown a decline since 1973; however, recent data supplied by the Public Health Service show that homicide has replaced accidents as the leading cause of death for young, nonwhite men.3 In addition, the homicide offense and victimization rates among black women have ranged from two to four times the rates of white men (Wolfgang, 1958; Shin, et al., 1977).

Since homicide is primarily an intraracial phemenon, high rates of black victimization indicate similarly high rates of black offending. However, as in the study of other types of crime, official homicide offense statistics vary in quality and reliability. The Uniform Crime Reports (UCR) of the Federal Bureau of Investigation provide arrest data for homicide offenders and for the last twenty years also provide some victimization data. Because of the methods for reporting crime used by the FBI, race-, sex-, and age-specific offense data have not always been readily available. Though the proportion of all homicides committed by nonblacks has increased over the last twenty years, the incidence among blacks is still four to five times greater than what one would expect given the relative size of the black population, i.e., 10%-12% during those decades (See UCR, 1960-80).

While these statistics raise a number of social, political and moral questions, the social scientist's task has been to provide an explanation for the disproportionately high rates of criminal homicide among black Americans.4 Are the rates accurate? If they are, what factors account for the black-white differentials observed? Many commentators have urged caution in using aggregate crime rates to propose a causal link between race and crime despite the obvious racial imbalance in statistics (e.g. Bonger, 1943, and Wolfgang and Cohen, 1964).

Patterning of Black Homicide

The notes of caution raised by Bonger (1943) and Wolfgang and Cohen (1964) emphasize the need for more detailed examination of homicide patterns among blacks. Which segments of the black population have the highest rates? Is the social patterning of homicide in the black community similar to that found among whites? While the black rate of arrests for all crimes is higher than the white rate, residential patterns are evident. Uniform Crime Reports data for 1975 show that blacks living in rural areas constituted 10% of the rural population and made up 10% of arrests for all types of crimes. The black suburban population was 15%, while only 12% of all suburban arrestees were black. A large discrepancy between population figures and arrest rates was evident only in urban areas.5 While this was not an analysis of homicide rates, a further examination of homicide statistics may yield similar findings.

Pettigrew and Spier (1962) found that black homicide rates differed by regions of the country. They conclude that a ranking of states on the basis of black homicide rates is similar to a ranking based upon white rates. A recent analysis of homicide rates in Atlanta found blacks and whites of similar socioeconomic status (SES) to have similar rates of family and acquaintance homicide (Centerwall, 1982). Blau and Blau (1982) report that while poverty, per se, does not explain rates of violent crime in urban areas, such rates are significantly related to income inequality between blacks and whites and to SES inequality among blacks themselves.

All of the studies reported above are ecological analyses. Consequently, they provide no data on the characteristics of individual offenders and victims, such as those required to examine the social patterning of black homicide in the United States. Indeed, a few non-ecological studies do exist (Pokorny, 1965a; Boudouris, 1970; and Lundsgaarde, 1977). However, the amount of data they provide on variables such as the SES of black or white homicide offenders and victims goes little beyond the kind of data provided in the pioneering work of homicide in Philadelphia by Wolfgang (1958). Most studies generally conclude that homicide victims and offenders are more likely to be black, poor, undereducated, and to reside in the South.

The Subculture of Violence: American Blacks

Analysts in the subcultural tradition appear to have proceeded on the basis of two rather plausible assumptions. First, they have noted that criminal homicide statistics in contrast to data for other types of crime are less subject to distortion by police and other criminal justice officials, e.g., by differing patterns of detection and prosecution. There are also high clearance rates for homicide cases in comparison to other crimes. Thus, they conclude that consistently high rates of black homicide represent a **real** phenomenon. Further, to the extent that whites and other racial groups do not display similar levels of violence, the cause does not lie within the whole of American culture.

Wolfgang and Ferracuti (1967) were among the first to propose the idea of a subculture of violence as a potentially integrating theory for explaining and predicting various patterns of criminal homicide. Certain subgroups in

111

America are said to live in a cultural and social milieu which encourages physical aggression, or at least does not actively discourage it. Wolfgang and Feracutti noted that on the basis of an awareness of social, economic and political disparities between whites and blacks, any diligent researcher would propose that the black crime rate would be higher than the white rate and that there would be a "large spread to the learning of, resort to and criminal display of the violence value among minority groups such as Negroes" (1967: 264).

Subculture of violence theory, therefore, tends to identify the value system of a given subculture as the locus of crime causation. Emphasis is also placed upon the role of social learning as the principal process by which aggressive behavior is acquired. While there is some attention paid to the social, economic and political deprivation within subcultures, such deprivation is itself seldom seen as a direct cause of crime. That is, the impact of deprivation on crime is mediated by social values--in particular the existence of a positive attitude toward the use of violence. Most subculture of violence theorists have focused on explaining the northern-southern differentials in homicide rather than black-white differentials. Hackney (1969), Gastil (1971), Erlanger (1974); Loftin and Hill (1974), Reed (1971) and Doerner (1975) have sought to provide explanations for the higher-than-average violent crime rates of the southern United States.

The high rates of both southern and black homicide have led to additional speculation. For example, it has been suggested that the high homicide rates of blacks may be related to their lower class, southern heritage. That is, blacks share with lower- class southern whites a common subculture of violence (Pettigrew and Spier, 1962). Block (1975) found not race but the percentage of residents who had migrated from the South to be the stronger correlate of violent crime in an analysis of Chicago data. City areas with large concentrations of southerners, whether black or white, tended to have higher rates of violent crime than those populated by non-southerners. Others have questioned this explanation for black homicide rates (Gastil, 1971), since black-white differentials appear to persist across regions and within similar socioeconomic strata (Wolfgang, 1958).

Recent studies have begun to look more specifically at the relationship between race, the history of blacks in the United States, and criminal violence but often continue to rely upon traditional subcultural explanations. Both Curtis (1974, 1975) and Silberman (1978) suggest that slavery and other slavery-linked factors may produce the observed high rates of black criminal violence. Like earlier analysts, Curtis (1975) linked black criminal violence to "a black poverty subculture" which potentially has both African and American slave origins. He relies partly on the subculture of poverty thesis of Lewis (1959). Silberman (1978), on the other hand, takes a subcultural approach but quotes Bohannon (1960) to argue that the propensity to violence is not part of the cultural heritage American blacks brought from Africa. Rather, he concluded that "violence is something black Americans learned in this country" (1978: 123). Silberman goes on to attribute present rates of criminal violence among blacks to the violence used by whites to perpetuate slavery and later violence used to maintain discrimination and white economic superiority. Like Blauner (1972), Silberman argues that the black experience has been different in kind not just degree from other American racial-ethnic groups.

Critique of Subculture of Violence Theory
and An Alternative Model

The empirical basis for subculture of violence theory has been extremely limited and unpersuasive. While it has often been asserted that blacks or white southerners possess distinct criminogenic subcultural values, few efforts have been made to adequately assess the nature of such values. In an empirical study of value orientations toward violence, Erlanger (1974) and Blumenthal, et al. (1971) found no support for the idea that the poor or nonwhites are more favorable toward violence than are more affluent persons and whites. Such evidence of a lack of empirical grounding has caused Loftin and Hill (1974) to assert that the idea of a cultural basis of regional variations in homicide is the result of an uncritical assessment of questionable research.

Fine and Kleinman (1979) have offered a general critique of the notion of subculture as it is used by social scientists. Many of their criticisms are relevant for understanding the limitations of subculture of violence theory. They note that problems in previous subculture research include: (1) a confusion of the ideas of subculture and subsociety, (2) the lack of a meaningful referent for subculture, (3) the homogeneity and stasis associated with the concept, and (4) the emphasis on defining subcultures in terms of values and central themes. They suggest that the subculture construct, to be of maximal usefulness, needs to be linked to processes of interaction among members of groups.

The usual problems of separating concepts of SES and subculture have also been evident in subculture of violence theory and research. That is, how much of a given homicide rate is attributable to each of these variables? How might one empirically separate the effects of each of these dimensions in a meaningful way? Wolfgang (1958) offered some limited evidence that black homicide rates in Philadelphia could not be accounted for on the basis of social class alone; but he could only speculate as to other possible causal factors. Though economic factors often determine the contours and boundaries of a given subculture, subcultural theorists have seldom attempted to link such conditions to homicide as Bonger (1969) has done. The concerns raised above point out several major weaknesses of subculture of violence theory: (1) There is an extreme emphasis on mentalistic value orientations of individuals--orientations which in the aggregate are said to produce a subculture. (2) The theory lacks empirical grounding and indeed is put in question by some empirical findings. (3) Much of the theory has tended to underemphasize a variety of structural, situational and institutional variables which affect interpersonal violence. For blacks, these variables range from historical patterns developed during slavery to the immediate social context of an individual homicidal offense to the operation of the criminal justice system, past and present. (4) Subcultural theory underemphasizes the effects of the law on patterns of criminal homicide. (5) There are other plausible ways apart from the inculcation of values by which the economic, political and social disadvantages of American blacks may produce high rates of homicide.

Gouldner (1974) has suggested that the study of criminology involves the critical understanding of both the larger society and of the broadest social

113

theory, as well as phenomena and theory peculiar to crime. Yet on the whole, criminological theory, including subculture of violence theory, has relied upon a rather limited subset of the broader body of social theory and research, e.g., see Taylor et al. (1974, 1975).

In the next part of the paper, I propose a series of general theoretical concepts which draw upon a variety of social science theory to explain rates of black criminal homicide. Diagram 1 is a summary of these concepts and provides a guide to the remainder of the paper. I begin with an historical-structural framework and rely upon studies of American race relations. This historical analysis is supplemented by a consideration of present situational, legal and sociocultural factors thought to affect rates of criminal violence. The framework as proposed will not meet all of the theoretical and methodological requirements demanded of a fully explanatory model and is not intended to do so. Rather, I attempt to integrate some of the important theoretical concerns raised by past studies of criminal homicide with those derived from non-crime research and theory in order to suggest plausible topics for future research.

Proposition 1. American Criminal Law: Black Life is Cheap but White Life is Valuable

Criminal violence is a legally defined and regulated phenomenon. The importance of that fact is most often underemphasized in sociological theories of crime etiology. Criminal violence and other categories of crime cannot be understood without consideration of the part played by criminal law and the criminal justice system in the attempted regulation of criminal behavior. Subcultural theory has ignored the historical and present day interaction between the legal and extra-legal factors that affect crime. There appears to be an assumption made in such theory that the official treatment of black and white crime and criminals is the same. Yet, an abundance of historical and contemporary data and theory refutes that assumption even for so serious an offense as criminal homicide.

Black (1976, 1979) argues that law is a form of governmental social control. It is also a variable and quantifiable aspect of social life. How the law behaves in any given situation is a function of the location of victims and offenders in the stratification system, organization, culture and so forth. He notes that law is affected by the distance between victims and offenders along various social dimensions such as social class, race, ethnicity and other similar factors. If criminal law and criminal justice in the United States are viewed in historical perspective, Black's theory is well grounded.

At the beginning of the slavery era, the killing of a slave by his master was not considered a criminal offense. Whites, including non-slaveowning whites, were permitted to injure slaves with impunity. At the same time, the killing of a white person by a black slave was considered one of the most heinous offenses. The constant fear of black insurrection led to swift and cruel punishment for blacks who offended against whites (see Hindus, 1980). Of course, since slaves were an economic investment, there was some incentive on the part of slavemasters to refrain from large scale executions or excessive punishment of offending slaves (see Fogel and Engerman, 1974; and David et al. 1976).

114

DIAGRAM 1

A CAUSAL MODEL OF BLACK HOMICIDE

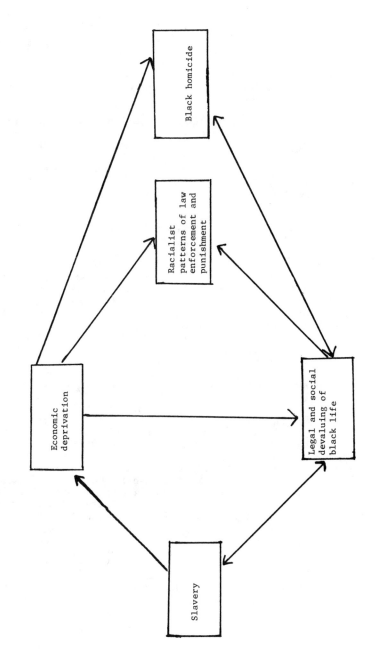

By the 1850s most southern states still had state statutes and local ordinances which made certain acts crimes only if they were perpetrated by slaves. Where crimes were not racially defined, there were nevertheless explicit, statutorily defined differences in punishment (Mangum, 1940). Capital offenses such as murder and rape were usually covered by such statutes. Murder was differentially punished based upon the racial identity of the victim and offender. Though there is some question regarding the extent to which these laws were actually implemented in given cases, the codified law was undeniably racist.

The legal cheapening of black life and the concomitant valuing of white life was not based primarily on racist ideas of inferiority and superiority. Rather, offenses against whites by black slaves were punished more severely because they came to represent an attack on the social order. The symbolic and non-symbolic structures of authority in the antebellum South were ones in which whites regardless of their social status had the right to control many aspects of the lives of black slaves.

Many analysts would suggest that the historical patterns described above are legal and social anachronisms today and have no impact upon the way the criminal law currently defines and punishes criminal behavior.[6] The various civil rights acts of the 1860s and 70s and the 14th Amendment specifically addressed the issue of differential punishment for crime. Despite legal reforms of that era and later which removed many of the obviously racist definitions of criminal behavior and provisions for punishment, there is evidence that some of these historical patterns have not been completely changed. Even where changed they may have set in motion certain historical-structural forces which affect the lives of blacks today. Consider for example the rank order of the seriousness of black and white homicides.

A Hierarachy of Homicide Seriousness

The idea of a racial hierarchy for the treatment of homicide offenders is not new in social science research. As early as 1941, Johnson proposed such a model. Follow-up studies have been conducted by Garfinkel (1949), Green (1964), Farrell and Swigert (1978) and Radelet (1981). These have been primarily studies of the extent to which the race of the offender and victim affect the amount of punishment administered. These studies assume the existence of antebellum origins for this racial hierarchy, but only Johnson attempts specifically to link it to pre- twentieth century social values. None of these studies suggests that such a hierarchy may be linked to rates of black homicide, as I do in the present discussion. That is, the legal cheapening of black life is seen to affect the behavior of the criminal justice system but not to have a causal effect on criminal behavior.

Johnson (1941) studied racial differences in sentencing in three states of the South during the 1930s and 1940s. He proposed that in the South black versus black homicides would be treated with undue leniency, while black versus white offenses would be treated with undue severity. The following ranking from most serious to least serious was hypothesized: "(1) Negro versus white, (2) white versus white, (3) Negro versus Negro and (4) white versus Negro.". Data from courts in Virginia, North Carolina, and Georgia tended to support this rank order of seriousness. A greater proportion of blacks who killed whites were executed once sentenced than was true of whites who killed whites. Least likely to be executed were blacks who murdered blacks. Only a small number of cases of whites murdering blacks were noted, thus few conclusions could be reached as to seriousness of this offense.[7] Garfinkel reported similar findings.

Kleck (1981) found racial bias to exist only in the South and asks whether previous findings apply to the non-South. Other researchers have warned that observed black-white differences in punishment for murder may be caused by a variety of unexamined factors. Among such factors are the social status of the offender and victim (Farrell and Swigert, 1978); the legal seriousness of the offense, e.g. degree of premeditation or the commission along with another felony (Green, 1964); and whether victim and offender are acquainted (Parker and Smith, 1979 and Smith and Parker, 1980). Lundsgaarde (1977) reported that Houston murderers charged with killing family persons (primary homicide) received less severe punishment than those charged with killing non-family persons (nonprimary homicide). Radelet (1981) controlled for some of these factors in a recent study of homicide sentencing.

Radelet found that overall there were no strong racial differences for his sample of 637 homicide cases in either the probability of being indicted for first degree murder or in the overall probability of being sentenced to death. However, blacks accused of murdering whites were more likely to be sentenced to death than blacks who were accused of murdering other blacks. This trend was due to the higher probability for those accused of murdering whites (whether black or white offenders) to be indicted for first degree murder. Significantly, nonprimary (stranger) homicides in which there were white victims were more likely to result in a first degree indictment than those nonprimary homicides with black victims. He concludes that the race of the victim, as well as the offender, must be considered in studies of sentencing disparities.

These studies suggest that a variety of factors convedge to determine the seriousness of a homicide. Many of these factors are not considered in recent studies of crime seriousness such as that of Rossi, et al. (1974). They also suggest that in a racially stratified society such as that in the United States, race remains a crucial determining variable. The response of the legal system toward black offenders and victims of homicide has created a racial hierarchy of homicide offenses. I suggest that such a hierarchy has direct and indirect effects on the etiology of homicide among blacks. These are discussed under the second proposition. Below, I suggest a scale of seriousness of homicide offenses which emerged from historical patterns of race relations in the American South. This scale assumes that where legally-relevant factors such as prior record and the brutality of the act are controlled for, racial differences will still be evident. There is also an assumption that social class differences alone will not fully explain levels of the hierarchy.

117

Rating	Offense
Most serious	Black kills White, in authority
	Black kills White, stranger
	White kills White, in authority
	Black kills White, friend, acquaintance
	Black kills White, intimate, family
	White kills White, stranger
	White kills White, friend, acquaintance
	White kills White, intimate, family
	Black kills Black, stranger
	Black kills Black, friend, acquaintance
	Black kills Black, intimate, family
	White kills Black, stranger
	White kills Black, friend, acquaintance
Least serious	White kills Black, intimate, family

Conclusions and Testable Hypotheses

Conclusion 1: Rates of criminal violence among American blacks, in comparison to other nonwhites and white ethnics, are attributable to their unique history of slavery and oppression.

Conclusion 2: The historical behavior of American law, especially in the South, created a hierarchy of the seriousness of criminal violence based primarily on the racial identity of and relationship between the victim and offender.

Conclusion 3: During slavery and in the immediate post-Reconstruction South, offenses committed by blacks against whites were seen as attacks on the racial social order.

Hypothesis 1: Past and present indices of official sanctioning of homicide offenders will reveal harshest penalties for offenses of blacks against whites, who are in positions of authority and/or who are strangers to the offender. Least severely sanctioned will be offenses occurring among interracial acquaintances or family members where whites are offenders.

Hypothesis2: Studies of black American public opinion will reveal blacks to believe that the behavior of the law protects the lives of whites more than the lives of blacks.

Proposition 2: Past and present racial and social class differences in the administration of justice affect black criminal violence.

Even if it can be shown that the historical patterns described above are accurately depicted, one must still explain how such patterns affect rates of black homicide today. The conclusions reached thus far do not rule out the possibility of a slavery- produced subculture of violence among blacks. However, as noted above, a simplistic pro-violence explanation may be inadequate for describing people's attitudes toward criminal violence. Violence, including homicidal aggression, is more acceptable under certain circumstances than it is under others. There are several plausible explanations of black criminal homicide that are not fully included in subculture of violence theory.

One such explanation is that blacks kill each other at higher rates because the legal system is seen as administering punishment unfairly. On the basis of the past behavior of the law, blacks may have come to believe that aggressive behavior of all types directed by blacks against each other will be tolerated and seldom severely punished. The only solution then becomes a kind of vigilantism for the handling of intraracial violence. Homicide becomes a form of conflict resolution (Levi, 1980).

This suggests that in addition to historical factors the present behavior of the law affects rates of black criminal violence. An assumption underlying any system of law enforcement is the idea that crime should not only be punished as a matter of just deserts but also that punishment serves to deter or prevent crime. Consequently, one plausible explanation for black homicide rates is that blacks kill blacks at a higher rate because there is less of a legal deterrent to such behavior among blacks than among whites. To the extent that homicide is a preventable or deterrable crime, one must

119

examine the role of law enforcement authorities in the genesis of black homicide, i.e., the official responses to homicide and pre-homicide behaviors. McNeeley and Pope (1981) provide recent analyses of black-white differences in the administration of justice.

Post-homicide Punishment as a Deterrent

Though blacks have higher rates of interracial homicide than whites, Silberman (1978) and others have noted that given the extent of racial oppression in the United States it is surprising that there is not more black violence directed at whites. Some would suggest that the historical patterns of swift and often cruel punishment for blacks who have murdered whites have served to deter such behavior. On the other hand, leniency in the treatment of black intraracial offenders may tend to encourage black-on-black aggression.

There is questionable empirical support for the deterrence effect on homicide of either a merely subjective perception of legal sanctions or of such perceptions with objective reinforcement, e.g., existence of a capital punishment statute as well as frequent use of the statute. Some studies have shown deterrent effects while others show none, e.g., see Gibbs (1975), Erlich (1975), and Kleck (1979). Few, if any, studies have looked at differential deterrence paeffects based on victim characteristics, such as that proposed in this discussion.

Parker and Smith (1979) attempted to assess the effects of punishment on homicide deterrence while controlling for the victim/offender relationship. They classified homicides into "primary," family and acquaintance, and "nonprimary," felony-murder, stranger and non-intimate offenses. Certainty of punishment was found to affect significantly nonprimary homicide rates but not primary rates. Etiological variables such as the level of poverty, were found to be better predictors of primary homicide rates. This finding supports the common speculation among law enforcement officials and criminologists that primary homicides are crimes of passion and are not deterred by perceptions of punishment.8 What is needed, however, is classification of past punishment for homicide into race and relationship of offender- victim categories in order to test possible race- related differences in deterrence.9

Even if it can be shown that patterns of punishment for homicide vary on the basis of racial characteristics and that punishment serves to deter homicide, one must still explain the large gap between black and white rates of intraracial offending. That is, why do blacks kill each other at much higher rates than whites kill whites? Why does expected punishment more effectively deter blacks from killing whites but not other blacks? Similarly, given the comparative leniency accorded white interracial offenders, why is this category of offending so small?

Some explanations may be offered. Most homicides involve family members or acqaintances and consequently are intraracial in a racially segregated society such as the United States. To the extent that there has been a devaluation of black life within a racially segregated society, such devaluation will result in homicide. Blacks will not murder whites both because white life is not similarly devalued and because of an absence of social interactions of the type that generally lead to homicide. On the other hand, despite the devaluation of black life, whites will seldom murder blacks because of limited interaction. All of these explanations, however, rely on social values and norms to explain the act of pahomicide. Below, I suggest that there are other factors to be considered.

Pre-Homicide Behaviors and the Lack of Deterrence

There is growing evidence that the way administration of justice agencies respond to various situational and circumstantial conditions preceding a homicide offense may profoundly affect the etiology of criminal violence. Much criminal homicide, for example, occurs among family members or acquaintances and is often preceded by somewhat predictable patterns of pre-homicide behavior.10 There is some evidence that the racial identity of the potential victim and offender may affect the way that the police, prosecutors, the courts, and other officials respond to pre-homicide events.

Because a given homicidal act usually occurs within the context of a social relationship, homicide may often be anticipated. In many instances, these pre-homicide events take the form of assault and may come to the attention of the public and/or law enforcement officials. Dunn (1976:10) suggests that to the extent that assaults among family members are reported, these may represent "attempted homicides nipped in the bud." He notes, however, that this is an inference and is not based on definitive data. The same effects of the reporting of assaults and other pre-homicide behaviors may also affect patterns of homicide outside the family. Studies of assault have shown patterns similar to those observed for homicide (Pittman and Hardy, 1964; Pokorny, 1965b; and Dunn, 1976). Assaults generally can be divided into primary and nonprimary categories, and are usually intraracial. Few, if any, studies have explored the link between a given homicide and assault as a prehomicide occurrence prior to the commission of the act.

In a society characterized by racial stratification, race may be a crucial factor in determining whether acts of aggression lead to death, and the response of law enforcement officials may be of importance. Several studies have probed the behavior of police in minority communities. Many of their findings support the conclusion that majority and minority relations with the police differ in crucial ways--ways that might affect the etiology of crime, such as homicide.

Bayley and Mendelsohn (1969) and Bernard (1978) cite data which show that (1) blacks have more negative perceptions of police than do whites; (2) blacks have more contact with police than whites, but these experiences are less satisfactory than those reported by whites; (3) in several large American cities minority groups filed by far the largest numbers of complaints about police misconduct. Barnard notes that factors other than racism mayexplain the findings; he also reports that the moreviolent the crime for which the person is suspected, the greater is the discrepancy between the treatment afforded white citizens and black citizens.11

A crucial question for the study of the etiology of homicide is whether black-white differences in perceptions and experiences with police lead to either a tendency for blacks to underreport prehomicide-type behavior or to differences in police response to black and white complainants. In a study of police service delivery in three cities, Ostrom (1978) reports that blacks do not differ from white respondents in their likelihood to report crimes nor in their reasons for not reporting crimes. However, black respondents were more likely than whites to report slower police response times to victimization calls for service. There are some questions regarding the conclusiveness and generalizability of Ostrom's findings, but they do provide a stimulus for further research on this question.

The police are not the only agents of social control who may influence patterns of homicide. Prosecutors and the courts also play crucial roles. Swigert and Farrell (1977) have provided some empirical bases for speculation regarding racial differences in homicide prosecution. These researchers, using data from a sample of persons arrested for murder, found that a stereotype of the violent offender, the "normal primitive" affects legal decision making. Blacks and individuals of lower occupational status were assigned this label more often than were whites or higher status persons. The eventual result of such a label was more severe convictions by the court. Garfinkel (1949) suggests a pasimilar typing of black offenders may result in less severe punishment when blacks kill each other.

I suggest that the official view of violent behavior as normal among blacks, especially lower class blacks, also affects the etiology of black homicide. This happens in several ways. First, pre- homicide behavior among blacks will be treated more leniently by public law enforcement officials than similar behaviors among whites or behaviors directed by blacks against whites. That is, the hierarchy of values for homicide perceptions also affects pre- homicide offenses. This means that police, prosecutors and courts will be more likely to arrest, charge and convict persons accused of interracial assaults or intraracial assaults among whites than those accused of black-on-black assaults.

Of course, many intraracial assaults mark domestic disputes. Such disputes account for 40-50% of all homicides in some studies. This poses many problems for both police and prosecutorial intervention in the pre-homicide behavior of whites and blacks. Police are sometimes unable and/or reluctant to intervene in family matters. However, for black lower class offenders who commit a disproportionate number of assaults and homicides, racial and class factors further reduce the probability of intervention. Such behavior may be seen as normal among such persons and as therefore unpreventable, or police may fear for their own safety when called to intervene in black lower class neighborhoods, whether such intervention involves domestic or non-domestic disputes. On the other hand, fear of police brutality may cause blacks to underreport assaultive behavior. This mutual distrust and fear will often lead to ineffective intervention in instances which are known to present the potential for homicide.

We need, then, studies (so far largely lacking) of such precursors to homicide as repeated assaults, verbal threats, and so forth. Such a longitudinal view is missing in past studies of homicide etiology and homicide patterning. Further, I argue that the way in which police and other public officials respond to instances of reported assault tends to mirror the historical hierarchy noted for official response to homicide. That is, racial and social class variables affect official responses and these race or class based differences may affect rates of criminal homicide.

Of course, assaults are much more numerous than homicides and occur in various contexts. While not all assaults lead to homicide, many homicides are preceded by patterns of reported assault, especially aggravated assaults. Criminologists must examine more carefully the patterns such prehomicide offenses tend to take and the link between them and acts of homicide.

There is also some evidence that other kinds of official response to aggressive behavior in minority communities may affect the etiology of homicide. For example, the extent to which emergency medical care is provided may mean the difference between an attempted murder or a murder statistic. The provision of emergency medical care, like medical care in general, may reflect patterns of racial and socioeconomic stratification. Thus, medical care must be seen as an important situational variable in the etiology of homicide.

In conclusion, I have suggested that official responses over time to situations of aggressive behavior in black, lower class communities may be a neglected variable in the study of causes of black homicide. A homicide statistic must be seen as more than the result of a discrete, time-bound act on the part of a criminal offender. Rather, aspects of the social context, such as prehomicide behavior, police response to citizen complaints, perceptions of police, actions of prosecutors and courts, and medical service delivery may determine whether relatively common incidences of aggressive behavior lead to murder. Official responses to black potential homicide offenders are influenced by patterns of both social class stratification and race bias.

Conclusions and Testable Hypotheses

Conclusion 1: The response of police, prosecutors and courts to prehomicide type behaviors affects the rate of homicide.

Conclusion 2: Official response to prehomicide behaviors, such as assault, are affected by such factors as the race and social class of victims and offenders.

Conclusion 3: Like homicide itself, prehomicide behavior among the poor and blacks is likely to be perceived by law enforcement authorities as "normal" and inevitable.

Hypothesis 1: Intraracial, prehomicide violence among blacks will be less likely to be reported to police than such offenses will be among whites.

Hypothesis 2: Where reported, proportionately more of such encounters among blacks will eventually lead to homicide. This difference will be partly due to the failure of police to intervene at the same level for black-white and white- white aggression.

Hypothesis 3: Measures of response time and other indices of police availability and cooperativeness will show greater availability and cooperativeness for interracial acts of criminal violence than for intraracial acts. Police will be less responsive to intraracial acts of violence among blacks than among whites. But social class variations will also be a factor. Greatest responsiveness will be to acts of violence among affluent whites and least responsiveness to lower class blacks.

Hypothesis 4: Patterns of punishment for prehomicide type behavior, such as aggravated assault, will mirror those for homcide. Most punishment will be given for black on white assaults involving a white authority person or stranger and least punishment will be given for black on black assaults among family or intimates.

Proposition 3: Economic deprivation creates a climate of powerlessness in which individual acts of violence are likely to take place.

While there may be some debate regarding the exent to which criminal statistics reflect the actual incidence of crime, there is agreement that persons arrested and charged with homicide are more likely to be not only a member of a minority group but also poor and undereducated. A recent survey conducted by the Law Enforcement Assistance Administration (LEAA) shows the extent of these trends for inmates sentenced and serving time in State prisons in 1974.12

The survey showed that of black inmates being held for all categories of crime, only 21% were high school graduates or higher. Of all black inmates with less than an eighth grade education, 24% were sentenced for murder and 10% were sentenced for manslaughter. Sixty-eight percent of all prisoners with less than an eighth grade education were charged with a violent crime.

Income and employment status data indicated similar disadvantage for black inmates in comparison to white inmates and to non-inmate blacks. For blacks sentenced in all categories of crime, the median family income was $4,100. One third of the inmate families earned less than $3,000 in the year prior to their initial arrest. Sixty-four percent earned less than $6,000. Only 9% of black inmates made more than $10,000. As expected, black inmates tended to come from lower status occupations and to have high rates of unemployment. Eighty-three percent of black inmates were employed as blue collar or service workers just prior to arrest. This compared to 74% of the entire black male population being employed in these occupations. Finally, 39% of all black inmates were unemployed or working only part-time in the year prior to arrest. The study concluded that there was little relationship between income and type of crime for which an inmate had been sentenced. However, the low SES of all, whether imprisoned for property or violent offenses, was far below national norms, including the official poverty level. paDespite the perennial debate among criminologists regarding the extent to which prison populations are representative of all criminal offenders and the extent to which official statistics distort the criminality of the poor and minorities, several conclusions appear warranted. First, "street" crimes of the type most likely to be included in official crime statistics are more likely to be committed by blacks and lower class persons than by other groupings. Second, the data above and those from numerous other studies of homicide provide reasonable support for the idea that poor and undereducated blacks are disproportionately represented among persons who have committed criminal violence, especially homicide.

If not subcultural factors (which I discussed later), what is the link between low SES and criminal violence among American blacks? Above, I argued that black poverty and crime must be seen in proper legal- historical perspective. However, historical data do not adequately explain why it is that present day criminal violence occurs more often among lower class than among middle class blacks. Almost all American blacks are descended from

124

families that were enslaved. Those who are not descendants of slaves have been nevertheless affected by the persisting patterns of prejudice and discrimination in the United States. The data on the SES of homicide offenders suggest that an adequate theory must explore the direct link between present-day black disadvantage and violent crime.

In the past, most often researchers have examined the relationship between economic condition and property crime. Blau and Blau (1982) have shown, however, that such factors also have an impact upon the murder rate within urban areas. They suggest that the traditional idea of relative deprivation might best account for such effects. A number of studies have shown that homicide offenders and victims, in comparison to suicide victims, have lower SES. Davis and Short (1978) have provided data and a theoretical model to examine black suicide in the United States. They note that integration into the community decreased the probability of suicide and that an increase in status was positively associated with increases in suicide. Social integration factors may also affect rates of homicide among blacks.

Rose (1978, 1981) has examined the relationship between aggregate measures of neighborhood stress and the black homicide rate. Although his approach is similar to that of earlier studies of ecological social disorganization, he provides new insight and data for understanding the wide variation in homicide within the black community. Since the work of Brearley (1932), it has been shown that the black homicide rate is much higher in some cities than in others. Rose shows that these rates are often correlated with various economic and related stress factors (overcrowding, health conditions, etc.). These conditions resulted in what he called "the geography of despair."

Unlike subcultural theory, I suggest that the path between black socioeconomic disadvantage and crime is not mediated by the intervening variable-- cultural values. Rather, such disadvantage generates sociopathological conditions in which violent crime among lower class blacks represents a socially disapproved, but predictable, effort to achieve some measure of control in an environment characterized by social, political and economic powerlessness. This type of psychologically oriented theory as an explanation for black criminal violence has been suggested by Fanon (1967, 1968) Grier and Cobbs (1968) and May (1972).

Fanon (1967, 1968) offered a psychoanalytic interpretation of the problems of blacks living under colonial rule. He suggested that intraracial violence represents a form of repressed aggression which will be reduced only when colonized peoples succeed in directing their aggression against the colonizer during acts of revolution. Grier and Cobbs (1968) described the almost constant state of rage found among blacks living in American society and noted the deleterious effects of such rage. May (1972) argues that powerlessness corrupts and that acts of violence under these conditions are merely pseudopower, an expression of impotence. A condition of relative powerlessness is precisely what characterizes the lives of blacks who are undereducated, unemployed or working in menial, low-paying occupations.

Dennis (1977) has attributed the extraordinarily high rates of homicide among young black men to a variety of social stresses caused by rural to urban migration, changes in the family and age structure, denial of employment opportunities, and so forth. Valentine and Valentine (1972) have noted that advocates of black self-destruction theory believe many homicides among blacks to be similar to suicides in that they are victim precipitated. They are responses to persisting patterns of oppression.13

These explanations for black aggression tend to suggest that a comprehensive theory of black criminal violence must consider the psychological dynamics at work under conditions of economic, political and social powerlessness.14 Many of the ideas proposed by Blauner (1972) to describe features of "internal colonialism" in the United States must be explored. Both Dennis (1977) and Valentine and Valentine (1972) have noted that patterns of black intragroup aggression, especially among young men, may be linked to increasing political awareness of oppression without concomitant means to affect social change or change in their own lives. The tendency of subcultural theory to focus on social values has led to an ignoring of such political concerns. The overemphasis on the causative role of attitudes toward violence has also led to an underemphasis on the more objective environmental conditions under which criminal violence is likely to occur.

These theories also suggest that the particularly lethal environment to be found among young, black males may be linked to age-related career and life- stage crises. The traditional subculture of youth explanations have most often concentrated on the anti- social values to be found among young adolescents. However, black criminal violence is also heavily concentrated in the young to middle age adult, 25-44 age range. This suggests that a variety of economic factors such as underemployment must be considered as causal factors, including the notion of a more or less permanent, minority underclass living in urban areas, e.g., see Glasgow (1980).15 Urban areas are also more likely than non-urban areas to offer the kind of economic contrasts that may lead to "relative deprivation" and inequality as causal factors in homicide.

Conclusions and Testable Hypotheses

Conclusion 1: To the extent that criminal violence is caused by economic deprivation and powerlessness, homicide rates will occur at a higher rate among the black underclass than among the black middle class.

Hypothesis1: Studies of attitudes toward violence will show no significant differences between lower-class and middle-class blacks.

Hypothesis 2: Studies of psychological adaptation will show higher rates of personal stress, rage, and feelings of powerlessness among black, lower-class males than among other comparable social groupings in American society.

Hypothesis 3: At the group level, improvements in the economic and social well being of blacks will lead to reductions in acts of criminal violence.

Summary and Conclusions

Although subculture of violence theory is most often used to explain black-white differentials in homicide, it is inadequate in many respects. In this paper I have suggested a number of alternatives and supplements to this theory that have not been adequately explored in previous research. The long range utility of these alternatives will be measured by future studies that attempt to test the proposed hypotheses. The section on pre-homicide behavior is likely to result in the most informative studies.

Though I have raised a number of theoretical and other issues in this paper, its purpose has been rather limited. In no way have I attempted to propose a general theory of homicide causation, either among blacks or among the public at large. A fully adequate theory of this sort would have to address issues of age and sex differences in homicide rates, rural-urban differences, regional differences, and so forth. Rather I have attempted to propose plausible theoretical direction for the analysis and understanding of the disproportionately high rates of homicide among American blacks. That is, why have American blacks consistently had higher rates of murder than other nonwhite and white Americans?

First, I offered a critique of subculture of violence theory and its sufficiency as an explanation for the consistently high rates of homicide among American blacks. Next, I suggested that etiological studies of criminal homicide must be broadened to include a variety of situational, structural and institutional variables not usually considered in studies of crime causation. These include the historical behavior of the law and the operation of the criminal justice system. I suggest that these factors must be considered along with cultural values to explain why blacks commit a disproportionate share of homicides.

In contrast to much of previous criminological research, I suggest that the study of racial discrimination and bias in the administration of justice cannot be separated from the study of homicide causation among American blacks. The propositions presented are an attempt to address this important social problem by combining some of the tenets of subcultural theory with those found in the theory of conflict oriented criminologists. The work of Quinney (1973, 1980), Turk (1969) and Taylor, et al. (1974) must be seen as contributing not only to an understanding of the processing of criminals in society, but as contributing also to the study of the cause of criminal behavior. The study of criminal homicide must include not only the actions of the criminal offender or victim but also the actions of officials of the state.

Notes

1. While white American rates are generally lower than those of blacks, there is evidence that various white ethnic groups have differing rates and trends of rates over time. Rates of crime, including homicide, have tended to be higher for recent immigrants than for more settled groups. Jews have reportedly lower rates of all crime than do most other white ethnics. However, few studies have provided data comparing rates of homicide among whites. Among nonwhites, Asian Americans have tended to have low rates of homicide and American Indians have relatively high rates.

2. There is nothing intrinsic in conflict theory that makes it inapplicable to questions of crime etiology. However, conflict oriented criminologists appear to have followed the lead of Karl Marx, who wrote very little about crime causation. An exception is Bonger (1969). Many conflict criminologists do talk of the extent to which the ruling class overcriminalizes the behaviors of the lower classes, thus making them appear more criminal. However, the cause of such **mala in se** offenses as homicide, is seldom probed from a conflict perspective.

3. The 1980 annual report on the nation's health status, **Health-United States: 1980**, by the Department of Health and Human Services gives causes of death among persons 15-24 years old. Among nonwhites the homicide rate was 43/100,000 compared to 25/ for motor vehicle accidents and 22/ for other accidents. Auto accidents was the leading cause of death for whites. Most homicide victims were black males.

4. For example, Shin et al. (1977), Dennis (1977, 1979) and Farley (1980) have all noted the extent to which homicide diminishes life expectancy probabilities for black males. A special issue of **Ebony** magazine (August 1979) detailed the social, economic and moral impact of black intraracial crime, especially homicide, on blacks.

5. FBI, **Uniform Crime Reports**, 1975, p. 210.

6. A number of recent studies of public perceptions of crime and official criminal justice responses suggests that actual or potential aggression by blacks against whites is thought to represent an attack on the social order. For example, research by Jacobs (1979), Jackson and Carrol (1980), Liska et al. (1981) and Loftin, et al. (1981) report that the percent nonwhite in American urban areas has an effect on papolice expenditures and strength. This is especially evident after the riots of the early 1960s.

7. The low incidence of reported white offender-black victim homicide in these studies is itself a manifestation of racism. Whites who kill blacks are also less likely to be prosecuted. The numerous lynchings of blacks from the 1890s through the 1960s are not reflected in official arrest statistics.

8. If expected punishment does prevent nonprimary (stranger) murders more than primary murders, the historical and current behavior of the law will have more impact on interracial offenses. That is, blacks will be more deterred from killing whites and whites will be more deterred from killing blacks than from killing members of their own race.

9. For example, will a jurisdiction with a reputation for being extremely lenient with black offender-black victim murderers but severe with black offender-white victim murderers show rates of these types of murders that are different from those found in jurisdictions with different punishment patterns?

10. By "pre-homicide behavior" I mean something more than a post facto detailing of all events leading up to the murder. Something more systematic and predictable is proposed. For example, much police department folklore may be useful in identifying such behavior.

11. Black (1971) found no evidence that police arrest decisions are affected by the race of the offender. However, further studies are needed, particularly of the effects of victims' and offenders' race on arrest and on other aspects of police response to crime.

12. See **Profile of State Prison Inmates, 1974,** published by the U. S. Department of Justice. SES data for all arrestees is not readily available.

13. The kind of "death wish" theory proposed by Valentine and Valentine (1972) suggests that a symbolic interactionist approach may be useful for describing aggressive encounters between blacks. Such a theoretical model for the study of violence has been proposed by Athens (1977).

14. Traditional psychiatric and psychoanalytic studies of homicide fail to consider the economic and social context within which most murders in the United States occur.

15. The ghettoization of various groups in America has, of course, included white ethnics as well as nonwhites. Many of these groups have resorted to crime as a means of responding to their deprivation and powerlessness. However, the ghettoization of blacks must be seen as occuring within the context of a slavery-influenced social system and persisting pattern of racial discrimination. To the extent that these historical-structural factors influence rates of homicide, blacks will have higher rates of homicide than oppressed whites.

References

Athens, Lonnie H. 1977. "Violent Crime: A Symbolic Interactionist Study." Symbolic Interaction 1(1): 56-70.

Bayley, David and Harold Mendelsohn. 1969. Minorities and the Police. New York: The Free Press.

Bernard, William. 1978. "Blacks and the Police: A Comparative Study of Police Relations with Black and White Citizens." Unpublished manuscript.

Black, Donald. 1971. "The Social Organization of Arrest," Stanford Law Review 23 (June): 1104-1109.

. 1976. The Behavior of the Law. New York: The Academic Press.

. 1979. "Common Sense in the Sociology of the Law." American Sociological Review 44 (February): 18-27.

Blau, Judith R. and Peter M. 1982. "Metropolitan Structure and Violent Crime." American Sociological Review 47 (February): 114-129.

Blauner, Robert. 1972. Racial Oppression in America. New York: Harper and Row.

Block, Richard. 1975. "Homicide in Chicago: A Nine Year Study (1965-1973)." Journal of Criminal Law and Criminology 66 (December): 496-510.

Blumenthal, Monica D., Robert L. Kohn, Frank Andrews and Kendra Head. 1972. Justifying Violence. Ann Arbor, MI: Institute for Social Research.

Bohannon, Paul (ed.). 1960. African Homicide and Suicide. Princeton, NJ: Princeton University Press.

Bonger, Willem. 1943. Race and Crime. New York: Columbia University Press.

. 1969. Criminality and Economic Conditions. Bloomington: Indiana University Press.

Boudouris, James. 1970. "Trends in Homicide, Detroit, 1926-68." Ph.D. dissertation, Wayne State University, Detroit, MI.

Brearley, H. C. 1932. Homicide in the United States. Chapel Hill: University of North Carolina Press.

Centerwall, Brandon S. 1982. "Race, Socioeconomic Status, and Homicide: Atlanta, 1961-62, 1971-72." Paper presented at annual meeting of Southern Sociological Society, Memphis, Tenn., April 1982.

Curtis, Lynn A. 1974. Criminal Violence: National Patterns and Behaviors. Lexington, MA: Lexington Books.

1975. **Violence, Race and Culture.** Lexington, MA: Lexington Books.

David, Paul, Herbert G. Gutman, Richard Sutch, Peter Temin, Gavin Wright. 1976. **Reckoning with Slavery: A Critical Study in the Quantitative History of American Negro Slavery.** New York: Oxford University Press.

Davis, Robert and James F. Short. 1978. "Dimensions of Black Suicide: A Theoretical Model." **Suicide and Life Threatening Behavior** 8 (Fall): 161-173.

Dennis, Ruth E. 1977. "Social Stress and Mortality among Nonwhite Males." **Phylon** 38 (September): 315-328.

. 1979. "The Role of Homicide in Decreasing Life Expectancy." In Harold M. Rose (ed.), **Lethal Aspects of Urban Violence.** Lexington, MA: D. C. Heath.

Doerner, William G. 1975. "A Regional Analysis of Homicide Rates in the United States." **Criminology** 13 (May): 90-101.

Dunn, Christopher S. 1976. "The Patterns and Distribution of Assault Incident Characteristics among Social Areas." Analytic Report 14. Law Enforcement Assistance Administration, National Criminal Justice Information and Statistics Service, Washington, D. C.: Government Printing Office.

Ebony Magazine. 1979. Special issue, "Black on Black Crime: The Causes; the Consequences; the Cure." 34 (August).

Erlanger, Howard S. 1974. "The Empirical Status of the Subculture of Violence Thesis." **Social Problems** 22 (December): 280-292.

Erlich, Issac. 1975. "The Deterrent Effect of Capital Punishment: A Question of Life and Death." **American Economic Review** 65 (June): 397-417.

Fanon, Frantz. 1967. **Black Skin, White Masks.** New York: Grove Press.

. 1968. **The Wretched of the Earth.** New York: Grove Press.

Farley, Reynolds. 1980. "Homicide Trends in the United States." **Demography** 17 (May): 177-88.

Farrell, Ronald A. and Victoria A. Swigert. 1978. "Legal Disposition of Inter-group and Intra-group Homicides." **Sociological Quarterly** 19 (Autumn): 565-76.

Fine, Gary A. and Sherryl Kleinman. 1979. "Rethinking Subculture: An Interactionist Analysis." **American Journal of Sociology** 85 (July): 1-20.

Fogel, Robert W. and Stanley L. Engerman. 1974. **Time on the Cross: The Economics of American Negro Slavery.** Boston: Little, Brown and Company.

Garfinkel, Harold. 1949. "Research Note on Inter- and Intra- racial Homicides." **Social Forces** 27 (May): 369-81.

131

Gastil, Raymond D. 1971. "Homicide and a Regional Culture of Violence." American Sociological Review 36 (June): 412-27.

Gibbs, Jack P. 1975. Crime, Punishment and Deterrence. New York: Elsevier.

Glasgow, Douglas G. 1980. The Black Underclass. San Francisco: Jossey-Bass Inc.

Gouldner, Alvin. 1974. Foreword in The New Criminology by Taylor et al., New York: Harper and Row.

Green, Edward. 1964. "Inter- and Intra-racial Crime Relative to Sentencing." Journal of Criminal Law, Criminology and Police Science 55 (September): 348-58.

Grier, William and Price M. Cobbs. 1968. Black Rage. New York: Basic Books.

Hackney, Sheldon. 1969. "Southern Violence." Pp. 505-27 in Hugh Davis Graham and Ted Robert Gurr (eds.)

Hagan, John. 1974. "Extra-Legal Attributes and Criminal Sentencing: An Assessment of a Sociological Viewpoint," Law and Society Review 8: 357-83.

Health-United States: 1980. 1981. DHHS Publication No. (PHS) 81-1232. United States Department of Health and Human Services, Public Health Service. Office of Health Research, Statistics and Technology. National Center for Health Statistics. National Center for Health Services Research. Washington, D. C.: Government Printing Office.

Hindelang, Michael J. 1969. "Equality Under the Law." The Journal of Criminal Law, Criminology and Police Science 60 (September): 306-13.

. 1981. "Variations in Sex-Race-Age-Specific Incidence Rates of Offending." American Sociological Review 46 (August): 461-74.

Hindus, Michael S. 1980. Prison and Plantation: Crime, Justice and Authority in Massachusetts and South Carolina, 1767-1878. Chapel Hill: University of North Carolina Press.

Jackson, Pamela I. and Leo Carrol. 1981. "Race and the War on Crime: The Sociopolitical Determinants of Municipal Police Expenditure in 90 Non-Southern U. S. Cities." American Sociological Review 46 (June): 290-305.

Jacobs, David. 1979. "Inequality and Police Strength: Conflict and Coercive Control in Metropolitan Areas." American Sociological Review 44 (December): 913-25.

Johnson, Guy B. 1941. "The Negro and Crime." Annals of the American Academy of Political and Social Science 217 (September): 93-104.

Kleck, Gary. 1979. "Capital Punishment, Gun Ownership, and Homicide."

American Journal of Sociology 84 (January): 882- 910.

. 1981. "Racial Discrimination in Criminal Sentencing." **American Sociological Review** 46 (December): 783- 805.

Levi, Ken. 1981. "Homicide as Conflict Resolution." **Deviant Behavior** 1 (April-September): 281-307.

Lewis, Oscar. 1959. **Five Families: Mexican Case Studies in the Culture of Poverty.** New York: Basic Books.

Liska, Allen E., Joseph J. Lawrence and Michael Benson. 1981. "Perspectives on the Legal Order: The Capacity for Social Control." **American Journal of Sociology** 87 (September): 413- 26.

Loftin, Colin and Robert H. Hill. 1974. "Regional Subculture and Homicide: An Examination of the Gastil-Hackney Thesis." **American Sociological Review** 39 (October): 714-24.

Loftin, Colin, David F. Greenberg, and Ronald C. Kessler. 1981. "Income Inequality, Race, Crime and Crime Control." Paper presented at annual meeting of the American Society of Criminology. Washington, D. C.: November 1981.

Lundsgaarde, Henry P. 1977. **Murder in Space City: A Cultural Analysis of Houston Homicide Patterns.** New York: Oxford University Press.

McNeeley, R. L. and Carl E. Pope (eds.). 1981. **Race, Crime and Criminal Justice.** Beverly Hills, CA: Sage Publications.

Mangum, Charles S. Jr. 1940. **The Legal Status of the Negro.** Chapel Hill: University of North Carolina Press.

May, Rollo. 1972. **Power and Innocence: A Search for the Sources of Violence.** New York: W. W. Norton and Company.

Ostrom, Elinor. 1978. "Race and the Equality of Police Service Delivery in Metropolitan Areas: A Preliminary Sketch of An Inquiry in Process." Paper presented at meeting of American Society of Public Administration, Phoenix, AZ, April, 1978.

Parker, Robert N. and M. Dwayne Smith. 1979. "Deterrence, Poverty and Type of Homicide." **American Journal of Sociology** 85 (November): 614-29.

Pettigrew, Thomas F. and R. B. Spier. 1962. "The Ecological Structure of Negro Homicide." **American Journal of Sociology** 67 (May): 621-29.

Pittman, D. J. and W. Hardy. 1964. "Patterns in Criminal Aggravated Assault." **Journal of Criminal Law, Criminology and Police Science** 55 (December): 462-70.

Pokorny, Alex D. 1965a. "A Comparison of Homicide, Aggravated Assault, Suicide and Attempted Suicide." **Journal of Criminal Law, Criminology and Police Science** 56 (December): 488-97.

133

Profile of State Prison Inmates: Sociodemographic Findings from the 1974 Survey of Inmates of State Correctional Facilities. NCJ-58257. United States Department of Justice, Bureau of Justice Statistics. Washington, D. C.: Government Printing Office.

Quinney, Richard. 1973. Critique of Legal Order: Crime Control in a Capitalist Society. Boston: Little Brown.

. 1980. Class, State and Crime. 2nd ed. New York: Longman, Inc.

Radelet, Michael. 1981. "Racial Characteristics and the Imposition of the Death Penalty." American Sociological Review 46 (December): 918-27.

Reed, John. 1971. "To Live-and-Die-in Dixie: A Contribution to the Study of Southern Violence." Political Science Quarterly 86 (September): 429-43.

Rose, Harold M. 1978. "The Geography of Despair." Annals of the Association of American Geographers 68: 453-464.

. 1981. Black Homicide and the Urban Environment. United States Department of Health and Human Services, National Institute of Mental Health.

Rossi, Peter H., Christine E. Bose and Richard E. Berk. 1974. "The Seriousness of Crimes: Normative Structure and Individual Difference." American Sociological Review 39 (April): 224-37.

Shin, Yongsock, Davor Jedlicka and Everett S. Lee. 1977. "Homicide Among Blacks." Phylon 38 (December): 398-407.

Silberman, Charles. 1978. Criminal Violence-Criminal Justice: Criminals, Police, Courts, and Prisons in America. New York: Random House.

Smith, M. Dwayne and Robert N. Parker. 1980. "Type of Homicide and Variation in Regional Rates." Social Forces 59 (September): 136-47.

Swigert, Victoria Lynn and Ronald A. Farrell. 1977. "Normal Homicides and the Law." American Sociological Review 42 (February): 16-32.

Taylor, Ian, Paul Walton and Jock Young. 1974. The New Criminology. 2nd edition. New York: Harper and Row.

. 1975. Critical Criminology. London: Routledge and Kegan Paul.

Turk, Austin. 1969. Criminality and Legal Order. Chicago: Rand McNally.

Uniform Crime Reports for the United States, 1960-1979. Federal Bureau of Investigation, United States Department of Justice, Washington, D. C.: Government Printing Office.

Valentine, Charles A. and Betty Lou Valentine. 1972. "The Man and the Panthers." Politics and Society (Spring): 273-86.

Voss, Harwin and John R. Hepburn. 1968. "Patterns in Criminal Homicide in Chicago." Journal of Criminal Law, Criminology and Police Science 59

(December): 499-508.

Wolfgang, Marvin E. 1958. **Patterns in Criminal Homicide**. New York: Wiley.

and Bernard Cohen. 1964. **Crime and Race: Conceptions and Misconceptions.** New York: Institute of Human Relations Press.

and Franco Ferracuti. 1967. **The Subculture of Violence: Towards an Integrated Theory in Criminology.** London: Tavistock.

and Marc Riedel. 1975. "Rape, Race, and the Death Penalty in Georgia." **American Journal of Orthopsychiatry** 45 (July): 658-68.

THE MASCULINE WAY OF VIOLENCE

Robert Staples

Some years ago the Civil Rights activist H. Rap Brown stated that violence is "as American as cherry pie."[1] The birth of the United States as a free nation was rooted in the violent overthrow of a dictatorial regime and this tradition of violence has permeated the social fabric of North America from that time to this day. By any statistical measure it outranks all countries in the world in the prevalence of violent acts. Its homicide rate is double that of all other industrialized nations. A number of its public officials have been victims of assassination or assassination attempts. Each hour of the day at least two Americans are homicide victims.[2] Such a pattern of violence led Sartre to label "that super- European monstrosity, North America, as a bastard child or satanic mutation of degraded Europe"[3]

Hence, black violence in the United States may be viewed as an exaggerated form of the normative pattern of violence in this cultural context. Although violent crime in this country is associated in the public mind with blacks, any review of history shows violence to be an institutionalized part of America's social structure. Beginning with the war against the Native American Indians, this country has rarely experienced a period without violent strife of some kind. Its wars alone have accounted for over four million American deaths, with even larger casualties for the enemy countries.[4] Labor strife, lynchings, riots, assassinations, mob violence are all part of this country's violent history.

The violent tradition in the United States is due partly to its frontier experience which cultivated a materialistic philosophy whereby sacred property rights superceded human rights, especially those of Native Americans and Chicanos.[5] Its contemporary cause may be found in the cultural supports for violence such as its anti-humanitarian values, prevalence of firearms, enshrinement of private property rights and a constant state of war- preparedness.[6] The latter is particularly important in creating a collective public predisposition toward violence. As Mills asserts, "war or a high state of war preparedness is felt to be the normal and seemingly permanent condition of the United States."[7]

In spite of its own combative history, this country is inordinately concerned and frightened over the violent acts committed by its men of color. While that is also the focus of this chapter, it should be noted that the incidence of violence in the United States is understood by the methods used to define it and by the methods used for law enforcement. Those acts of violence used in the interest of the political and economic elite are what might be called "legitimate" violence. Violence committed by members of America's underclass is regarded as illegitimate violence. Thus, the mass killings of workers, students or blacks by the police is seen as a necessary force. The murder of millions of non- combatants in a war is seen as necessary for national security. It we accept as a definition of violence any behavior designed to inflict physical injury on people,[8] it is clear that the greatest perpetrators of violence are American manufacturers. Each year over 30 million Americans are hurt and 30 thousand killed because of unsafe consumer products other than automobiles.[9]

It is because the people who run the government serve the interests of the manufacturers that laws are designed to punish only those who commit "illegitimate" acts of violence. For the most part they will be members of America's underclass, the poor and blacks. Therefore, it would be more accurate to see violence as a political act because its definition and the penalties for it reflect one's status in the society, not the objective fact of physical injury inflicted upon another person. The power to define and enforce laws against violence is contingent upon one's standing in a society stratified along class and racial lines.

Violence Against Blacks

Before examining the types of black male violence, it is necessary to note that in most instances of interracial violence, blacks have been the victims of white violence--not the reverse.[10] This has been true since the beginning of the slave trade, a practice itself which was responsible for the deaths of an estimated 100 million black people.[11] During the period of slavery, violence was normally used to intimidate and control the bondsman. There were no laws to protect a slave against the wrath of a white person. Except for his value as human capital, the slave could not escape acts of violence by any white person, and the free Afro-American was often the victim of white mob violence.[12]

After the end of slavery, blacks were still subjected to white violence. In the South it was frequently in the form of lynching. According to Wertham:

> Between 1882 and 1939 more than 5,000 Negroes were lynched in the United States, more than 1,800 since the year 1900. These statistics are incomplete, inasmuch as they do not include the countless and unaccounted persons who have been lynched in a clandestine way and just disappeared without getting into the statistics.[13]

Outside the South the most tyical form of white violence against blacks was the white-dominated race riot. Between 1865 and 1940 over 500 blacks were killed in race riots and massacres.[14] It was rare to have white casualties in these disturbances since the violence originated with, and was controlled and directed by whites. In most cases the principal purpose was to inflict personal injury or death on Afro-Americans. Lynching and race riots are examples of black powerlessness. These were occasions when the entire white adult population of certain communities in the United States collectively violated the law by attacking whole communities of blacks. The unilateral character of these riots led Myrdal to comment that "it was more a one-way terrorization than a two-way riot."[15] Yet, white law officials not only failed to enforce the laws which were violated but in some instances participated in the terrorism.

Collective white violence against blacks has declined in the last decade.[16] In turn black-on-black violence has increased along with the incidence of black violence against whites. It is the latter phenomenon that the law-and-order political campaigns exploit to gain white votes. But, the overwhelming majority of black acts of violence are directed at other blacks. It is the purpose of this chapter to examine those acts of intra-group antagonism and to analyze the forms of family and sexual violence, which dominate/terrorize/characterize black life today.

Theories of Black Male Violence

Various theories attempt to explain the reason for the high rate of black male violence. In an earlier period criminologists leaned toward a genetic explanation. Using a social Darwinist approach, Lombroso asserted that criminality was an atavistic throwback to an earlier evolutionary stage. Thus, "primitive" people (or those originally from "primitive" societies) possessed a predisposition toward criminal behavior.[17] This theory is largely discredited in most scientific circles today. The history of violence throughout the world reveals a pattern of violent subjugation of non-white peoples by white settlers, therefore suggesting that centuries- old patterns of miscegenation and amalgamation tend to violate any assumption of racially defined groups as biologically unique.[18]

A more prominent theory is that of Wolfgang and Ferracuti, who believe that differences in attitudes towards the use of violence exist in specific populations and are organized into a set of culturally transmitted norms. Undergirding this theory is the assumption that lower class blacks have a culturally trasmitted value system which approves the use of violence for conflict resolution more so than is found in other American groups.[19]

Another theory of black violence is the regional tradition explanation of Pettigrew. He noted that Afro-Americans were primarily descendents of the Southern region of the United States and that this area has a markedly higher degree of violence than other parts of the country. This tradition of violence found in the South was, he asserted, responsible for the greater proclivity to commit homicide among blacks. Although the highest murder rates exist in large Northern cities, he thinks this can be explained by the large number of black migrants from the South in those locations.[20] In their migration to the North, Southern blacks carried values related to violence that they had learned as long ago as the era of slavery. Elkins has argued that the slave's only values were derived from the slavemaster. By identifying with the slaveholder's beatings, torture and rape of women, these values were internalized by Afro-Americans who bring a predilection toward violence with them to Northern states.[21]

Other theories of black violence are: (1) Violent acts are associated with relative deprivation. Rates of violence will be highest in areas where the occupational and income gap between blacks and whites is the greatest.[22] (2) Since means of masculine expressions are often denied to Afro-American males, they rechannel these expressions into violent forms. A major reason for this need for violence to prove manhood is the lack of a male role model in the family. Uncertain of his masculinity, he adopts a tough, violent life most closely associated with the dominant culture's definition of maleness.[23]

Some of these theories are of questionable validity, others are deficient in failing to acknowledge the political economy of violence. The former is typical of the theories of black violence as deriving from regional mores and as a form of masculine expression. Violence in America is concentrated in Northern urban ghettos, not the South. Only three Southern cities are represented of the ten with the highest homicide rate and the majority of black violence in the North is not committed by Southern immigrants.[24] To contend that black violence in the North is a reflection of Southern ethos

139

presumes a tenacity of the norms of violence which is transmitted intergenerationally.

The argument that violence is a form of masculine expression that black men need because of a deficit of male role models in their lives is limited as a unitary explanation. This theory is part and parcel of the matriarchy myth, which attempts to blame blacks for their own oppressed condition. Almost all black males have masculine role models, even if there is no legal husband or biological father within the nuclear family context. Men from broken homes dominate the violence statistics partly because fatherless black families represent the poorest of the poor, the most oppressed of the oppressed, and the men act out their frustration and anger. It is the relationship between racial oppression and black violence that should be examined.[25]

Stress and Family Violence

The subject of violence in family relations has been neglected as an area of study by behavioral scientists until recent years. Most of the research has been carried out by criminologists and not by family sociologists. A primary reason for this void in the family literature on family violence has been the prevailing ideology of the family as a unit characterized by affection and cooperation between its members. Yet, it has been known for some time that the largest group of homicides in the United States involves spouses, kinsmen and close friends. In the Wolfgang study of homicide in Philadelphia during the period 1948-1952, over fifty percent of all homicides involved an altercation between family members and close friends. And one fourth of all homicides were family killings.[26]

It is difficult to discuss violence of any kind in America without noting the over-representation of blacks in the official statistics on violent crimes. In 1972 they were recorded as committing 60 percent of the homicides, 45 percent of the aggravated assaults, and 50 percent of the rapes in the United States.[27] Although there has been an increase in interracial acts of violence, the aggressor and victim in most acts of black violence are black. Most black violence is perpetrated against family and friends. It should be noted, however, that the proportion of homicides involving strangers is sharply on the increase.

Blacks are very prominent in those groups most likely to commit acts of family violence: the lower- class, large families, and the unhappily married. Hence, it is not surprising to find that romantic triangles or marital arguments add to the large number of violent crimes committed in the black community. One-fourth of all black homicides in 1972 took place among family members. A majority of them consisted of spouse killing spouse, and the others involved killings of a parent or child.[28]

While it may be simple to dismiss black violence as the result of that group's predisposition to it, the cross-cultural evidence does not support such an assumption. Bohannon's data from African societies illustrate that cultural, not biological factors, account for the high homicide rate among Afro- Americans. This is evident from his studies which show that African rates tend not only to be lower than Afro-American rates but also lower than rates for the general American population.[29]

While I do not uncritically accept the theory of Frantz Fanon about the therapeutic effects of violence among oppressed peoples, he does provide a guideline for understanding black violence in his supposition that the colonized man will initially be violent against his own people and that the development of violence among the oppressed colonial subjects will be proportionate to the violence exercised by the colonial regime.[30] Thus, it is understandable that the victims of black violence are primarily other blacks and that the white majority and its government leaders have set an example of violence by historical acts of aggression against Third World peoples in the United States and throughout the world.

Socialization Into Violence

Lower-income black children are exposed to violence at very early ages. In housing projects, for instance, it is not at all uncommon for young children to have been shot at, robbed and raped by the time they reach the age of ten. The structure of low- income public housing projects is conducive to certain forms of crime such as rapes on the stairwell, robberies in elevators and sniper shooting from windows. Hence, children living in these areas that are relatively unprotected by the police, must learn to protect themselves.[31] Other forms of resolving conflicts are subordinated to physical skills which will prevent one from being overwhelmed by those who will test a person's toughness.

The status-conferral system in black life initiates the youth into acts of aggression. In the ghetto, the highest level of esteem and respect is reserved for the best streetfighter in the neighborhood. Older males in this environment encourage children to develop aggressive tendencies by their philosophy that a "real" man is supposed to fight. Claude Brown comments that in Harlem the people everyone respected were the men who had killed somebody. And, the children respected by the adults in their neighborhood were those who did not let anybody beat them.[32]

The black ghetto, however, is nothing but a microcosm of the entire society. Violence is endemic to the American social structure and America easily deserves its reputation as the most violent country in the world, while public officials decry violence by oppressed minorities. The public support for former President Carter's invasion of Iran to free American hostages is but one example of the cultural supports for violence in this country. Americans are the most heavily armed citizenry in the world.[33]

Sexual Aggression

Sexual attacks against women are pervasive and sharply increasing in this country. The typical rapist is a black male and his victim is most often a black female. However, the most severe penalties for rape are reserved for black males accused of raping white women. Although 50 percent of those convicted for rape in the South were white males, over 90 percent of those executed for this crime in that region were black. Most of their alleged victims were white. No white male has ever been executed for raping a black woman.[34]

One of the most salient aspects of internal colonialism is the status of women and the question of sexual access. Historically, the white male has had both black and white women available to him. This is one of the privileges of white males in a racist society, and it contributes to the domination of black men. While white women have been unavailable to black men, there was no such protection for black women who were subjected to habitual abuse and sexual prostitution by white males.[35] The rape of black women by white men, has, historically, not been a punishable offense in American common law or by community standards. Most cases of interracial rape reported today involve black men and white women.[36] As has been noted, "no black woman would report being raped by a white man to the police in Oakland. They might report it to the Panthers but never to the police."[37]

The prohibition of unions between black men and white women is an important aspect of majority rule. Myrdal is in agreement with this idea when he states: "what whites ask for is a general order according to which all Negroes are placed under all white people and excluded from not only the white man's society but also from the ordinary symbols of respect. No Negro shall ever aspire to them, and no white shall be allowed to offer them."[38]

Regardless of white society's taboo on black aspirations to white privileges, it is precisely the wish of the black male to take the Euro-American male's place. At least, it is Fanon's contention that the African male is an envious man who covets all the European's possessions; to sit at his table, to sleep in his bed and to sleep with his wife.[39] The rape of white women by Afro-American men often reflects this desire of the African. Cleaver thus explains his past history of crime:

Rape was an insurrectionary act. It delighted me that I was defying and trampling upon the white man's law, upon his system of values, and that I was defiling his women--and this point, I believe was the most satisfying to me because I was very resentful over the historical fact of how the white man had used the black woman. I felt I was getting revenge.[40]

And, it was due to this fear of the black male invading his domain, destroying his property, that the settler punished severely any black man who attempted to become familiar or intimate with the symbol of white privilege--the white female. Many of the lynchings in the South were brutal reminders to black men that intermingling with white women was regarded as an unmentionable crime.[41] In recent years the function of lynch mobs has been transferred to the political state. From 1930 to 1964, 89 percent of the 455 men officially executed for rape in the United States were black. Bowers reports that 85 percent of all executions for rape have involved black men and white victims.[42]

However most contemporary rape cases are intra- racial. Despite white fear of the omnipresent black rapist, only ten percent of all rape cases involve a black man and white woman. In fact, it is the black woman who should be wary of rape since her chance of being assaulted is much higher than that of a white woman.[43] The protection that is denied black women from white male sexual attack often is not provided from black men either. Hammond found that what is often considered as strong-arm methods or even "rape" in the middle class terms was often quite a commonplace practice in the housing projects in Saint Louis.[44]

142

As is probably true of white females, the incidence of rape of black women is underreported. Ladner reported than an eight year-old girl has a good chance of being exposed to rape and violence if she is a member of the black underclass.[45] The examples of black males who have "taken it" from black women are probably known to us all. Widespread incidents of this kind are rooted in the sexist socialization of all men in this society. It is pronounced among black men who have other symbols of manhood blocked to them. Various explanations have been put forth to explain why black men rape their women. Poussaint attributes it to the tendency for black men to adopt the attitudes of the majority group toward black women. Because white men have historically raped black women with impunity, many black males believe they can do the same.[46] That they are often correct in this assumption is depicted in the saying of Sapphire that she realizes that "it is useless to report being raped because no one will believe that she didn't just give it away."[47]

Sexual violence is also rooted in the dynamics of the black dating game. The majority of black rape victims are familiar with their attacker, who was a friend, relative, or neighbor. Many of the rapes occur after a date and are what Amir describes as misfired attempts at seduction.[48] A typical pattern is for the black male to seek sexual compliance from his date, encounter resistance which he thinks is feigned, and proceed forcibly to extract sexual gratification from her. Large numbers of black men believe sexual relations to be their "right" after a certain amount of dating. A truly reluctant black woman is often victimized by the tendency of some black women to play a coquettish role in resisting male sexual demands, when they actually are willing to engage in sexual intercourse. Such a pattern of assault is defined as situational and led feminist Germaine Greer to label seduction as a four letter word--rape.[49]

Rape, however, is not regarded as the act of a sexually starved male but rather as an aggressive act toward females. Students of the subject suggest that it is a long-delayed reaction against authority and powerlessness. In the case of black men, it is asserted that they grow up feeling emasculated and powerless before reaching manhood. They often encounter women as authority figures and teachers or as the head of their households. These men consequently act out their feeling of powerlessness against black women in the form of sexual aggression.[50] While such a characterization of black rapists may be fairly accurate, rape should be viewed as both a sexual and political act because it is an externalization of social repression, such as racial prejudice, which is a barrier to normal expression of manhood for black males.

Manhood in American society is closely tied to the acquisition of wealth. Wealth is power--power to control others. Men of wealth rarely rape women because they gain sexual access through other means. The secretary or other female employee who submits to the sexual demands of a male employer, in order to advance in her job, is as much an unwilling partner in this situation as is the rape victim. The rewards for her sexual compliance are normatively sanctioned, whereas the rapist does not often have the resources to induce such sexual compliance. Moreover, it is the concept of women as sexual property that is at the root of rape as a crime that is, ipso facto, a male transgression. This concept is peculiar to capitalistic, European societies rather than African nations where the incidence of rape is much lower. For black men, rape is often an act of aggression against women because the kinds of status men can acquire through success in a job is not available to them. This act of aggression affords a moment of power, and, by extension, status.

Marital Conflict

Homicides and assaults committed by spouses are rather pervasive in lower class black communities. At one time the murder of a spouse constituted one-fourth of all the homicides committed in this country. It is primarily a crime of the lower class as reported in official crime statistics. While domestic quarrels occur quite often among middle and upper class couples, they do not report them with the same frequency as the poor. Despite the underreporting of spousal violence by the upper classes, it is probably still more common among lower class blacks for reasons associated with their socio-economic and racial status. Strauss and his associates found the rate of wife abuse to be higher among blacks than in any other racial group, and that wife abuse was nearly 400 percent more common in black families than in white families.[51] When Cazanave and Strauss established a control group to study income, it was revealed that family violence occurred less frequently in middle- income black families than in middle-income white families.[52]

Contributing to spousal violence in lower class black families is the normative expectation that some physical violence against the wife is natural or necessary. In Chicago, for instance, a good "old man" is defined as one who "may slap or curse his old woman if he's angry but definitely not beat on her all the time when he's sober or endanger her life when drunk."[53] The husband is expected to use his physical superiority over his wife on occasions and frequent reference is made by lower class black men to the belief that they are supposed to treat women roughtly to keep them in line. The study by Cazanave and Strauss revealed that black respondents reported more approval of spouse slapping than white respondents. Black husbands were also three times as likely as white husbands to have slapped their wives and engaged in severe violence within a given year.[54] A major class difference, without regard to race, is that physical domination by a spouse is seen as an intolerable behavior pattern by many middle class wives. The first blow struck by a husband is taken by some of them as a symbol of gross abuse and it alone can result in divorce action.

Among the reasons for violent marital conflict are disputes over money, jealousy or drunken behavior. Jealousy is most likely the primary cause of spousal violence. Because of a community norm that encourages extramarital affairs, a liaison with another man or woman may ensue in a violent conflict between spouses.[55] Black families may be particularly subject to this stress in a marriage because of the belief by black husbands that a wife will seek sexual gratification elsewhere if relations do not go well. Such a belief may not be without foundation since one study revealed that one-half of their black female subjects condoned extramarital relations for the wife under certain conditions.[56] Men who are only living with, but not married to, a woman are even more prone to violence motivated by jealousy. One man commented that, "I figure if you are just staying with a woman and you're not married to her, she's as much somebody else's as she is yours." Sometimes, being married to a woman is regarded as a license for physical domination of her. According to this man, "If that's your wife, can't nobody say nothing." If you want to whip her, you can whip her."[57]

An unusual characteristic of black spousal violence is the incidence of black female aggression. In African societies, men are almost always the aggressor in domestic homicides.[58] But the American black women "has a reputation for using razor blades and lye to take care of business when he pushes her too far."[59] Boudouris in his analysis of homicides among family relations in Detroit during the period 1926-1968, found black women were the defendant in 44 percent of the court cases."[60] According to Cazanave and Strauss, black wives were twice as likely to have engaged in serious violence against their husbands as white wives.[61]

Upon further investigation of these family homicides, it appears that the high rates of murder for black women can be explained as acts of self-preservation when attacked by their spouses. Such an explanation is borne out by the findings of Wolfgang that one-third of the homicides he analyzed showed that it was the victim who committed the first aggressive act.[62] However, it can also reflect the low status of black men in their family relations because of their inability to find jobs or because they are employed at jobs which pay very low wages.The class characteristics of individuals involved in violent marital conflict are a natural result of their racial status. High rates of unemployment and underemployment automatically consign the majority of blacks to the underclass and several factors influence the incidence of marital violence. In the higher social classes, both black and white, men are able to exercise control over their wives in other than violent ways. Middle class men have more prestige, money and power than lower class men. Hence, they possess greater resources with which to achieve their aims with intimates.[63] The balance of power in marriage belongs to the partner bringing the most resources to the marriage. In general, money has been the source of power that sustains male dominance in the family. As has been noted elsewhere, "money belongs to him who earns it, not her who spends it, since he who earns it may withhold it."[64]

Lower class black males often find themselves at a disadvantage vis-a-vis their wives within the family. As a result of their consignment to the underclass, they are often unable to provide for their families properly and have a problem maintaining status in the eyes of their wives and children. Because they are aware of their role failure, they are inclined to counter-attack any perceived challenge to their manhood with violence. Rainwater observed that beatings and arguments precipitated by a husband seem to occur particularly when there is a discrepancy between the demands on him as a provider and his ability to meet those demands.[65] Hence, he responds violently in an attempt to regain status and respect for his role as head of the family.

The incidence of domestic violence is probably higher among lower class blacks than poor whites. A major reason for this interclass difference is due to the strictures of racism. It is the internal devaluation of their self-worth as individuals that precipitates much of the black violence. Comer reports that violent behavior against other blacks is often a displacement of anger toward whites. Since many blacks have little power to affect change, overwhelming obstacles and hopeless surrender produce high levels of frustration.[66] In the words of psychiatrist Alvin Poussaint, "Frustrated men may beat their wives in order to feel manly. These violent acts are an outlet for a desparate struggling against feelings of inferiority." It has only been in recent times that this rage and anger has been turned against whites.

Marital violence among blacks is primarily related to the poverty, oppression and cultural values found in a racially stratified society. Blacks are not predisposed toward violence any more than other groups. But, in a society which dehumanizes them, as well as economically exploits them, psychological controls are broken and violent rage against the safest and most accessible person ensues. Environmental factors place such stress on blacks so as to make the incidence of marital violence much higher than among the white majority population.

Parent-Child Violence

Parental abuse of children is nothing new. In earlier periods it was believed that children were inherently sinful and this evil must be violently exorcised. Among Americans of African descent, however, children have historically avoided much of the abuse heaped upon their white counterparts. The love of the African and Afro-American mother for her children is strongly documented in the historical records.[68] However, in recent years an increasing trend in parental injury to children has been evident among blacks. In fact, in the years 1967-68, the child abuse reported for black children was 21.0 per 100,000 in comparison to 6.7 per 100,000 white children.[69] Much of the racial difference in the statistics can be attributed to reporting bias but it also reflects the effect of environmental stress on black parent-child relationships.

Among the factors responsible for black child abuse are the conditions of poverty under which many children are reared. Child abuse is primarily concentrated in the lower class. These families, especially if they are black, are much larger than middle class families. Black families with four and more children were twice as likely to have a reported case of child abuse than similar white families.[70] Morever, those families have less living space in which to rear their children than more affluent families. Many of them are headed by a woman, who must often work outside the home and take care of her children afterwards. Such a difficult set of factors frequently leads to abusive behavior toward children.

The child-rearing methods of low-income parents are cited as an important cause of child abuse. While middle class parents tend to use verbal reasoning and psychological techniques with their children, lower class parents often use physical punishment to exact child obedience. As was true of their parents, most lower class parents believe that the way to make a child learn is to beat him. While alternate forms of punishment may also be used, a beating is eventually employed to force the child to conform to parental instructions.[71] However, some authorities believe that middle class child rearing techniques can be just as violent (although only verbal) and as psychologically damaging to children as those in the lower class.[72]

Many of the studies that deal with the discipline of the black child are limited. They typically measure attitudes toward the use of corporal punishment, but do not assess actual incidents. The findings of Cazanave and Strauss indicate most black and white parents are very similar in their frequency of their approval of slapping or spanking a 12 year- old. They discovered, however, that blacks were less likely to report actually having

146

done so within a given year. Black and white families also reported very similar rates of severe violence against children. One reason, they say, that blacks practice less child abuse than expected on the basis of their low income, high unemployment and rejection by the rest of the society, appears to be the aid and support, particularly in the care of children, provided by black extended families.[73]

At any rate, the physical method of child behavior control can and does lead to excessive injuries to some children. But, in exacting child obedience, many lower class parents are without other effective means of accomplishing this objective. They cannot offer the more significant status rewards to their children. They are unable to reward their children for good behavior because they lack the educational and social privileges of the middle class.[74] Very few of these resources are available to black children in the underclass. The conventional wisdom is that women are the main offenders in child abuse. But, abuse by men is often far more frequent and severe, considering the amount of time they spend with the children. During periods of layoffs and economic recession, fathers are increasingly put in contact with their children for many more hours a day and some are driven to hurt them physically. Increased unemployment is definitely correlated with incidences of child abuse as socio- economic circumstances lead to heightened stress in the family's life. The Cazanave and Strauss study found economic factors to be paramount in the causes of child abuse. Their data revealed a child abuse rate in families where the husband is a manual worker which is 41 percent higher than in families where the husband is a white collar worker. Among husbands who are dissatisfied with their standard of living, the child abuse rate was 61 percent greater than the rate for other husbands.[75]

While most people conceive of parent-child violence as commonly involving the parent as the aggressor, there are a number of incidents in which the parent is the victim. An increasing number of violent acts, including homicide, are committed by youth under the age of 15.[76] The lack of status and economic resources among lower class black families means that many parents are unable to control a child's aggressive behavior toward them. An enormously high unemployment rate among black teenagers in the inner cities is also a contributing factor.[77] Being a poor, uneducated young black male in an oppressive environment without any means of escape, and having observed violence throughout his childhood, are explosive forces which erupt in aggression against those who are physically accessible, namely the parents.

Summary

In this chapter I have tried to show how acts of black male violence and environmental stress factors are inextricably linked. While other forces operate in the incidence of family conflict that may transcend race, the crucial variable in intra-family violence among blacks has been their status as a devalued racial group. There is no reason to believe that the lower class black male is any more prone to violence than males in the middle class or general white population. Yet, they are so over-represented in the official statistics on crimes of family violence as to preclude any explanation other than that racial and economic forces are responsible for the amount of violence in their family constellation.

While the most pronounced trend currently is the increase in stranger assaults and homicides, this does not necessarily reflect a decrease in the number of intra-family acts of violence. With the attendant fragility of marriages, female-headed households and parent-child tensions, violence continues to be a primary source of conflict resolution in the family. It is a pattern of violence that was introduced to Afro-Americans during slavery and has persisted throughout their existence in this country. While a greater emphasis on family solidarity, respect for women, and value of children can do much to reduce the amount of violence within the black family, only by eliminating the cause of, and cultural support for, violence in the larger society can we expect to live free from danger in an environment that is safe and free from harm.

Footnotes

1. H. Rap Brown. 1969. **Die, Nigger, Die.** New York: Dial Press.

2. Hugh Graham and Ted Gurr (eds.). 1969. **Violence in America.** New York: Grove Press, p. 22.

3. Frantz Fanon. 1963. Preface **The Wretched of the Earth.** New York: Grove Press, p. 22.

4. Alphonso Pinkney. 1972. **The American Way of Violence.** New York: Random House, p. 26.

5. Joe B. Frantz. "The Frontier Tradition: An Invitation to Violence" in **Violence in America,** op. cit., pp. 119-143.

6. Pinkney, op. cit.

7. C. Wright Mills. 1956. **The Power Elite.** New York: Oxford University Press, p. 184.

8. Eugene Genovese. 1975. **Roll, Jordan, Roll.** New York: Random House, pp. 458-475.

9. Report of the Consumer Produce Safety Commission quoted in **Newsweek,** October 15, 1973, p. 91. This is three times the number of homicide victims in a year.

10. Marvin Wolfgang and Bernard Cohen. 1970. **Crime and Race.** New York: Institute of Human Relations Press, p. 44.

11. Basil Davidson. 1959. **The African Slave Trade.** Boston: Little, Brown and Co.

12. Stanley Elkins. 1959. **Slavery.** New York: Grossett and Dunlap.

13. Frederic Wertham. 1966. **A Sign for Cain: An Exploration of Human Violence.** New York: MacMillan, p. 91.

14. Bureau of the Census. 1960. **Historical Statistics of the United States, Colonial Times to 1957.** Washington, D. C.: U. S. Government Printing

Office, p. 218.

15. Gunnar Myrdal. 1944. **An American Dilemma.** New York: Harper and Brothers, p. 567.

16. The pendulum has turned again. At the beginning of the eighties, there were a rash of white attacks on blacks in some American cities.

17. Gina Lombroso, Ferrers. 1911. **Criminal Man According to the Classification of Cesare Lombroso.** New York: Putnam.

18. Ashley Montague. 1964. **Man's Most Dangerous Myth: The Fallacy of Race.** New York: World.

19. Marvin Wolfgang and F. Ferracuti. 1967. **The Subculture of Violence.** London: Social Science Paperbacks.

20. Thomas Pettigrew and Rosalind Spier. 1962. "The Ecological Structure of Negro Homicide." **American Journal of Sociology** 67 (May), pp. 621-629.

21. Elkins, op. cit.

22. P. Everts and K. Schwirian. 1968. "Metropolitan Crime Rates and Relative Deprivation." **Criminologica** 5, pp. 43- 52.

23. Walter Miller. 1958. "Lower Class Culture as a Generating Milieu of Gang Delinquency." **Journal of Social Issues** 14 (Fall), pp. 5-19.

24. Leonard Savitz. 1973. "Black Crime" in Kent Miller and Ralph Dreger, eds., **Comparative Studies of Blacks and Whites in the United States.** New York: Seminar Press, pp. 467- 516.

25. Robert Staples. 1970. "The Myth of the Black Matriarchy." **The Black Scholar,** (January), pp. 8-16.

26. Marvin Wolfgang. 1958. **Patterns in Criminal Homicide.** New York: John Wiley and Sons, pp. 200-207. More recent studies have come up with similar figures.

27. Federal Bureau of Investigation. 1973. "Crime in the United States, 1972." Crime Reports, Washington, D. C.: U. S. Government Printing Office, Table 36, p. 131.

28. Ibid.

29. Paul Bohannon, ed. 1967. **African Homicide and Suicide.** New York: Atheneum, p. 237.

30. Frantz Fanon. 1963. **The Wretched of the Earth.** New York: Grove Press, pp. 29-74.

31. Graham B. Spanier and Carol Fishel. 1973. "The Housing Project and Familial Functions: Consequences for Low Income Families." **The Family Coordinator,** 23 (April), pp. 235-240.

32. Claude Brown. 1965. **Manchild in the Promised Land**. New York: Macmillan, pp. 263-271.

33. Alphonso Pinkney. 1972. **The American Way of Violence**. New York: Random House, pp. 2-27.

34. William J. Bowers. 1974. **Executions in America**. Lexington, Mass.: Lexington Books, p. 78.

35. Winthrop Jordan. 1968. **White Over Black: American Attitudes Toward the Negro 1550-1812**. Durham, N. C.: University of North Carolina Press.

36. John M. Macdonald. 1971. **Rape Offenders and Their Victims**. Springfield, Ill.: Charles C. Thomas.

37. Michael W. Agapian, et al. 1972. "Interracial Rape in a North American City: An Analysis of 66 Cases," a paper presented to the Inter-American Congress of Criminologists. Caracus, Venezuela, November, p. 13.

38. Myrdal, op. cit., p. 65.

39. Fanon, Wretched of the Earth, op. cit., p. 32.

40. Eldrige Cleaver. 1968. **Soul on Ice**. New York: McGraw- Hill, p. 26.

41. Ralph Ginzburg. 1962. **100 Years of Lynching**. New York: Lancer Books.

42. William J. Bowers, loc. cit.

43. Savitz, op. cit, p. 482.

44. Boone Hammond. 1965. "The Contest System: A Survival Technique." Masters thesis, Washington University, p. 38.

45. Joyce Ladner. 1971. **Tomorrow's Tomorrow: The Black Woman**. Garden City, New York: Doubleday, pp. 51-52.

46. Bernette Golden. 1974. Cited in **The Ugly Crime of Rape. Essence**, 6 (June), p. 37.

47. Carolyn Jetter Greene. 1973. **70 Soul Secrets of Sapphire**. San Francisco: Sapphire Publishing Co., p. 6.

48. Menachim Amir. 1974. "Sociocultural Factors in Forcible Rape," in **Sexual Behavior** (Leonard Gross, ed.). New York: Spectrum Publications, p. 12.

49. Germaine Greer. 1973. "Seduction is a Four Letter Word." **Playboy**, January, pp. 220-223.

50. Dotson Rader. 1973. "The Sexual Nature of Violence." **The New York Times**, October 22, p. 231.

51. Murray Straus, et al. 1980. **Behind Closed Doors: Violence in the**

American Family. Garden City, New York: Anchor.

52. Noel Cazanave and Murray Strauss. 1979. "Race, Class, Network Embeddedness and Family Violence: A Search for Potent Support Systems." Journal of Comparative Family Studies 10 (Fall), pp. 281-300.

53. St. Clair Drake and Horace Clayton. 1945. Black Metropolis. New York: Harcourt, Brace and Co., pp. 566-67.

54. Cazanave and Straus., op. cit.

55. B. D. Cohen. 1973. "Home Fights Hurt Hundreds." The Washington Post, March 25, pp. 81-3.

56. C. f. Robert Staples. 1973. The Black Woman in America: Sex, Marriage and the Family. Chicago: Nelson-Hall, pp. 114.

57. David A. Schutz. 1969. Coming Up Black: Patterns of Ghetto Socialization. Englewood Cliffs, N. J.: Prentice- Hall, p. 107.

58. Bohannon, op. cit., p. 244.

59. Greene, op. cit., p. 45. pa60. James Boudouris. 1971. "Homicide and The Family." Journal of Marriage and the Family, Vol. 33, November, p. 671.

61. Cazanave and Straus, loc. cit.

62. Wolfgang, loc. cit.

63. William Goode. 1971. "Force and Violence in the Family." Journal of Marriage and the Family, Vol. 33 (November), p. 33.

64. Reuben Hill and Howard Becker, eds. 1975. Family, Marriage and Parenthood. Boston: D. C. Heath, p. 790.

65. Lee Rainwater. 1970. Behind Ghetto Walls. Chicago: Aldine, p. 163.

66. James D. Comer. 1969. "The Dynamics of Black and White Violence," in Violence in America, Hugh Graham and Ted Gurr, eds. New York, p. 434.

67. Alvin Poussaint. 1972. Why Blacks Kill Blacks. New York: Emerson-Hall, p. 72.

68. Staples. The Black Woman in America, op. cit., Chapter 6.

69. Davis Gil, 1971. "Violence Against Children." Journal of Marriage and the Family, 33 (November), p. 640.

70. Ibid.

71. Constance K. Kamis and Norma J. Radin. 1971. "Class Differences in the Socialization Practices of Negro Mothers." The Black Family: Essays and Studies, Robert Staples, ed. Belmont, Calif.: Wadsworth, pp. 230-247.

72. Gil, op. cit., p. 648.

73. Cazanave and Straus, loc. cit.

74. Allison Davis and John Dollard. 1940. **Children of Bondage.** Washington, D. C.: American Council on Education, pp. 264- 267.

75. Cazanave and Straus, loc. cit.

76. "Crime in the United States." 1972. Op. cit., p. 132.

77. Robert Staples. 1975. "To Be Young, Black and Oppressed." **The Black Scholar.** December, pp. 2-9.

HOMICIDE AMONG YOUNG BLACK ADULTS:
LIFE IN THE SUBCULTURE OF EXASPERATION

William B. Harvey

"It's like a jungle sometimes...it makes me wonder
how I keep from going under."
"Don't push me 'cause I'm close to the edge...
I'm trying not to lose my head."

Grandmaster Flash and the
Furious Five

The comparatively high incidence of crime, including homicide, among Black people should come as no surprise to anyone who is familiar with the patterns of racial discrimination and repression that have been a fundamental part of the American culture. The eminent criminologist, Marvin Wolfgang, (1964:31) offered the following observations on the subject of crime in the Black community. He wrote that

. . . if a careful detached scholar knew nothing about crime rates but was aware of the social, economic and political disparities between whites and Negroes in the United States, and if this diligent researcher had prior knowledge of the historical status of the American Negro, what would be the most plausible hypothesis our scholar could make about the crime rate of Negroes? Even this small amount of relevant knowledge would justify the expectation that Negroes would be found to have a higher crime rate than whites.

Statistics reveal that the expectation is realized. Black people, as an aggregate, commit crimes at a greater rate than their White counterparts. The variability in the rate differs depending on the particular crime, but for homicide, recent data indicate that the comparative figures per 100,000 are more than six times greater for Blacks than for Whites. (Statistical Abstracts, 1986;) Attempts to provide an explanation for Black-White differences in homicide rates have generated spirited discussion and a variety of hypotheses. The most likely reason seems rather apparent though, for as Palmer so gingerly remarks, "the difference is probably explained on the basis that social pressures on Negroes are greater than on whites." (1962:4).

These social pressures--racial discrimination, underemployment, substandard housing, inadequate health care and inferior education--continue to impact adversely upon Black Americans. It has generally been recognized that there are identifiable conditions which tend to be related to a high homicide rate, and these criminogenic conditions are more likely to be found among Blacks than among Whites. Wolfgang notes (1967: 8) that whenever a culture is racially heterogenous with a minority that is subservient and suppressed, the minority group is likely to be considered socially inferior and to have high proportions of its people in the lower socio-economic classes. Elaborating on this point, he cites data from a study he conducted (1967: 275) which purports that "the rate of homicide rises in certain race- sex-age specific groups, and this fact in turn suggests an equivalent rise in the value of violence found in the subculture from which these groups emerge. The single race-sex-age group with the highest rate of homicide is among Negro males, aged 20-24, whose rate is 92.5 compared to 24.6 for all Negroes and 1.8 for whites."

These comments are interpreted in this paper as suggesting that the dominant culture places a substantial portion of Black Americans in a situation where they are encapsulated in unfavorable living environments and afforded significantly less opportunity to attain the rewards that are available to others in the society, thus increasing the likelihood that they will commit criminal acts.

Similarly, Bensing and Schroeder (1960:vii) have pointed out that Black people

"live for the most part, in those areas of greatest social need, poorest health (care), and most sub-standard housing, which characteristics...correlate so highly with the homicide rate...they, on the whole, acquire less formal education and earn less money than the general population, factors which may also play a role in producing those tensions and needs which tend to explode into homicides."

The Genetic Argument

Inferences have been made from time to time that the high homicide rates among Black Americans are due to a transmission of attitudes and behavioral traits from their forebearers in Africa, where life is thought (by Westerners) to have been lightly regarded. The reasoning goes that if Blacks were frequently engaged in homicidal activities in their African homelands, then biological inheritance may be an explanation for high homicide rates among Blacks in America. Such suggestions gain attention only because of the racist strain of biological and cultural determinism that has long been an acceptable theory in American and European scholarship. Fortunately, this issue has been addressed in a thorough and precise manner, and has been called into question by cross- cultural evidence. Bohannon (1960: 237) has concluded on the basis of studies conducted in several African societies, that "here is overwhelming evidence that it is cultural and not biological factors which make for a high homicide rate among American Negroes." Indeed, he also noted that the homicide rates for Africans tended not only to be lower than those of Black Americans, but to be lower than those of white Americans as well. One might reasonably conclude from these findings that the repressive treatment of Black people in American society, along with the high level of cultural acceptance, and even affinity for violence in this country, are the major factors that account for the high incidences of homicide among Americans who are of African heritage and descent.

Taking into account the significance of environmental factors and the inapplicability of the genetic transmission theory in regards to Black homicide rates, a more thorough scrutiny of the particular conditions in which Black Americans live seems more useful for explaining the levels of violent behavior found among Black Americans.

154

Subculture of Exasperation

The combination of oppressive environmental conditions and minimal opportunities for escape or improvement make the poor Black neighborhoods places in which the prospect of conflict between individuals becomes extremely high, relative to Black or White middle and upper class residential areas. Researchers (Bensing and Schroeder, 1960; Danto, 1982; Kirk, 1982) have long recognized that structural conditions in the Black community impinge on both the organizational and interpersonal activity that takes place there. Wolfgang (1967: 19) also acknowledges that the territorial area he describes as encompassing the highest rate of homicide is one which "is characterized by poor housing, high density of population (and) overcrowded conditions." It is my contention that (Wolfgang and Ferracuti (1967: 140) inappropriately label this territory and the social patterns of the residents as a **subculture of violence**. To be sure, violence occurs with unfortunate regularity in these circumstances, but figuratively speaking, it is the **symptom** of and not the disease. The dearth of opportunities that are available for Black people to accrue reasonable incomes through socially sanctioned employment, to live in dignity and self-respect, and to realize the same benefits and pleasures as Whites, inevitably results in displays of discontent and outward directed aggression.

In this situation, the White American dream becomes the Black American nightmare. The oppressive nature of their living conditions could conceivably be tolerated by young Black men in these settings if they were able to secure employment that would begin to address some of their economic needs, while also satisfying their psychological need to meet the societally constructed definition of a "real" man as someone who works. The inability to realize this need, through no fault of their own and certainly not because of a lack of interest, pushes young Black men into a situation where an alternate expression of masculinity becomes necessary. The expressive act(s), if conducted in a setting where it is interpreted by another male as threatening to his own masculinity, can result in argument, conflict, and even homicide. For example, Staples (1986: 72) writes of "incursions to be punished by death [which are] many and minor...[and] include stepping on the wrong toe, literally; cheating in a drug deal; simply saying 'I dare you' to someone holding a gun; crossing territorial lines in a gang dispute." Given a framework of social conditions such as this, it would be more appropriate to label the circumstances as a **subculture of exasperation**, rather than one of violence. Here are individuals who have little hope or reason to expect that their lives will improve; who have experienced serial poverty across generational lines; whose living conditions are piteous; who are likely to be functionally illiterate with no marketable skills; and who know the shame and pain of racism.

Kirk (1982: 146) posits that the constant pressures of institutionalized racism and oppression leave Blacks with a sense of frustration, hopelessness and powerlessness and a resultant anger that is internalized and long simmering (Grier and Cobb, 1968). The manifestation of that anger is often aggression, usually directed against those who are in close proximity to the aggressor. Often, the triggering incident is a seemingly insignificant issue, but the importance of any given situation often is dependent on the wider sphere of activities in which an individual is involved. In other words, a

155

steadily employed person with comfortable living quarters and modest possessions may pay little attention to an intentional personal slight or small insult, whereas the unemployed, more transient individual with few posssessions, might consider the same situation to be of major importance to his pride and honor. Unfortunately, many analysts of Black aggression appear to describe these acts of violence triggered by trivial events as **causes** of homicide. Instead they are merely **symptoms** of a larger social- structural pattern of pathology.

Wolfgang's analysis of the people who, unwittingly, find themselves in this situation, and his **subculture of violence** characterization seem to be, in essence, a means of blaming the victim. He presents this notion as a socio-psychological theory which stakes its validity in what is deemed to be the value system of this group. In fact, the value system of the group is not at variance with that of the larger culture (Merton, 1968). Its members would like to have the highly paid job, the big house in the suburbs, two cars and an annual vacation in the Caribbean as much as their middle and upper class counterparts would. And with the accumulation of such items, it is likely that the violence that Wolfgang claims they value would decline to the comparable level of their wealthier fellow citizens.

It is the denial of opportunity to realize those "mainstream" values, and the aggravation that is manifested as a result of that denial that leads to the violent, sometimes homicidal acts within this subculture. The ultimate causes, of violence, generally, and of homicide particularly, within Black communities, do not rest fundamentally with those persons who are themselves victims of their environment or with those symptomatic acts of aggression that tend to escalate into lethal acts. Rather the causes must be traced to the social structure that generates such interpersonal encounters. To present the conditions in which poor young Blacks usually live, and considering the forces that impact on them as a **subculture of exasperation**, rather than one simply of violence, is not to offer a defense of destructive or antisocial activity that is perpetrated within Black communities. Such a label, I suggest, focuses attention on the nature of the relationship between minimal employment possibilities, low social status, and substandard environmental conditions as factors that directly affect the number and rate of homicidal activities carried out by young Black adults.

It is also important to note that the race and class specific housing patterns that prevail in America mean that, in almost all cases, poor Blacks will kill other poor Blacks. Nearly 95 of Black homicides were committed by Blacks, while only 10 percent of White homicide victims were killed by Blacks (Whitman, 1986: 22). The following table (Table 1) illustrates the various components of the **subculture of exasperation**.

Carried to its tragic extreme, the pathos of this situation in which young men have no sense or belief that their lives will be appreciably better or different regardless of the intensity of their efforts to make it so, was captured by Pouissant (1972) when he wrote that, "It is as if, in a mood of sheer desperation, blacks seem to become a part of the white mainstream and obtain so-called manhood by turning to physical brutality and crimes against one another. Reacting to the futility of his own life, the individual derives an ultimate sense of power when he holds the fate of another human being in his hands." Staples (1986: 72) adds that "killing is only **machismo** taken to the extreme."

These statements clearly capture the imbued fury of the people who comprise the **subculture of exasperation**, and establishes, to some degree, a connection between deprivation, poor self-concept, and the resulting sense of futility that then becomes the impetus for hostile actions against others. The inherent flaw in the mode of analysis that results in the conceptualization of a **subculture of violence** is that it overlooks the root causes of the anger, the frustration, the anxiety and the dissatisfaction that is felt by persons who are the victims of stigma and discrimination. The highly significant effects of environment and the degree of social acceptance and treatment, with consequent effects on individual attitude and value formation are substantially understated. Though the rates of homicide among young Black adults are inordinately high, simply taking the figures out of their cultural context and attaching a sinister group value orientation to them, presents a distorted and oversimplified view of what is obviously a complex and difficult problem--one which has profound implications for the larger society.

TABLE 1

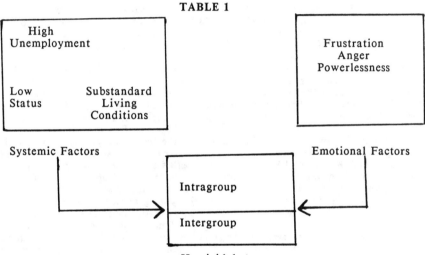

PROBLEMS FACING YOUNG BLACK MEN

Unemployment and Self Image

Disadvantageous living conditions obviously affect all segments of the Black poor, but the focus thus far in this paper has been particularly on young Black men, who, as a group, are more likely to be unemployed, have the least likelihood of attaining postsecondary education, and have the greatest chances of spending time in prison than any other sub-group in America (Hare, 1985). The following figures provide a glimpse of the unemployment situation as it pertains to Black men.

TABLE 2

Unemployed Total in Thousands

Blacks

	1983	1982	1981
16-19 years old	392	396	357
20-24 years old	591	565	483

Unemployment Rate (Percent)

Married men, wife present			
White	6.0	6.0	4.0
Black	11.3	11.5	8.6
White Teenagers (16-19)	19.3	20.4	17.3
Black Teenagers (16-19)	48.5	48.0	41.4

(Statistical Abstracts (1985:406)

According to Swinton's (1986: 14) research, Black men over 20 have averaged 12.9% unemployment since 1975 and 15.4% unemployment during the last five years. In the first three quarters of 1985, their unemployment rate was 13.1% Black teenagers have had unemployment rates that have averaged 41.3% since 1975, 44.1% for the last five years and 40.1% during 1985.

In America, as in many other countries, the period of young adulthood is one in which the individual feels a strong need to demonstrate capability and maturation. Kimball (1962: 86) refers to this phenomenon by which young people are compelled to acknowledge their adulthood as the "forced abandonment of childhood." The societally imposed need to abandon childhood is made more difficult for the young person by the absence of clearly defined and socially recognized rites of passage that symbolize movement into the more desirable category of manhood. These feelings bring with them a kind of anxiety that is especially stirring to young men operating in a male-dominated society such as this one, so that they are compelled to demonstrate that the process of their physical maturation has been completed. Young Black men, who are mostly urban based, find that the individualistic ethos of modern American society leaves it largely to their own discretion to determine ways in which they will "demonstrate" their self- perceived arrival into adulthood. In earlier times, and perhaps in less complex societies even today, the successful hunting of an animal or the cultivation of a plot of land might have served as a means of satisfying this concern. But contemporary America has not only minimized such outlets, it has failed to provide constructive means for the simultaneous affirmation of their manhood and the release of the pent-up energy of these young men. Although such problems of adolescence-to-adulthood plague all American youth, regardless of race, the socioeconomic conditions under which young Black men are forced to live lead to even greater problems among this cohort. Whitman (1986: 22) posits that "with no job--and few prospects of employment--the uneducated black man of the ghetto is witness to his own economic impotence."

What might be called the "exasperation factor" among young Black men is quite high, and there is no way it could be reduced in the absence of some specific activity or ritual in which they can receive confirmation of their masculinity and affirmation of their adulthood. Sporting events, of various kinds, have been used as both an outlet and a diversion by young men, and these episodes receive attention that is far greater than their actual significance. Male adolescents, white and Black, actively participate in them as an expressive act and a demonstration of individual development. But, as much as sports are celebrated in this culture, athletic achievements don't satisfy the social standard for adult accomplishments, unless they are performed by professional athletes.

While personally fulfilling, sports are remunerative activities for only a very miniscule percentage of those involved. Despite their level of personal excellence, very few young men are compensated monetarily or otherwise for their athletic skills. The significance which is attached to sports perhaps underscores the absence of any socially sanctioned activity, other than working, that can be used as an indication of having reached a certain plateau of maturation. However, the primary avenue for athletic participation is through the schools and young Black men are more prone than students from other groups to drop out or be "pushed out" of the education system. The anxiety that young Black men feel stems in part from their inability to translate their sense of having reached a significant stage in their lives into some validating act or set of actions, and the apparent impossibility of their obtaining those trappings of the "good life" that are teasingly flashed before them every day in shop windows and through the mass media. From the dawning of their manhood, American society denies to young Black men the ability to carry out one of the most important traditional roles that has been used to define masculinity in the social order--the role of worker and provider (Harvey, 1977).

If the society was seriously concerned with the fullest development of all of its citizens, this expression of self-worth might be satisfied through gainful employment, with its accompanying material and psychological benefits. Goodman observes that, "It's hard to grow up when there isn't enough man's work." (1960: 17) This statement reflects the essence of the dilemma that has been forced upon young Black men. Among members of this group, unemployment is consistently at a rate that is substantially higher than the national average, ranging upward to fifty percent when economic circumstances are depressed. There is an old adage in the Black community that when white America catches a cold, Black America catches pneumonia; and among young Black men the negative effects of the highly stratified American economic system are especially severe and even lethal. The significance of gainful employment leading to positive self-esteem and normative social interaction and behavior patterns cannot be overstated when assessing the dynamics of the Black community, and the actions of young Black males. The opposite situation also holds true because people who have nothing, have nothing to lose, and they behave accordingly.

In this cultural system, where political determinations allow for massive numbers of young Black men to be unemployed and a racist ideology denies them the kind of humane and dignified treatment that they know Whites are provided, resentment builds like a time bomb within those persons who are affected negatively by this double standard. According to Joe (1983: 20), "between 1960 and 1982, the black male population over age 16 nearly doubled, from 5.6 million to 10.73 million. But the number of employed Black males increased by only 1.79 million, from 4.15 million to 5.94 million. **Thus, the number of unemployed black males grew by 3.34 million during this period.**" (Emphasis added) This process of economic emasculation has profound effects on every aspect of Black life and explains why despite some gains in the educational, political, and social arenas over the past few decades, life has not improved, and in some ways has worsened, for large numbers of Black people. Thus, the problems of young Black males cannot be fully described as purely age-related but must be linked to the plight of the larger Black community in the twentieth century.

Viewing the Broader Context

Young Black male adults are perhaps the most systematically deprived group in the nation, and no meaningful plan for the improvement of their lives exists, nor apparently is one being officially considered. As an antidote to the problems faced by poor Black people generally, the contemporary wisdom is that providing a stimulus for business and industry through tax cuts and other fiscal incentives will ultimately result in the expansion of the economy, with resultant increases in employment, income and benefits for all. Until this situation is realized however, if it ever is, the aggression and frustration that develops in the legions of the underclass fosters and continues to grow like a cancerous tumor, feeding on anger, dissatisfaction and disappointment.

To develop a clearer understanding of the disproportionately high rates of homicide among Black young adults, it is necessary to broaden the analysis past this particular group, to get a better view of the whole culture. In America, the definition of a satisfactory life style is tied to the consumption and acquisition of goods and services, and the prevalence of the mass media results in the transmission of continuous visual representations of the fruits of the world's richest economic system. As a result, all of the benefits that are being enjoyed by those who have the economic means to acquire them are paraded before those who do not receive a proportionate share of the "goodies." Meanwhile, the consumption directed advertising messages constantly urge everyone, including those who are excluded from the social mainstream, to get more goods, so that they can experience a happier existence. The paradox is that many Black people have no way to acquire these items unless they do so through illegal or extra-legal means. Black teenage males who were surveyed in an inner city admitted that about one-fourth of their income was from crime (Whitman, 1986: 20). The nagging frustration of constantly being reminded of all the things that one does not have and can not get is aggravated by the obvious and significant differential in opportunities that are open to Blacks and Whites to participate in the socio-economic system.

The realization that they are denied from enjoying the benefits of America's wealth because of a social structure that relegates them to its lowest levels is not lost on Black young adults. It is a major source of the rage that they feel so stridently. Unable to strike back at those in power, whom they feel are responsible for their societal positions and for their inability to obtain the possessions that are considered most desirable, many males in this category manifest their aggression through criminal activity and demonstrable expressions of bravado or "toughness." These actions can take either an individual or group format, with examples of the latter being youth gangs, or even loosely affiliated mobs of people striking out to protest perceived mistreatments. When the activity takes on a large scale collective form, it becomes the riot that has frequently erupted in American cities over the past twenty years, almost all of which have started in poor Black neighborhoods. Here, one sees efforts on the part of those involved to accumulate goods first, as they have been socially conditioned to do, then to destroy the property of those who are regarded as their victimizers and exploiters.

Considerably more frequent than these group occurrences, though, are situations in which aggressive actions are directed against someone who is close, from the standpoint of either relationship and/or geography. Because homicide is such a markedly intraracial crime, as well as one which is most often committed against persons who are in the immediate proximity, the victim is quite likely to be a friend, relative, or loved one of the perpetrator. And, though these actions may be labeled deviant from a White middle-class perspective, fundamentally they are attempts by the persons involved to express some measure of control over their lives, their circumstances, and their destiny.

It is not simply the luxuries of life, but often the necessities, that are outside the reach of the members of the underclass. Young Black men who have spouses and families are effectively denied the opportunity to carry out the provider function that has traditionally been expected of the male as a result of gainful employment. Simultaneously, government policies dictate that they not receive financial assistance, despite their joblessness. These formidable impediments of economic discrimination and inequalty prevent young Black men from executing the standard male role in the society, and so they attempt to find alternative ways in which they can express and demonstrate their masculinity. For most Black youths, only two avenues are open--the military services or the streets. Those who take the former option escape their stultifying environment for a time, but many of them find themselves right back in the same situation a few years later, and gaining access to the services is becoming increasingly difficult as they impose additional restrictions on entrants. The ones who take the second choice usually spend their time with a fraternity of their peers and involve themselves in a hustle of some kind or another to try to secure funds as opportunities present themselves (Whitman, 1986: 22).

These factors are all destructive to the operation of the Black family unit. Further, the scope of the problem is increasing, rather than diminishing, as revealed by the increase in unemployment figures that were cited earlier, figures which impinge most heavily on young Black male adults. Swinton (1986: 14) notes that "the devastating unemployment experience of the last eleven years has affected all black demographic groups, adult males, adult females, and teenagers." In addition, even when Blacks are employed, they still find themselves in an unfavorable situation when compared to Whites, since Black family income in 1984 was only about 56 percent of that earned by White families (Statistical Abstracts: 1986: 450). This is not a new situation, because "on measures of income, poverty and unemployment, wide disparities between blacks and pawhites have not lessened or have even worsened since 1960." (Joe, 1983: ii.)

These findings seem to invalidate the applicability of Henry and Short's (1954: 60) conclusions that there is a direct positive correlation between the

161

business cycle and homicide among non-White people. Arguing that homicide is often the outcome of an act of aggression that has its source in frustration, they contend that as business improves, the rate of homicide among Blacks increases because at such times they tend to lose status relative to Whites who are also enjoying the benefit of the economic prosperity. The crux of their argument is that homicide is directly related to the frustration caused by loss of status relative to others in the same status reference system. However, they also point out that "if our assumptions are correct, Negroes who commit homicide rank at the bottom of our hierarchy of status since they are lower class members of the lowest ascriptive category." For young Black adult males, the business cycle would seem to bear little relationship per se to their involvement in homicidal activities since they are so likely to be unemployed even during the best of economic times. It would appear that persons in this category develop their status reference considerations on factors other than employment, since it is the exceptional situation, rather than the norm.

Prevailing indexes that determine the level of status appear to include the amount of contact with peers, the frequency of interaction with females and a capacity for spontaneous vocal elocutions, also known as "rapping." The ability to acquire cash is also looked upon favorably. Status considerations are an important factor for persons in this group, who are continuously reminded of their positions at the bottom of the social hierarchy. Glasgow believes that the anger and despair that these young men feel arises, to a large degree, from their contact with mainstream institutions, which almost imperceptibly and very impersonally, reject them (1980: 10). Certainly, the economic institution offers them only the most miniscule of prospects--these are emphatically the people who are the last hired and the first fired. But, business and industry are not alone in turning their backs on them. In similar fashion the schools, social service agencies, the legal and criminal justice institutions, also tend to treat them with contempt and disrespect. The frustration-aggression hypothesis advanced by Henry and Short is given credence and support by the kinds of interaction that occur between the members of the Black underclass and the mainstream institutions, and more generally by the very tenor of the **subculture of exasperation.**

The **subculture of exasperation,** then, encompasses those who have not simply fallen out, but who have been pushed out of mainstream American society. Suffering from chronic unemployment, substandard living conditions, and facing an unsympathetic bureaucratic colussus, its victims look backward at failed band-aid approaches to meeting their needs and forward to increasing conservatism and clearer statements of concern for corporate profits than for the needs of poor people. The worsening indicators of the quality of life experienced by many Blacks come at a time when the federal government refuses to champion its most disadvantaged citizens, preferring to rely instead on private initiative and personal compassion to provide services for that portion of the population. Young Black men have fallen through the proverbial "safety net for the truly needy" in large numbers, which indicates either that the categories which are currently being used as operational determinants to define need are different from what they have ever been before, or that there is a very large hole in the net.

Technological Expendability

Historically, black Americans have been exploited for their labor, receiving lower wages than their white counterparts and suffering from the results of being "last hired and first fired" when jobs were made available. But the parallel developments that have occurred nationally, from an agricultural to an industrial to a technologically based economy, and from a rural to an urban to a suburban centered residence scheme have combined to push Black people into a situation where their labor is of lesser need to the financial viability of the country than it has ever been before (Wilhelm, 1976). The inordinately high rates of unemployment that exist for Black people are ultimately, a function of racism, even when secondarily attributed to such causes as: (1) the paucity of demonstrable job skills that they hold which are suitable for the kinds of positions now being developed; (2) and the abysmally low level of education skills that they are receiving in urban school systems (Renick and Harvey, 1985). The collective impact of these phenomena have combined to entrap large numbers of young Black people into what is increasingly being called "an underclass."

Whitman (1986: 18) estimates the number of Blacks living in the underclass at about 2 million to 3.5 million, or about one-third of all poor Blacks. He considers this group to be an irreducible core of poor inner-city Blacks who are trapped in an unending cycle of joblessness, broken homes, welfare, and often drugs and violence. Glasgow (1980: 10) believes that "this entrapment into underclass status is clearly affected by many factors, primarily the lack of real opportunities to succeed and the limited alternatives provided by socialization patterns of the inner city."

In this same vein, McDonald (1961: 29) points out that,

> . . .the extremely low economic status of the lower class Negro is productive of living conditions conducive to homicide. The combination of low income, restrictive zoning and shortage of housing brings about severe overcrowding, ...(and) it may be said that the lower class Negro is only a marginal participant in the society. His participation in the legal and social institutions of the community is partial and largely passive.

The persons who are trapped in the kind of living conditions to which these scholars make reference do not feel as though they have a stake in the established order. To the contrary, it is the prevailing social order and its policies that they consider to be responsible for their positions at the bottom of the social hierarchy. The members of this group have a pronounced lack of commitment to the society, which is not at all surprising given their near total exclusion from the social and economic benefits produced by this country. While discrimination and racism impact on all Black people to some degree or another, it does not seem unreasonable to suggest that those persons who are at the low end of the economic scale within the Black community are likely to be most affected by these dehumanizing conditions and forces. It is that most impoverished section of the Black lower class that makes up the underclass. The paucity of income for members of this group is matched by their absence of political, lineal, or affiliational leverage. If American society is a family, then these are the orphans, existing as best they can and scarcely gaining notice from those who lead a more favored existence. The crucial link here is a recognition that not only does the underclass exist, as

163

an identifiable, if not altogether discrete unit of the Black lower class, but that the operation of the society seems designed to produce and reproduce it (Tabb, 1970: 106).

Because no precise indexes have been established as to where "lower class" ends and "underclass" begins, no body of substantive data exists that can positively identify members from the latter group as individuals who are involved in most of the homicidal activity that occurs in the Black community. It is clear, however, that they are subjected, to a much greater degree than others, to the environmental circumstances that are correlated with high homicide rates. What is also known is that young Black men are involved in homicides at a rate that is highly disproportionate to their numbers in the total population and that they are unemployed at similarly disproportionate rates. Lack of income usually leads to depressed living conditions and the absence of opportunity can provide the spark for an explosion of frustration generated aggression--and homicide. Class separation and racial segregation are situational determinants that come into play such that young Black men who commit homicide usually find their victims in the same racial group and socioeconomic circumstances as themselves.

Declining Family Life

There is still another factor that has been proposed as being significant in regard to the high homicide rate among young Black men. Fattah (1977: 69) suggests that "one of the major causes of the homicide of young Black men was the destruction of the Black family life." Major changes have been identified in the structure of the Black family over the past two decades which have resulted in a downward push for many Blacks from the lower class to the underclass. Wilson (1982: 121) zeroes in on the particular economic vulnerability faced by members of this group when he points out that "in underclass families, unlike other families in the Black community, the head of the household is almost invariably, a woman. The distinctive makeup of the underclass is also reflected in the very large number of adult males with no fixed address--who live mainly on the streets, roaming from one place of shelter to another." There is a definite relationship between the inability of young Black men to find employment; the increasing number of female-headed households in the Black community; the economic and psychological trauma endured by the Black poor; and the high rates of homicidal activity among young, impoverished Black males.

From a rhetorical standpoint, the future inclusion of Blacks as full partners in the American social system is governmental policy and there is professed optimism among many politicians that this goal can be realized. But past expectations have failed to materialize for large portions of the Black population, and often they have been contradicted by subsequent realities. For example, a 1967 government study reported that the "incidence of poverty among nonwhite families remains high, with about one of three classified as poor. Still, just six years ago one of two of the nonwhite families were poor." (Tabb, 1970: 82) Yet, a decade and a half later, updated information based on a broader range of data reveals that "the gap between the average incomes of whites and blacks is as wide today (1983) as it was in 1969 primarily because the proportion of black families headed by women rose from one-fifth to nearly one-half and the proportion of black men with jobs dropped sharply in that period." (Herbers, 1983: 8).

The present national policies do not offer any meaningful improvement in the lives of the people who find themselves in this underclass. Neither is there any reason to believe that the future will be substantially different. As a result, the pattern of social relations is often at variance with that practiced by white middle-class Americans who expect and who have reason to believe that their reasonably comfortable lifestyles will remain stable, or perhaps even improve. The underclass is distinguished even from the lower class, principally by the lack of mobility of its members (Glasgow, 1980: 8). According to classical definitions, the lower class is a variation of middle-class adaptation and striving, but such pretentions do not exist in the underclass. The kinds of aspirations and attitudes that go along with the expectation of mobility are not held by young people from the underclass. Certainly, this group is among the lowest status cohorts in America, and as Lester (1975: 235) has pointed out, "homicide...is characteristic of low status persons, whereas suicide is characteristic of high status persons."

Differential Interpretations of Behavior

As noted previously, social interactions in poor Black neighborhoods are often different from those that occur in higher income Black and white areas. The key focus is on survival and for young men, it can be what Glasgow calls "a harrowing social and psychological existence." (1980: 88) The various modes of adaptation are likely to be more visibly aggressive than those in middle and upper class areas because the standards of politeness and civility that mark middle-class standing do not hold sway there. But, violence is not a basic, integral component of underclass behavior. The particulars that lead to confrontation between people who are members of the underclass might seen inconsequential to someone from a different background. Within the subculture of exasperation, certain actions and statements take on an importance that they would not have in other settings, but this phenomenon is true of many sub- groups at various income and class levels. When people respond to stimuli that have negative meanings and connotations within their ethnic or social groups, that response hardly indicates that they value violence for its own sake. For example, some upper class males have been known to fight over discrepancies in their golf scores, and while this action may not be approved of by others in their circles, it nevertheless merits an in-group understanding of that situation as having a particular kind of significance that others might have great difficulty in comprehending.

This process of aggressive response to certain behaviors is what Wolfgang observed when he wrote that

> ...the significance of a jostle, a slightly derogatory remark, or the appearance of a weapon in the hands of an adversary are stimuli differentially perceived and interpreted by Negroes and whites, males and females. Social expectations of response in particular types of social interaction result in differential "definitions of the situation." A male is usually expected to defend the name and honor of his mother, the virtue of womanhood...and to accept no derogation about his race (even from a member of his own race), his age or his masculinity (1958: 188).

165

While the incidents cited can certainly be cause for violence, in this particular example they are lifted out of the historical and cultural contexts which would provide a fuller understanding of why they are flashpoints, not simply for lower class Blacks, but for those in higher income ranges as well. They more likely reveal the difference and distance between Black and White cultures in America than they do the existence of a subculture of violence.

Further, Kirk (1982: 144) posits that imitative learning may play a role in the developmental processes of young people, and makes them more tolerant of violence than they would be otherwise. He considers media presentations of violence as an especially influential force. Noting that many low income Black people spend an extremely large amount of time watching television, where they are fed a steady diet of crime and violence, he speculates that such programming may have an influential effect on the viewers, and especially young people, such that it encourages similar behavior in their daily lives. This theory has gained support in recent years when certain crimes that were perpetrated closely resembled similar ones that had been broadcast on television programs. Homicide is usually an impulsive crime and so would not likely occur as a direct influence of media presentations, but a predilection to violent behavior which could lead to homicide could conceivably be spawned from media presentations. Again, what is particularly noteworthy here is the absence of opportunities for underclass persons to put their energies to productive use that would minimize a media-violence link in the first place.

As far as the issue of behavior analysis is concerned, Bohannon makes an eloquent statement for the examination of statistics only against a background which will provide their true meaning and significance. He writes that:

> It has been the battle cry of the anthropologists for over half a century that the procedure of lifting social or cultural facts out of context and comparing them with other facts also lifted out of context is inadmissable procedure. Until now, that battle cry has never been directed toward criminologists, who are still lifting rates of specific crimes--like homicide--in particular, or occasionally of classifying crimes by "motive." (1960: 252)

When the homicide statistics of young Black adult males are put back into the larger cultural context, as Bohannon argues, then the picture of their victimization by the social order becomes clearer and the harshness of Wolfgang's labelling of a subculture of violence seems, at the very least, to be a mischaracterization. The term is also unfortunate in regard to its impact on the prioritizing of social policies because it implicitly suggests that these poor Black people will continue to kill only each other, which then reduces the urgency of the problem to White and middle class populations. Such a conclusion may be both misleading, and of very temporary comfort to those populations that do not feel the direct impact of these activities. There is no accurate or precise way to predict when or where some of the anger felt by these young men might spill out of their own neighborhoods, and into other areas. While not predicting such activity, Kirk (1982: 147) intimates that "we know from history that the oppressed ultimately direct their aggressive actions toward the oppressors."

Even this warning will be missed by some because they will refuse to see the system or themselves as oppressors. Those who believe that American society is truly a meritocracy and that those who work hard will get ahead, discount or completely dismiss the prevalent and pernicious effects of racism. Certainly, there are various factors that are contributory to the unfavorable circumstances in which many young Black people find themselves, but the root cause of their condition can be easily identified, and perhaps with sensitive leadership and determination, eventually eliminated. According to Glasgow, (1980: 11) "Racism is probably the most basic cause of the underclass condition." The options in dealing with this issue appear to be obvious and distinct. America's leaders can introduce programs to help poor people create meaningful lives by developing productive work opportunities at reasonable wages for a growing body of angry, frustrated young men who currently have no stake in the existing economic- political system. Or, with prevailing practices of exclusion from the mainstream, the continued oppression and discrimination of the Black underclass can continue, with the hope that the violence and homicide that these policies breed will remain confined to Black neighborhoods. The approach that is selected may very well impact on the quality of life that is experienced, not only for those persons who are located within the **subculture of exasperation,** but for significant numbers of other Americans as well.

The Plight of Black Females

Though the primary focus of the material presented thus far has been on Black males because their homicide rates are higher than all other subgroups, it seems inappropriate to address the subject of homicide without also making some reference to the problems faced by Black females. While their homicide rates are considerably lower than those for Black males, they are, nevertheless, higher than those for White females, **and those for White males.** Obviously, young Black women are also trapped within the **subculture of exasperation,** and suffer from some of the same problems that bedevil their male counterparts. While they do not have the "macho" cross to bear that Black men have, such that they feel compelled to prove their femininity in the same way that their male counterparts must validate their masculinity, Black women have to contend with the reality that their social status is very low. They face the double discrimination of racism and sexism and the manifestation of these two forces is felt in various ways, so that they feel the anger, frustration and disappointment of second class citizenship from two perspectives. Given these factors, the lower incidences of homicide among Black women than among Black men is likely due to socialization, which in America denies to females the sanction of aggressive behavior.

Probably the most serious of several difficulties faced by Black women is one of economic deficiency--as a group, they have lower average incomes than white women, and than men, white or Black. This point has become increasingly significant with the growing number of households that are headed by women. In addition, cultural factors have shaped a set of attitudes about Black women that have not been favorable and have led to their being held in low esteem. Further, the circumstances, both physical and emotional, that many Black women live in are highly stressful and anxiety producing. Finally, there is the scapegoat effect in which the Black female becomes the repository of the anger and frustration of the Black male. In

167

these situations, she kills, to escape her tormentor, usually a husband or lover, or is killed by him.

The economic plight of Black women is absolutely staggering. In 1978, the median income of Black female headed families was $5888, and 74 percent of all poor Black families were headed by women (Wilson, 1982: 121). As previously stated, in a Black underclass family the head of the household almost invariably will be a woman, and families headed by women are almost twice as likely to be poor as two parent families, regardless of race. (Herbers, 1983: 8). The paucity of their incomes forces these Black women into the kinds of living environments that correlate with high homicide rates, thus completing the cause and effect relationship from the economic and residential standpoints.

The income levels for Black female headed- households in 1983 was $8190 (Statistical Abstracts, 1986: 447), and while this figure represents some gain, it is unadjusted to account for the inflationary increases in prices that occurred during that period. Since Black female headed-households are the most rapidly increasing proportion of all Black families, the fact that they have gained little economic ground is very distressing. Black women from the underclass are especially vulnerable to violence because racism and their meager incomes limit their housing options to a very few areas. These locations will invariably be marked by high crime rates and the accommodations themselves will be substandard. Just as important, police protection of citizens and their response to criminal acts is notably deficient in these areas as well. Within this setting, the Black women, if she does not share her residence with a male, has little to protect her save her own wiles. The net effect of their minimal incomes is that Black women are virtually imprisoned in settings where they are most likely to be victimized and where the personal and institutional safeguards that they would be privy to in other places may not exist.

A direct connection can be made between the lack of protection afforded Black women by social institutions and agencies, such as the police and the courts, and their absence of status within the social system. The various stereotypes that have been generated about Black women have placed them in a position of low esteem in both the white and Black communities.

Though they must also contend with sexism, white women are characterized as members of the "weaker" or "gentler" sex and, as a result, generally are viewed with a protective eye by the remainder of the society. Black women, though, have been depicted as wanton, lustful beings on the one hand and harsh, emasculating creatures on the other hand. Thus, they are cast into a "blaming the victim" situation where any violence that is perpetrated against them, including homicide, is considered to be, if not deserved, then at least understandable. These negative images of Black women and the corresponding attitudes about them along with the virtual absence of societal protective mechanisms and the historical domination and abuse of women by men have combined to make Black females victims of homicide at a much higher rate than Whites, male or female.

Black women are not just homicide victims, but are perpetrators of that act as well. Remembering Wolfgang's initial comment that knowing the history of Blacks in America would lead one to conclude higher crime rates among members of that group, it should hardly be surprising that Black females have a high incidence of homicide. When one realizes the high levels of stress that they endure and the tremendous amount of anxiety which they face, it is not difficult to imagine their frustrations turning into aggression and erupting in some violent action. Within the subculture of exasperation, many Black females live out their lives with bitter feelings about the conditions in which they live, their inability to change them and the absence of any indicators of probable improvement. Like their male counterparts, they are likely to be undereducated and unemployed or underemployed. Unlike the males, however, they are likely to also have one or more children living with them, which magnifies both the severity of their economic shortcomings and their exasperation with the status quo as the force which perpetuates a substandard existence for them and their offspring.

The Black female, especially when she is involved in a relationship with a male from the underclass, also stands the danger of becoming the scapegoat for his failure to achieve success. The unfortunate tendency of people under oppression is to strike out in frustration, not against their oppressors who may be far removed from them, but against people who are near to them. These people are likely to be dear to them as well--they are often family, lovers, or friends--but they become the targets of the pent-up feelings of exasperation that characterizes members of this subculture. These scapegoating encounters can lead to a homicidal outcome from either of two directions. The male might, in a fit of rage over his circumstances, wind up killing the female; or the woman, usually as a measure of self-defense, could commit homicide against the man. Black women, when they do commit homicide, are more likely than men to have a spouse or family member as the victim.

Black women from the subculture of exasperation then, have problems that are similar to, but at the same time, different from their male counterparts. The systematic exclusion of the members of this group from opportunities to participate fully in the society can only lead to continued social upheaval and additional deaths. American society has promised equality of opportunity for all its citizens, but it has failed miserably in delivering on that promise. The discrepancies between the lifestyles enjoyed by more favored groups and their own are not lost on people from the underclass. If the people, both male and female, from the subculture of exasperation do not find their needs being addressed by social planners and government officials, then the rates of intergroup homicide will likely show dramatic increases, and poor black neighborhoods may be turned into virtual battlegrounds.

Bibliography

Bensing, Robert and Oliver Schroeder. 1960. **Homicide in an Urban Setting.** Springfield, IL: Charles Thomas.

Bohannon, Paul. 1960. **African Homicide and Suicide.** Princeton, NJ: Princeton University Press.

Danto, Bruce. 1982. "A Psychiatric View of Those Who Kill." In **The Human Side of Homicide.** Bruce Danto (ed.), New York: Columbia University, pp. 3-21.

Fattah, Falaka. 1977. Quoted in "Juvenile Delinquency, Juvenile Justice and Black Youth," by Alex Swan. In **Black Perspectives on Crime and the Criminal Justice System.** Robert L. Woodson (ed.). Boston: G. K. Hall.

Glasgow, Douglas. 1980. **The Black Underclass: Poverty, Unemployment and Entrapment of Ghetto Youth.** San Francisco: Jossey-Bass.

Goodman, Paul. 1960. **Growing Up Absurd.** New York: Random House.

Grier, William and Price Cobbs. 1968. **Black Rage.** New York: Basic Books.

Hare, Bruce. 1985. "No Place to Run, No Place to Hide: Comparative Status and Future Prospects of Black Boys" in **Beginnings: The Social and Affective Development of Black Children,** M. Spencer et al.,(ed.) Hillsdale, NJ: Lawrence Erlbaum Associates.

Harvey, William. 1977. **The Black Male: Attempted Victim of Cultural Assasination.** (Unpublished paper)

Henry, Andrew and James Short, Jr. 1954. **Suicide and Homicide.** London: Free Press.

Herbers, John. "Income Gap Between Races Wide as in 1960, Study Finds," **The New York Times,** July 18, 1983, p. 1.

Joe, Tom. 1983. **A Dream Deferred: The Economic Status of Black Americans: A Working Paper.** Washington, D. C.: Center for the Study of Social Policy.

Kimball, Solon. 1974. **Culture and the Educative Process.** New York: Teachers College Press. Kirk, Alton. 1982. "Black Homicide," in **The Human Side of Homicide,** Bruce Danto (ed.). New York: Columbia University, pp. 138-150.

Lester, David and Gene Lester. 1975. **Crime of Passion.** Chicago: Nelson-Hall.

McDonald, John. 1961. **The Murderer and His Victim.** Springfield, IL: Charles Thomas.

Merton, Robert. 1968. **Social Theory and Social Structure.** New York: Free Press.

Palmer, Stuart. 1962. The Psychology of Murder. New York: Thomas Y. Crowell, Co.

Pouissant, Alvin. 1972. Why Blacks Kill Blacks. New York: Emerson Hall.

Renick, James and William Harvey. 1985. "On the Way to Tomorrow: Institutional Racism and Black America in the Technological Society," in Institutional Racism and Black America, ed. by Donald Tryman. New York: Ginn Press.

Shin, Yongsock, Davor Jedlick, and Everett Lee. 1977. "Homicide Among Blacks," in Phylon, 38, No. 4, pp. 398-407.

Staples, Brent. 1986. "A Brother's Murder" in New York Times Magazine, March 30, 72.

Statistical Abstracts. 1978, 1979, 1980, 1981, 1982, 1986. Washington, D. C.: U. S. Government Printing Office.

Swinton, David. 1986. "Economic Status of Blacks 1985," in The State of Black America 1986. New York: National Urban League.

Tabb, William. 1970. The Political Economy of the Black Ghetto. New York: W. W. Norton & Co.

U. S. Department of Commerce. 1980. The Social and Economic Status of the Black Population in the United States. Washington, D. C.: U. S. Government Printing Office.

Whitman, David. 1986. "A Nation Apart," in U. S. News and World Report, 100, No. 10, March 17.

Wilheim, Sidney. 1976. Who Needs the Negro? Garden City, N. Y.: Anchor Books.

Wilson, William. 1982. "Race-Oriented Programs and the Black Underclass," in Race, Poverty, and the Urban Underclass, Clement Cottingham (ed.). Lexington, MA: Lexington Books.

Wolfgang, Marvin. Patterns in Criminal Homicide. 1958. Philadelphia: University of Pennsylvania Press.

and Bernard Cohen, 1964. Crime and Race: Conceptions and Misconceptions. New York: Institute of Human Relations.

. 1967. Studies in Homicide. New York: Harper and Row.

and Franco Ferracutti. 1967. Subculture of Violence. London: Tavistock Publications.

Woodson, Robert (ed.). 1977. Black Perspectives on Crime and the Criminal Justice System. Boston: G. K. Hall.

PART III
PUNISHMENT AND PREVENTION

PART III

PUNISHMENT AND PREVENTION

Introduction

The essays in this section address two important public policy-related concerns. The punishment of homicide offenders across racial lines has been a significant sociopolitical issue for most of the history of this country. Blacks have been acutely aware of a double standard for the punishment of homicide and other crime based on the race of the victim. For example, Charles Owens (1977: 3) cites a black folktale, "A Fine for Killing Two Negroes" from the work of Dorson (1967) to illustrate black views of the low value placed on black life in the United States. A rapidly growing body of social science literature supports the conclusion that the race of the victim is the most important factor affecting the processing of homicide cases by the criminal justice system (Baldus et al., 1983; Bowers and Pierce, 1980; Garfinkel, 1949; Gross and Mauro, 1984; Johnson, 1941; Paternoster, 1983, 1984; and Radelet, 1981, 1985).

The two essays by Radelet and Vandiver and Lundsgaarde discuss racial differentials in punishment. Radelet and Vandiver report that despite efforts during the last decade to define clear and firm criteria for the imposition of the death penalty, racial biases remain evident. They find that both overt racism by individuals and institutional racism lead to bias. The race of the offender and victim greatly affects legal decision-making. Lundsgaarde attempts to provide a more global and historical view of the differential punishment of homicide offenders in contemporary American society. He argues that punishment is a function of the social costs and benefits associated with the taking of a human life. This is a persuasive argument when one considers notions of the devalued status of black life in the United States; however, Lundsgaarde does not provide sufficient discussion of the **particular** problems associated with black-white punishment for homicide. As in other areas of social life in the United States, a purely economic model such as that proposed by Lundsgaarde does not fully account for the effects of racial prejudice and discrimination on public policy. Nevertheless, his discussion provides a grounding for future research designed to explain black-white rates of punishment for homicide and other crime.

The last two articles address another current public policy concern--efforts by the federal government to prevent homicide among young black males. Hawkins argues that past research on homicide among blacks has ignored various aspects of the phenomenon that might be useful for devising successful intervention and prevention strategies. In the final essay Davis and Hawkins assess the papers presented in this volume in terms of their usefulness for meeting the challenge of reducing black homicide rates. They suggest that homicide among blacks must be viewed as a public health

175

concern and remedies must be devised accordingly.

References

Baldus, David C., Charles Pulaski and George Woodworth. 1983. "Comparative Review of Death Sentences." **The Journal of Criminal Law and Criminology** 74: 661-753.

Bowers, William J. and Glenn L. Pierre. 1980. "Arbitrariness and Discrimination Under Post-Furman Capital Statutes." **Crime and Delinquency** 26 (October): 563-635.

Dorson, Richard. 1967. **American Negro Folktales.** Greenwich, Conn.: Fawcett Publications.

Garfinkel, Harold. 1949. "Research Note on Inter- and Intra- racial Homicides." **Social Forces** 27 (May): 369-381.

Gross, Samuel R. and Robert Mauro. 1984. "Patterns of Death: An Analysis of Racial Disparities in Capital Sentencing and Homicide Victimization." **Stanford Law Review** 37 (November): 27-153.

Johnson, Guy B. 1941. "The Negro and Crime." **Annals of the American Academy of Political Science** 217: 93-104.

Owens, Charles E. 1977. "What Price Justice." Introduction to **Blacks and Criminal Justice,** edited by Charles E. Owens and Jimmy Bell. Lexington, MA: D. C. Heath.

Paternoster, Raymond. 1983. "Race of Victim and Location of Crime: The Decision to seek the Death Penalty in South Carolina." **Journal of Criminal Law and Criminology** 74: 754- 785.

_____. 1984. "Prosecutorial Discretion in Requestioning the Death Penalty: A Case of Victim-Based Racial Discrimination." **Law and Society Review** 18: 437-478.

Radelet, Michael L. 1981. "Racial Characteristics and the Imposition of the Death Penalty." **American Sociological Review** 46 (December): 918-927.

_____. and Glenn L. Pierce. 1985. "Race and Prosecutorial Discretion in Homicide Cases." **Law and Society Review** 19 (4): 587-621.

RACE AND CAPITAL PUNISHMENT:
AN OVERVIEW OF THE ISSUES*

Michael L. Radelet and Margaret Vandiver

Introduction

Consider the following four cases:

JOHN GRAHAM - In March of 1931, a young white girl was raped near Ocala, Florida. John Graham, a black man, was arrested for the crime, and was removed to Jacksonville to avoid lynching. He was returned to Ocala for a trial which lasted half an hour. The jury deliberated for three minutes. After Graham was condemned to death, the sheriff again had to rescue him from the assembled mob. The prosecutor at once telegraphed Governor Doyle Carlton, requesting "assurance of speedy execution date." Carlton replied by telegram promising a warrant as soon as he received the record in the case. The superintendent of the prison where Graham was being held wrote to the head of the Florida prison system, saying he hoped "the governor will issue the death warrant as quickly as possible and let us make an example out of this man." Carlton issued a death warrant two days after the trial, and Graham was executed six days later.

LEE JACOBS - Scarcely six months had passed when a similar case occurred near Ocala. In October of 1931, a white woman accused a black man of rape. The **Ocala Evening Star** headline of October 8th proclaimed "SHERIFF AND POSSE ON TRAIL OF BLACK FIEND." The defendant was arrested, tried, found guilty, and condemned, despite testimony from the doctor who examined the alleged victim that he could not positively say that she had been assaulted. The jury in this case deliberated for 17 hours, one juror holding out for mercy. As the prosecutor wrote to Governor Carlton, "Never, at any time, did any of the jury doubt that the crime had been committed, but this one juror felt that the woman had consented..." The Judge called the jury back and explained that Jacobs could be convicted of rape even if the woman had consented to intercourse. The jury retired and within a few minutes returned with a guilty verdict. The Governor, troubled by the case, delayed a full five months in signing the death warrant. This annoyed the white citizens in the area, and they presented the Governor with a petition declaring "...the delay has already caused a change in the demeanor of the negroes in our section ... they are showing signs of departing from the humble and restrained position they have recently assumed." The Governor complied, and Jacobs was electrocuted.

SIE DAWSON - Dawson was a middleaged, illiterate, mentally retarded mentally ill, one-legged man who had the misfortune to be a black living in the Florida panhandle. He worked for the Claytons, a poor white family. On April 13, 1960, Mrs. Clayton and her two year old child were murdered by someone who beat them with a hammer. Dawson was arrested. For more than a week he was driven around the panhandle from jail to jail; during

---

*We would like to thank Hugo Adam Bedau and Werner Einstadter for their helpful comments on an earlier draft.

that time, he was not taken before a judge or allowed to see a lawyer. After a week alone with white officials, Dawson gave a confession to the murders. He was tried, convicted and condemned to die by an all white, all male jury.

Except for his confessions given to the police, Dawson always maintained his innocence. He said that Clayton had killed his own wife and child, and had threatened Dawson if he told anyone about it. Dawson's version of the events was ignored, however, and he was executed May 12, 1964.

TOM BROOKS - Tom Brooks and Charlie McCray were two black farmworkers who were employed by the same man. In 1933, Brooks killed McCray, and was condemned to death. Brooks' employer appealed for clemency: "He just got a little too much bad licker (sic) in him and ... killed one of his contemporaries." And the clerk of the court where Brooks was tried wrote to the Parole Board: "This is just another case of one negro killing another..." Brooks not only received clemency, but was later paroled (Vandiver, 1983).

Examples like these make it difficult to believe that some still claim that the use of capital punishment in the United States is not and never has been a racist instrument of injustice. Even Walter Berns, one of America's most articulate advocates of capital punishment today, admits that its history "is surely one that should give us pause" (1980:41), and suggests that the question of whether states should be permitted to carry out executions "depends on our ability to restrict the use of the death penalty to the worst of our criminals and to impose it in a nondiscriminatory fashion, on white as well as black, on rich as well as poor (1980:55-5). This paper will examine the principal issues relating to race and capital punishment. It will begin with a brief overview of the history and present status of the death penalty in America, and will then review the research that has explored the impact of race on this form of punishment. Most examples will be taken from the state of Florida, where there are at present more people under sentence of death than in any other state. The paper will conclude with an examination of the question of whether present (post-1972) death penalty statutes have eliminated caprice and racism in the imposition of capital punishment and whether new patterns of racial bias now operate under these laws. We will argue that race of the defendant and especially race of the victim have influenced the societal reactions to homicide, and continue to do so today. When blacks are killed, the criminal justice system does not give high priority to the crime, but when a white is killed, especially by a black, the crime is treated with the highest priority and vigor. The result is that racial variables remain strong predictors of who is chosen to be executed.

Before turning directly to the debate on capital punishment, a point made by Black (1978; 1980a) is worthy of consideration. He argues that there are really two distinct forms of death penalty debates at present. The first type discusses, in theory or in the abstract, whether the death penalty should be used and whether some criminals might "deserve" to die. Black argues that such a debate, because of its speculative and theoretical nature, is irrelevant as a basis for public policy or informed public opinion. Instead, he argues that only the second type of debate, in which the issue is whether the death penalty is supportable **as it is actually applied today**, raises the real question. In his words:

We are not presently confronted, as a political society, with

178

the question of whether something called "the state" has some abstract right to kill "those who deserve to die." We are confronted by the single unitary question posed by reality: "Shall we kill those who are chosen to be killed by our legal process as it stands?" ... Strictly, for this purpose, it doesn't really make any difference at all what I think about the abstract rightness of capital punishment. There exists no abstract capital punishment" (1980a:166).

According to this logic, debates over whether a person (real or imaginary) should be sentenced to death for some crime are irrelevant. Each state in fact has only one system of deciding who should die, and the only issue is whether that system, including its shortcomings and faults, should be permitted to make life and death decisions (see also Vidmar and Ellsworth, 1982).

Historical Context

Capital punishment has been used in response to a variety of crimes in America. North Carolina had 26 capital offenses on its law books in 1837 (Bowers, 1984: 140). Before the Civil War many southern states developed "Slave Codes," or separate sets of laws which carefully governed the activities of most blacks. These codes often made a crime capital or not according to the race of the defendant. In Virginia, for example, in the 1830s there were five capital crimes for whites but 70 for black slaves (Bowers, 1984: 140). In 1848, Virginia passed a law that required the death penalty for blacks if convicted of any crime that was punishable by three or more years of imprisonment for whites (Bowers, 1984: 140). Some states also explicitly considered the victim's race, making certain offenses capital crimes when the victim was white and the offender black, while stipulating lesser penalties for other racial combinations. In 1816, for example, Georgia required death for a black who raped or attempted to rape a white, but imposed a two year sentence on whites convicted of rape (Bowers, 1984: 140).

There was some reluctance to execute a slave, however, "for the obvious reason that he represented an investment" (Franklin, 1974: 141). Florida law expressly recognized this and provided that "in all capital cases, the owner of any slave who may be executed shall be entitled to such valuation as the jury trying him or her shall affix, to be paid to him by the Territorial Treasurer" (Section 62, Session Laws, Acts of the Legislative Council of the Territory of Florida, 1829).

After the Emancipation of the slaves, disparate treatment of black offenders based on the race of their victims continued. While no longer written into the law, the race of the victim was openly considered as one of the factors that should influence the disposition of homicide cases. A black person convicted of murdering another black was likely to be treated leniently by the courts, particularly if he had a respected white person to speak on his behalf (Dollard, 1949: 212). The murder of a white by a black, however, was perceived by whites as an assault upon their whole caste (Myrdal, 1944: 535). The response to blacks who were convicted of killing whites was intended not only to punish individual offenders, but also to keep other blacks "in their places." The law was used as a powerful means of

179

intimidation. A researcher studying police before World War I was told by an official that southern police departments recognized three types of homicide. "If a nigger kills a white man, that's murder. If a white man kills a nigger, that's justifiable homicide. paIf a nigger kills another nigger, that's one less nigger" (Fosdick, 1969: 45).

A case which occurred in Florida during Reconstruction illustrates the lack of seriousness attributed by officials to murders of black victims. A white man named John Denton shot and killed a black man for "insolence" in Micanopy on April 6, 1966. Denton was arrested by United States troops; however, a white mob met the soldiers in nearby Gainesville and freed the prisoner. Some time later Denton was tried, and found guilty of manslaughter. He was sentenced to pay court costs and to serve **one minute** in jail (Shofner, 1974: 88).

Historical data on the number of executions in American history are incomplete, but Watt Espy, America's foremost death penalty historian, has documented over 12,000 legal executions in the United States since 1622 (Espy, 1980a; 1980b). He estimates the actual number to fall between 18 and 20 thousand (1980a: 164). The federal government's data on executions date from 1930. Between 1930 and 1967, 3,859 people were executed under civil authority in the U. S., and another 160 were put to death by the U. S. Army (U. S. Department of Justice, 1982). Of the 3,859, 54 percent were black (N=2,066), 32 were women, and about 60 percent were in the south. There were 455 executions for rape, and 405 of these defendants (89 percent) were black (U. S. Department of Justice, 1982). Of the thousands of cases in his files, Espy records only two in which a white was executed for killing a black, both in the late 1800s (1980a: 172). Myrdal (1944: 1345, fn. 23) mentions one other case, occurring in 1936 in North Carolina. No cases are known in which any white man was executed for the rape of a black woman.

The table below indicates the percent who were black of all persons executed by the eleven states of the Confederacy (excluding federal cases) during the years for which information is available.

In addition to these legal executions, White (1948: 42) reports that over 5,000 people in the United States were lynched in the thirty year period ending in 1918. Egerton (1983) reports that between 1900 and 1962, 1,799 blacks and 196 whites were lynched, most often in southern and border states. These extra-legal killings were closely connected to judicial executions. Law enforcement personnel were involved in some lynchings (Cash, 1941: 32), such as that of Jesse Payne, delivered to a mob by the sheriff of Madison, Florida, and Sam McFadden, beaten and drowned by the police chief of Branford, Florida, both in 1945 (Patterson, 1970: 59-60). At times an acquittal or reversal of sentence for a black defendant led to a lynching. In Roseland, Louisiana, Meredith Lewis was acquitted of murder by an all white jury. A few days after the acquittal Lewis was seized by a mob and hanged (Wells-Barnett, 1969: 36).

Even if mob attack was averted, the legal proceedings which followed in some cases were little better than lynch law. As John Dollard wrote, frequently "the difference between the trial and the lynching is more formal than factual" (1949: 326). Lynchings were also given approval by persons in authority. Cole Blease, Governor of South Carolina from 1911 to 1915,

180

EXECUTION BY RACE IN THE SOUTHERN STATES

STATE	YEARS	#BLACK	#WHITE	UNKNOWN AND OTHERS	TOTAL	%BLACK
Alabama	1927-65	126	27		153	82.35
Arkansas	1913-64	129	41	2	172	75.00
Florida	1924-64	131	65		196	66.83
Georgia	1924-64	338	83	1	422	80.09
Louisiana	1957-61	10	1		11	90.90
Mississippi	1955-64	24	7		31	77.42
N. Carolina	1910-61	280	77	5	362	77.35
S. Carolina	1912-60	194	47		241	80.50
Tennessee	1910-60	90	44		134	67.16
Texas	1924-64	228	109	24	361	63.16
Virginia	1908-62	204	33		237	86.08
TOTAL		1754	534	32	2320	75.60

SOURCE: Figures computed from Teeters and Zibulka data in Bowers, 1984.

defended lynching: "Whenever the Constitution comes between me and the virtue of the white women on the South, I say to hell with the Constitution" (Cash, 1941: 248). Governor Catts of Florida responded to NAACP criticisms with a statement saying that he himself would engage in lynching if a member of his family was raped:

> If any man, White or Black should dishonor one of my family he would meet my pistol square from the shoulder and every white man in the South, who is a red-blooded American, feels the same way I do (McGovern, 1982: 12).

Judicial executions were used as a substitute for lynchings, and officials tried to avert lynchings with promises of swift executions. After the brutal lynching of Claude Neal in Florida in 1934, Governor Sholtz said, "This lynching was not only deplorable but absolutely unnecessary in this state under the present administration, where crimes of this character are so speedily and summarily dealt with." He went on to cite the example of a black man who recently had been executed 45 days after the commission of a crime (McGovern, 1982: 110). As time went on, lynchings dramatically declined in number, but executions continue to serve as outlets for feelings of revenge and hatred against those persons, particularly black males, charged with serious crimes.

Present Status

Executions were successfully blocked beginning in 1967 pending Supreme Court review of issues related to the death penalty (see Meltsner, 1973). In 1972, in the landmark case of **Furman v. Georgia** (408 U. S. 238), the U. S. Supreme Court ruled 5 to 4 that the death penalty was arbitrarily applied, and hence was "cruel and unusual" punishment in violation of the Eighth Amendment. Each of the nine justices wrote a separate opinion, and the

Court was divided 5-4. The five justices in the majority rejected the death penalty as applied for a number of reasons; they were in agreement that "infrequency, arbitrariness, and discrimination in the administration of the death penalty" violated the Constitution (Bedau, 1977: 91). The 633 persons then condemned to death in 32 states had their sentences reduced to life imprisonment. Of those prisoners, 364 (57.5 percent) were nonwhite (Meltsner, 1973: 293).

The abolitionist victory was short lived. By 1985, thirty seven states had again enacted operative capital punishment statutes, and thirty-two of these jurisdictions housed prisoners awaiting execution (Legal Defense Fund, 1985). The other thirteen states and the District of Columbia remained abolitionist. The movement to reinstate capital punishment was led by Florida, where immediately after the 1972 **Furman** decison a special session of the legislature was called for the purpose of enacting a new death penalty law (see Ehrhardt et al., 1973; Ehrhardt and Levinson, 1973). In 1976, the U. S. Supreme Court upheld the constitutionality of the new Florida statute (**Proffitt v. Florida**, 428 U. S. 242), as well as those in Georgia and Texas (**Gregg v. Georgia**, 428 U. S. 153 (1976); **Jurek v. Texas**, 428 U. S. 262 (1976)). Under Florida's law, nine aggravating and seven mitigating circumstances are listed to guide judges and juries in their sentencing decisions. At the same time (1976) that the Supreme Court approved these "guided discretion" statutes, the Court also ruled that statutes requiring a mandatory death sentence were unconstitutional (**Roberts v. Louisiana**, 428 U. S. 325 (1976); **Woodson v. North Carolina**, 428 U. S. 280 (1976)). The death penalty for rape was declared unconstitutional by the U. S. Supreme Court in 1977 (**Coker v. Georgia**, 433 U. S. 584).

In the time between the 1976 Supreme Court decisions and September 1, 1985, 46 men and one woman were executed in the U.S. The Texas execution of Charlie Brooks, the first post-**Furman** black defendant to be executed, was cheered by a group of boisterous whites outside the prison waving a Confederate flag (see picture in Reavis, 1983: 104). When James Adams, the first Florida black to be put to death under the new law was executed (May 9, 1984), two whites drove their pickup truck by protesters standing outside the prison and yelled "Fry the nigger." Only four of the 47 executed defendants had black victims (one other had both white and black victims). Except for three consensual executions, all of these post-**Furman** executions occurred in states of the former Confederacy. As of August 1985, there were 1,520 men and 20 women sentenced to death in the United States. Of these, 1,540 inmates, 783 (50.85 percent) were white, 640 (41.56 percent) were black, 113 (7.34%) were other minority, and the race of four defendants was unknown (Legal Defense Fund, 1985). Between 1930 and 1967, 50.09 percent of those executed for homicide were nonwhite and in August 1985 49.50 percent of those on death row were nonwhite, a difference of less than 2 percent. Despite all the emphasis on formal standards after **Furman**, it appears that the racial composition of the condemned population has changed very little (Riedel, 1976; Black, 1980b). Florida had more condemned persons (221) than any other state, followed by Texas (201), California (173), and Georgia (110). It is noteworthy that 877 (56.95 percent) of today's death row prisoners are in the eleven states of the former Confederacy--states which in 1983 accounted for 41 percent of all homicides in the United States (U. S. Department of Justice, 1984).1 It is unknown how many of the defendants, sentenced to death, either before or after **Furman**, had black victims, but as will be discussed below, the proportion is substantially lower than the proportion of black homicide victims.

Statistical Literature

Blacks have composed between 10 and 12 percent of the American population since 1930. The disproportionate number of blacks who have been executed or are awaiting execution, however, does not in itself necessarily indicate disparate treatment of homicide defendants by race. The homicide rate is higher for blacks than for whites (Dollard, 1949: Chapter 8; Silberman, 1978), and thus any misunderstanding of the problem of race and capital punishment must consider the racist history of the United States and the way this leads to a higher proportional involvement of blacks in criminal homicides. The higher rate of death sentences among blacks than among whites could reflect differential response by the criminal justice system, or both. To explore this question, statistical research has focused on three points in the criminal justice process: presentencing, sentencing, and postsentencing.

A. Presentencing

Garfinkel (1949), looking at potential capital cases that occurred in North Carolina between 1930 and 1940, found that both the defendant's and victim's race correlated with the grand jury's decision to indict for first-degree murder (rather than other degrees of murder) and the prosecutor's decision not to reduce first-degree murder charges. Blacks accused of killing whites were the most harshly treated. Similarly, Radelet's study (1981) of Florida homicide cases from the mid-1970s found that even after restricting the sample to homicides against strangers, those accused of killing whites were more likely than those accused of killing blacks to be indicted for first-degree murder (rather than second- or third- degree murder). More recently, Radelet and Pierce (1985) compared police and court records of 1017 Florida homicides. Each homicide was classified as felony, possible felony, or nonfelony by both the police and the prosecutor. Of these cases, 174 (17.1 percent) were classified differently by the two sources. Among these 174 cases, blacks accused of killing whites were the most likely to be harshly classified by the prosecution. Even before the trial takes place, defendant's and victim's race begin to correlate with the way the prosecution classifies a homicide case. Paternoster (1984), looking at South Carolina data, found similar patterns: those who killed whites were more likely than those who killed blacks to have the death penalty requested by the prosecutor, even after several legally relevant factors were taken into account.

Prosecutors have tremendous power in shaping homicide cases. An excellent illustration is given in a report of the so-called "Dawson Five" case in Georgia in 1977 (Bedau, 1983a). Five black youths were accused of the robbery-murder of a white victim. Defense attorneys mounted an effort to have Georgia's death penalty statute ruled unconstitutional. But, after 20 minutes of expert testimony concerning capital punishment, the prosecutor simply announced that he did not intend to ask for the death penalty. What led to this decision, of course, is not public, but in the hands of a different prosecutor the outcome might have been quite different.

Other examples of prosecutorial discretion are abundant. For example,

183

prosecutors make decisions about 1) the way in which homicides are investigated and presented, 2) whether to give the defendant a chance to plead guilty to a noncapital offense, and 3) whether to seek a death sentence if the plea offer is refused. Although some of these decisions are correlated with defendant's and victim's race, this empirical finding does not prove the existence of overt or conscious radical discrimination, at least as narrowly defined. Faced with a heavy workload and forced to make priority decisions, prosecutors could downgrade cases because of an unwillingness or perceved inability to substantiate the aggravating factors necessary to secure conviction of the gravest degree of criminal homicide. Prosecutors might believe that black witnesses of the murder of a black would not make a convincing presentation to a jury. Cases with white victims might stimulate more public attention and community pressure than cases with black victims, and so downgrading such cases would be politically difficult. In an effort to be responsive to the community, prosecutors will use their discretion to allocate resources to the most publicly visible cases. In short, bureaucratic and political variables affect what in theory is a purely legal decision. The cause is not conscious intent by the prosecutor to be racially biased or capricious; rather it is the tacit bias built into the structure of the criminal justice system.

In addition to prosecutorial discretion, jury selection is a second important presentencing activity that works against blacks (Mullin, 1980). In a 1985 Gallup Poll, 72 percent of Americans favored the death penalty for persons convicted of murder and 20 percent stood opposed (Gallup, 1985). The question simply asked whether respondents favored the death penalty for persons convicted of murder (thus it ignored the crucial distinction, mentioned earlier, between abstract but irrelevant theoretical support and the more important question of informed support for the death penalty as actually applied. Nominal support for capital punishment has risen dramatically since 1966, when 42 percent of Americans supported it for murder and 47 percent stood opposed. In the 1985 poll, 75 percent of whites and 57 percent of blacks voiced approval, while 18 percent and 35 percent respectively were opposed (Gallup, 1985). These notable differences by respondents' race, which have always been found (Zeisel, 1982: 136), have implications not yet thoroughly explored for the racial makeup of juries in capital cases.

According to a 1968 ruling by the U. S. Supreme Court (**Witherspoon v. Illinois**, 391 U. S. 510), potential jurors may be excluded from capital juries for cause if their opposition to capital punishment is so strong that they would never vote to impose the penalty. This applies even in states were the jury vote on punishment is only an advisory recommendation to the judge, who alone has the authority to make the final life-or-death decision. Florida is one of these states; a prospective juror may be excluded for cause because of an anti-death penalty attitude despite the fact that in 87 post-**Furman** cases, Florida judges have overridden jury recommendations of life imprisonment and sentenced the defendant to death (Radelet, 1985). Even if the potential jurors are racially representative of the community, the effect of the **Witherspoon** ruling is to exclude a disproportionate number of prospective black jurors (see Mullin, 1980; Winick, 1982).

B. Sentencing

Many studies have examined racial disparities at the sentencing stage (for reviews, see Bowers and Pierce, 1980; Sellin, 1980; Dike, 1981; Bowers, 1984; Gross and Mauro, 1984). This is where the brunt of the attack on racial discrimination in the imposition of death penalty has been concentrated. Such disparities are particularly evident in the punishment for rape; 89 percent of the 455 men executed for rape since 1930 were black (Wolfgang and Reidel, 1973). In their analysis of 1,265 rape convictions in seven southern states between 1945 and 1965, Wolfgang and Riedel found that 13 percent of the 823 blacks convicted of rape were sentenced to death, whereas only 2 percent of the 442 convicted whites were condemned. Of the 317 black defendants with white victims, 113 were sentenced to death (36 percent), compared to only 19 of the 921 defendants (2 percent) with all other victim-defendant racial combinations. Even the Solicitor General of the United States, in arguing in support of the death penalty in the **Gregg** case, did not question the conclusions of this study (see Bedau, 1983b: Note 32).

Research on the application of the post-**Furman** capital statutes continues to find significant differences in the probability of condemnation correlated with the race of defendant and victim. In one study, which examined over 16,000 homicide cases in Florida, Georgia, Texas, and Ohio, Bowers and Pierce (1980) found that black defendants convicted of killing whites were more likely to receive the death penalty than were defendants in any of the other three racial combinations. Similar patterns emerged when their analysis was restricted to homicides involving felony circumstances. Rather than restricting the analysis to homicides with felony circumstances, the determination of which itself may be affected by race, Radelet (1981) examined homicides occurring between strangers. Like Bowers and Pierce, he found in a sample of Florida cases that those defendants with white victims were more likely to be indicted for first-degree murder and more likely to be sentenced to death. When only homicides between strangers involving a first-degree murder indictment were examined, 16.5 percent of the cases with white victims ended with the imposition of the death penalty, whereas only 10 percent of the cases with black victims ended this way. In a third post-**Furman** study, Jacoby and Paternoster (1982) reached similar conclusions. Examining 205 homicide cases from the first twenty-nine months of South Carolina's new death penalty statute, they found that "(d)efendants who were charged with killing whites were 3.2 times more likely to have prosecutors seek the death penalty than those charged with killing blacks" (1982: 384). While defendant's race in itself did not make a significant difference, blacks who killed whites were far more likely to find themselves facing execution than were blacks who killed other blacks.

Two recent projects have extended this line of inquiry. First, in the most extensive social science study ever conducted on capital sentencing patterns, Baldus et al. (1983) found that blacks accused of killing whites in Georgia were more likely to be sentenced to death than were other defendants. This difference remained after considering the possible effects of over 200 control variables (for response of Court, see **McCleskey v. Kemp**, 753 F.2d 877 (1985). Second, Gross and Mauro (1984) used the FBI's Supplemental Homicide Reports to examine sentencing patterns in eight states (Arkansas, Florida, Georgia, Illinois, Mississippi, North Carolina, Oklahoma, and Virginia). They found "remarkably stable and consistent" discrimination, based on victim's race, in all the states. Again, these results held when several other factors which might affect sentencing decisions were statistically controlled.

The principal concern of social science research on racial disparities now has shifted to the impact of victim's race on the application of the death penalty. Relatively few individuals convicted of killing blacks are sentenced to die, particularly if the defendant is white. In 1926, Britt Pringle, a white man, was sentenced to die in Florida for killing a black man, but he was never executed (Shofner, 1981). The second case in the history of Florida in which a white was sentenced to die for killing a black did not occur until 1980 (Zeisel, 1981: 466); between then and early 1985 seven other whites have been condemned for killing blacks (files on all people sentenced to death in Florida are maintained by the authors). Further, although official crime statistics show that since 1973 blacks have been 44 percent of the homicide victims in Florida, only 10.2 percent (38/371) of the death sentences handed down in Florida under its post- **Furman** statute have involved defendants convicted of killing blacks (Radelet, 1985). Even if one argues that homicides with white victims are more likely to involve additional felony circumstances or are less likely to occur among family or friends, analysis controlling for these factors fails to explain this racial disparity (Bowers and Pierce, 1980; Radelet, 1981; Gross and Mauro, 1984).

In Florida, the disparity based on victim's race has declined somewhat in recent years, but still remains substantial. In the first five years of the new Florida statute (1973-77), only five defendants (all of them black) were sentenced to death for killing black victims. In the next five years 25 or more defendants with black victims received death sentences. The proportion of black homicide victims was 49.34 percent between 1973-77, and fell to 41.26% in 1978-82. Despite the rise in death sentences for crimes against black victims and the decline in the overall proportion of black homicide victims, the number of people on death row for killing black victims remains very low. Under Florida's present death penalty law, 331 persons have been given death sentences for killing white victims, compared to the 38 for black victims (two other men had victims of both races).

So far, there is little quantitative research on the impact of socioeconomic variables on the imposition of capital punishment. Such research is badly needed and related to the issue of race, as throughout our history black Americans have received relatively lower incomes than whites. A study by Judson et al., using California data, found that juries "exhibited a significant economic bias" against blue collar defendants (Judson et al., 1969: 1367). Qualitative research also strongly indicates that such a correlation is substantial (e.g., Johnson, 1981). In part this absence of research reflects the difficulty of accurately measuring the social class of prisoners: official records of defendant's income are nonexistent or unreliable, even affluent defendants might have earned their wealth through illegal or "shady" occupations (e.g., drug trade), and defendants with prior imprisonments often will not have an income in the community to report. The few death row inmates who did have financial resources when indicted for capital homicide spent their savings on trial fees, and thus very few have anything left with which to mount appeals.

Inmates on death row are usually socially as well as economically marginal to their communities. In describing the only whites known to have been executed for killing blacks Espy notes:

186

Both of these white men were more or less outcasts, thoroughly despised by their white neighbors, one because he was a gambler and whiskey dealer, the other because he was considered a rogue in general, and both because they chose blacks for their closest friends (1980a: 172-3).

Socioeconomic factors will exert their strongest impact on the death penalty through its correlation with the quality of the defendant's lawyer and strength of community ties. As one former Florida Supreme Court Justice wrote:

> The result is an old story, often repeated in this jurisdiction where the subconscious prejudices and local mores outweigh humane, civilized understanding when certain segments of the population are up for sentencing for murder (Spinkellink vs. State, 313 So.2d 666, Justice Erwin dissenting, at 674). Thus, socioeconomic variables appear to be strong factors in the determination of who is sentenced to death.

C. Postsentencing

Few studies have focused specifically on correlates of decisions made after a death sentence has been imposed by the trial court. The existing studies indicate that post-sentencing decisions do not correct the earlier arbitrariness; in fact some disparities are exacerbated. In one study, Wolfgang et al. (1962) examined the records of 412 persons sentenced to death for first-degree murder in Pennsylvania between 1914 and 1958. The authors found that 82.77 percent of these men eventually were executed and that 17.23 percent of the sentences were commuted. White offenders were significantly more likely than black offenders to have their death sentences commuted, even after controlling for whether or not the homicide was classified as a felony murder. In fact, of the 308 cases for which complete data were available, nearly three times as many white felony murderers as black felony murderers had their sentences commuted. Another study examined the records of the 660 capital offenders sent to death row in North Carolina between 1909 and 1954 (Johnson, 1957). Of the 650 cases reported, 42.94 percent of the 170 whites were eventually executed, compared to 57.92 percent of the 480 blacks. Similarly, looking at a sample of post-**Furman** cases in Florida and Georgia, Bowers and Pierce (1980) found no evidence to suggest that the appellate review process was correcting the racial disparities in treatment found at earlier points in the capital sentencing process. Radelet and Vandiver (1983) found the same lack of corrective action in their study of the first 145 post-**Furman** capital cases reviewed by the Florida Supreme Court.

Conclusion

The rights of black citizens have gained much formal recognition in recent years. Nonetheless, racism still influences the treatment received by persons accused of capital crimes. As well as overt individual racism, there are inherent structural biases in the criminal justice system which lead to disparate treatment by race.

Statistical research indicates that under pre- **Furman** discretionary statutes, juries and judges were influenced by the race of defendants and victims. In an attempt to eliminate racial disparities, guided discretion statutes were enacted and mandatory reviews by higher courts in each state were required. Recent research leads to the conclusion that the attempt at reform has been unsuccessful. Numerous studies indicate a continuity of bias under different forms of the law. These studies also demonstrate that bias exists at various levels of the system, and is compounded rather than corrected at each successive level.

Overt bias by racist individuals may be less prevalent under the present statute, but it still exists. The following examples illustrate this point. Judge William Lamar Rose of Ft. Myers, Florida disagreed with the U. S. Supreme Court's ruling in **Furman v. Georgia** (1972), which invalidated all but a few death penalty statutes. Judge Rose called a press conference to express his disapproval publicly. The Judge threw a rope with a noose over the limb of an oak tree outside the courthouse to demonstrate "how they did it in the old days" (Ft. Myers News-Press, July 1, 1972). Less than two years later, Judge Rose presided over a trial under Florida's new death penalty statute. The defendant was a black man charged with the rape and murder of an elderly white woman. The all white jury recommended a life sentence. Judge Rose, however, used his power under Florida law to reject the jury's recommendation, and imposed death (Magee, 1980: 27).

Millard Farmer, a Georgia attorney, succeeded in having seven trial judges disqualified for prejudice in a 1977 case involving a black man charged with killing a white police officer. An excerpt from the questioning of one judge follows:

Q. How do you feel about having a black person into your home for a meal?

A. I wouldn't like it.

Q. How would you feel if your son came home before he was married with his girlfriend and his girlfriend was black?

A. I'd kick them out of the house.

Q. Do you think Blacks have been given an equal education to whites, historically, in the South?

A. Listen, most of them don't want an education.

Q. Is the black man equal to you?

A. No, I don't think so (Gettinger, 1979: 223-4).

Willie Darden, on trial before an all-white jury in Citrus County, Florida in 1973 for crimes against white victims, was called an "animal" by the prosecutor. The prosecutor went on to say:

He (Darden) shouldn't be out of his cell unless he has a leash on him ... I wish (the victim) had had a shotgun in his hand when he walked in the back door and blown his (Darden's) face off. I wish I could see him sitting here with no face, blown away by a shotgun (**Darden v. Wainwright**, 699 F.2d 1031, at 1646-7, footnote 14).

In another Florida case, one of the authors testified in the sentencing phase of a 1984 case shortly after a black man had been convicted of first-degree murder. After the guilt phase, the trial judge, referring to the defendant's family, suggested that the sentencing phase should begin immediately, "while those niggers are in town." After an outcry by the defense, the overtly racist judge recused himself from the case, but another judge, after disallowing testimony on the racial bias in the application of Florida's death penalty as irrelevant, promptly sentenced the defendant to death.

Finally, although statements by racist individuals in support of the death penalty are not difficult to find, it is crucial to reiterate that inequities in the application of the death penalty do not always, or even usually, reflect conscious intent by officials in the criminal justice system. There is more variation in penalties for homicide, ranging from probation to death, than for any other criminal category. This necessitates arranging homicides in numerous categories, which by definition means that some cases will be treated with more priority than others. And, as long as the general social position of blacks remains lower than that of whites, crimes against them will not be treated with equal priority. The criminal justice system need not consciously make decisions based on race or even recognize race as a crucial variable for its hierarchy of homicide cases to parallel race and class lines. The problem is not so much the conscious intent to be racially biased or capricious, but rather a more tacit bias built into the structure of the criminal justice system. As such, removing bigoted prosecutors, judges, and jurors can only be a partial solution to the problem.

In recent years many have come to believe that racism no longer influences the imposition of death sentences (Kleck, 1981). Some will still argue that the statistical patterns which show a clear tendency for blacks and those who kill whites to be sentenced to death and executed at higher rates than other convicted murderers are explainable by legally relevant facts (see, e.g., **McCleskey v. Kemp**, 753 F.2d 877 (1985)). For example, some argue that black defendants and those who kill whites have a longer criminal record, and are more likely to participate in homicides against strangers or homicides with felony circumstances. Even when the effects of such factors are statistically controlled, however, racial biases remain evident, despite strong efforts in the last deeade to define clear and firm criteria for the imposition of the death penalty. Ignoring the long history of racism in the United States, some choose to believe that the death penalty has been and continues to be evenly applied. But as Black notes:

> I submit that in such a country, with such a history, a virtually irrebuttable presumption should be set up that, in the United States, what **looks like** raw racial discrimination is raw racial discrimination (1980a: 34; emphasis in original).

Equality for blacks has not yet been achieved in American society, least of all in the criminal justice system. The idea that all of us are born with an equal chance of eventually dying in the electric chair remains a myth.

189

Footnotes

1. These eleven states had a homicide rate of 11.6 per 100,000 population in 1983, compared to a national figure of 9.1 per 100,000 (U. S. Department of Justice, 1984). This suggests that even a high rate of death sentencing in these states is not bringing their homicide rates down to the national average.

Cases Cited

Coker v. Georgia, 433 U.S. 584 (1977).

Darden v. Wainwright, 699 F.2d 1031 (1983).

Furman v. Georgia, 408 U. S. 238 (1972).

Gregg v. Georgia, 428 U. S. 153 (1976).

Jurek v. Texas, 428 U. S. 262 (1976).

McCleskey v. Kemp, 753 F.2d 877 (1985).

Proffitt v. Florida, 428 U. S. 242 (1976).

Roberts v. Louisiana, 428 U. S. 325 (1976).

Spenkellink v. State, 313 So.2d 666.

Witherspoon v. Illinois, 391 U. S. 510 (1968).

Woodson v. North Carolina, 428 U. S. 280 (1976).

REFERENCES

Baldus, David C., George Woodworth, and Charles Pulaski. 1983. "Discrimination in Georgia's Capital Charging and Sentencing System: A Preliminary Report."

Bedau, Hugo Adam. 1977. The Courts, the Constitution, and Capital Punishment. Lexington, MA: D. C. Heath.

. 1983a. "Witness to a Prosecution: The Death Penalty and the Dawson Five." Black Law Journal 8: 7- 28.

. 1983b. "Berger's Defense of the Death Penalty: How Not to Read the Constitution." Michigan Law Review 81: 1152-1165.

Bedau, Hugo Adam and Michael L. Radelet. 1985. "Miscarriages of Justice in Homicide Cases." Paper currently under preparation.

Berns, Walter. 1980. "Retribution, Morality and Capital Punishment." Pp. 41-58 in The Penalty of Death. Washington, D. C.: The Roscoe Pound - American Trial Lawyers Foundation.

Black, Charles L. Jr. 1978. Capital Punishment: The Inevitability of Caprice and Mistake, Second Edition. New York: W. W. Norton Co.

. 1980a. "Caprice and Racism in the Death Penalty." Pp. 21-39 in The Penalty of Death. Washington, D. C.: The Roscoe Pound - American Trial Lawyers Foundation.

. 1980b. "Objections to S.1382, A Bill to Establish Rational Criteria for the Imposition of Capital Punishment." Crime and Delinquency 26: 441-52.

Bowers, William J., with Glenn Pierce and William McDevitt. 1984. Legal Homicide: Death as Punishment in America, 1864- 1982. Boston: Northeastern University Press.

Bowers, William J. and Glenn L. Pierce. 1980. "Arbitrariness and Discrimination under Post-Furman Capital Statutes." Crime and Delinquency 26: 563-635.

Cash, Wilbur J. 1941. The Mind of the South. New York: Alfred A. Knopf.

Dike, Sarah T. 1981. "Capital Punishment in the United States Part II: Empirical Evidence." Criminal Justice Abstracts 13: 426-47.

Dollard, John. 1949. Caste and Class in a Southern Town. Garden City, NY: Doubleday.

Egerton, John. 1983. "A Case of Prejudice: Maurice Mays and the Knoxville Race Riot of 1919." Southern Exposure 19: 4, 56-65.

Ehrhardt, Charles W., Phillip A. Hubbart, L. Harold Levinson, William M. Smiley, Jr., and Thomas A. Wills. 1973. "The Future of Capital Punishment in Florida: Analysis and Recommendations." Journal of Criminal Law and Criminology 64: 2-10.

Ehrhardt, Charles W. and L. H. Levinson. 1973. "Florida's Response to Furman: An Exercise in Futility?" Journal of Criminal Law and Criminology 64: 10-21.

Espy, Watt. 1980a. "The Historical Perspective." Pp. 163-74 in Doug Magee, Slow Coming Dark. New York: Pilgrim Press.

. 1980b. "Capital Punishment and Deterrence: What the Statistics Cannot Show." Crime and Delinquency 26: 537- 44.

Florida. 1829. Acts of the Legislative Council of the Territory of Florida. Tallahassee: William Wilson.

Fosdick, Raymond Blaine. 1969. American Police Systems. Montclair, NJ: Patterson Smith.

Franklin, John Hope. 1974. From Slavery to Freedom, 4th Edition. New York: Alfred A. Knopf.

Gallup, George. 1985. The Gallup Report, 232 and 233 (January/February).

Garfinkel, Harold. 1949. "Research Note on Inter- and Intra- Racial Homicides." Social Forces 27: 369-81.

Gettinger, Stephen H. 1979. Sentenced to Die. New York: Macmillan Publishing Co.

Gross, Samuel R. and Robert Mauro. 1984. "Patterns of Death: An Analysis of Racial Disparities in Criminal Sentencing and Homicide Victimization." Stanford Law Review 37: 27-153.

Jacoby, Joseph E. and Raymond Paternoster. 1982. "Sentencing Disparity and Jury Packing: Further Challenges to the Death Penalty." The Journal of Criminal Law and Criminology 73: 379-87.

Johnson, Elmer H. 1957. "Selective Forces in Capital Punishment." Social Forces 36: 165-9.

Johnson, Robert. 1981. Condemned to Die. New York: Elsevier.

Judson, Charles, James Pandell, Jack Owens, James McIntosh, and Dale Matschullat. 1969. "A Study of the Penalty Jury in First Degree Murder Cases." Stanford Law Review 21: 1297-1431.

Kleck, Gary. 1981. "Racial Discrimination in Criminal Sentencing: A Critical Evaluation of the Evidence with Additional Evidence on the Death Penalty." American Sociological Review 46: 783-805.

Legal Defense Fund. 1985. "Death Row, U. S. A." New York: Legal Defense Fund, March 1.

Magee, Doug. 1980. Slow Coming Dark. New York: Pilgrim Press.

McGovern, James. 1982. Anatomy of a Lynching: The Killing of Claude Neal. Baton Rouge: Louisiana State University Press.

Meltsner, Michael. 1973. Cruel and Unusual: The Supreme Court and Capital Punishment. New York: Random House.

Mullin, Courtney. 1980. "The Jury System in Death Penalty Cases: A Symbolic Gesture." Law and Contemporary Problems 43: 137-54.

Myrdal, Gunnar. 1944. An American Dilemma. New York: Harper and Brothers.

Paternoster, Raymond. 1984. "Prosecutorial Discretion in Requesting the Death Penalty: A Case of Victim-Based Racial Discrimination." Law and Society Review 18: 437-478.

Patterson, William L. (ed.). 1970. We Charge Genocide: The Historic Petition to the United Nations for Relief from a Crime of the United States Government against the Negro People. New York: International Publishers.

Radelet, Michael L. 1981. "Racial Characteristics and the Imposition of the Death Penalty." American Sociological Review 46: 918-27.

Radelet, Michael L. and Margaret Vandiver. 1983. "The Florida Supreme Court and Death Penalty Appeals." Journal of Criminal Law and Criminology 74: 401-414.

Radelet, Michael L., Margaret Vandiver, and Felix M. Berardo. 1983. "Families, Prisons, and Men with Death Sentences: The Human Impact of Structured Uncertainty." Journal of Family Issues 4: 593-612.

Radelet, Michael L. and Glenn L. Pierce. 1985. "Race and Prosecutorial Discretion in Homicide Cases." Law and Society Review 19 (4): 587-621.

Radelet, Michael L. 1985. "Rejecting the Jury: The Imposition of the Death Penalty in Florida." University of California- Davis Law Review 18: 1409-1431.

Reavis, Dick J. 1983. "Charlie Brooks' Last Words." Texas Monthly 11 (February): 100-105+.

Riedel, Mark. 1976. "Discrimination in the Imposition of the Death Penalty: A Comparison of the Characteristics of Offenders Sentenced Pre-Furman and Post-Furman." Temple Law Quarterly 49: 261-87.

Sellin, Thorsten. 1980. The Penalty of Death. Beverly Hills: Sage.

Sherrill, Robert. 1983. "Death Row on Trial." New York Times Magazine, November 13, 80-116.

Shofner, Jerrell H. 1974. Nor Is It Over Yet. Gainesville: The University Presses of Florida.

1981. "Judge Herbert Rider and the Lynching at LaBelle." Florida

Historical Quarterly LIX: 292- 306.

Silberman, Charles. 1978. Criminal Violence, Criminal Justice. New York: Random House.

U. S. Department of Justice. 1982. Capital Punishment, 1981. Washington, D. C.: U. S. Government Printing Office.

. 1984. Crime in the United States, 1983. Washington, D. C.: U. S. Government Printing Office.

Vandiver, Margaret. 1983. "Race, Clemency, and Executions in Florida, 1924-1966." Unpublished Masters Thesis, Florida State University.

Vidmar, Neil and Phoebe C. Ellsworth. 1982. "Research on Attitudes Toward Capital Punishment." Pp. 68-84 in Hugo Adam Bedau (ed.), The Death Penalty in America, 3rd Ed. New York: Oxford University Press.

Wells-Barnett, Ida B. 1969. On Lynchings. New York: Arno Press.

White, Walter. 1948. A Man Called White. New York: The Viking Press.

Winick, Bruce J. 1982. "Prosecutorial Peremptory Challenge Practices in Capital Cases: An Empirical Study and a Constitutional Analysis." Michigan Law Review 81: 1-99.

Wolfgang, Marvin E., Arlene Kelly, and Hans C. Nolde. 1962. "Comparison of the Executed and Commuted Among Admissions to Death Row." Journal of Criminal Law, Criminology, and Police Science 53: 301-11.

Wolfgang, Marvin E. and Marc Riedel. 1973. "Race, Judicial Discretion, and the Death Penalty." Annals of the American Academy of Political and Social Science 53: 301-11.

Zeisel, Hans. 1981. "Race Bias in the Administration of the Death Penalty: The Florida Experience." Harvard Law Review 95: 456-468.

. 1982. "The Deterrent Effect of the Death Penalty: Facts vs. Faith." Pp. 116-138 in Hugo Adam Bedau (ed.), The Death Penalty in America, Third Edition. New York: Oxford University Press.

PUBLIC POLICY AND THE DIFFERENTIAL
PUNISHMENT OF HOMICIDE

Henry P. Lundsgaarde

Introduction

Every known system of law grades offenses in accordance with criteria that specify degrees of culpability. Ideally, therefore, a rational system of justice would ascertain relative culpability and punishment in accordance with the principle of treating "...like cases alike and different cases differently" (Hart, 1961: 155). It is evident, however, that offenders who commit seemingly equivalent amounts of harm may in actual fact be treated unequally. The differential judicial sanctioning of homicide offenders may best be explained as the product of social norms, values, and attitudes embedded in public policies and not, as many theoretical jurists perhaps would like to see it, as the equitable distilate from a rational system of distributive justice (see, also, Black, 1976). While this paper presents three different explanatory models of official sanctioning behavior in homicide cases, it is assumed that the generalizations apply to other serious offenses against the person.

The first observation to be made is that homicide per se may not be viewed as threatening to the achievement of the common good. In Anglo-Saxon England, for example, every person's life was equated with a fixed monetary value or wergild. The monetary compensation for homicide was payable to the deceased person's kindred. The exact amount owed a victim's surviving kinsmen was based upon a fixed rate determined by the social status of the victim. This seemingly simple system of retributive justice only proved workable in principle, however. Many homicides reportedly led survivors to seek revenge through reciprocal acts of violence that further threatened both the public peace and social order. At first, therefore, the King imposed a fine, or wite, to act as a penalty for disturbing the public peace (see, e.g., Taswell-Langmead, 1946). Gradual evolution of early Anglo-Saxon law into the present common-law tradition has completely transformed the early view of homicide as a tort or a personal wrong against the victim and his surviving kinsmen to its modern version as a crime or offense against the state. Stig Iuul's (1949 and 1969) discussion of Danish law exemplifies parallel developments in Scandinavian criminal law (see, also, Maine, 1963).

The gradual official conceptualization of homicide as a crime or public wrong has thus extinguished all former survivor's rights to both financial indemnity and vegeance. The criminal laws of both federal and state governments in the United States today discriminate between lawful and unlawful acts of homicide, provide explicit statutory and procedural guidelines for the apprehension and prosecution of offenders and, most significantly, empower only government officials to punish persons convicted of unlawful conduct. These officials--who serve as bureaucratic functionaries in law enforcement, prosecutorial, and correctional agencies--nominally exercise their official responsibilities in accordance with the broad guidelines of public policy. Government thus has come to symbolize the legal rights and duties of the extinct victim.

These government officials, unlike the authority figures among the traditional kinship groups of pre- industrial societies, are not supposed to view homicide offenders with any feelings of revenge or moral outrage. As illustrated by Goldschmidt's (1966: 173-190) theory of sanctioning behavior, officials themselves in many ways contribute directly to the differential apprehension, prosecution, and punishment of criminal offenders.

Victim compensation and restitution for surviving relatives also has been eliminated from the offense- punishment equation; public officials may apprehend and possibly prosecute persons who allegedly have committed an act of unlawful homicide; convicted offenders are variously punished or "rehabilitated" by the state; the state shoulders the direct economic costs associated with both adjudication and punishment. The benefits to society, if any, are equated with the removal, either permanent or temporary, of lawbreakers from participation in normal community life. These general cost and benefit considerations, which are implicit in public policy, play such a fundamental part in the system of criminal justice that the differential sanctioning of homicide offenders is now accepted as axiomatic.

THREE EXPLANATORY MODELS

To explain the connections between social policy and distributive justice (or differential punishment), let us examine three different models of justice: (1) the arbitrary justice model, (2) the discriminatory justice model, and (3) the economic justice model.

First, it is possible to assume that the system of criminal justice is arbitrary. Judicial outcome, for any particular offender, approaches arbitrariness if it is impossible to predict whether he or she may be excused from any from of legal sanctioning. The unpredictability of judicial outcome may be attributed to a host of subjective factors such as the relative skills of both prosecutors and defense attorneys, the relative and selective interests on the part of public officials in punishing a particular person, or the processing of routine homicide cases in accordance with principles of expediency. The mathematician Norbert Weiner's caricature of a system like the arbitrary justice model helps clarify why one convicted murderer may be given a minimum two year prison sentence while his cellmate may have to come face to face with the executioner: "At present the criminal law speaks now in the language, and now in another. Until we in the community have made up our minds that what we really want is expiation, or removal, or reform, or the discouragement of potential criminals, we shall get none of these, but only a confusion in which crime breeds more crime. A code which is made, one-fourth on the eighteenth century British prejudice in favor of hanging, one-fourth on the removal of the criminal from society, one-fourth on a halfhearted policy of reform and one-fourth on the policy of hanging up a dead crow to scare away the rest, is going to get us precisely nowhere" (Wiener, 1954: 110). The validity of the arbitrary justice model depends upon our ability to demonstrate empirically that "like cases" are in fact treated arbitrarily. This has never been done in civil society.

Second, one of the simplest ways to reduce judicial arbitrariness is to group offenders and offensive acts into categories. This is accomplished by

198

discrimination. Offenders, for example, may be categorized on the basis of any number of discriminants: Age, sex, race, ethnicity, social status, or clinical sanity. Infants, children, juveniles, and incompetents are not held to be responsible or culpable to the same degree as are "normal" adults. Legal culpability, similarly, is not the same for persons hold to be sane as for persons declared to be insane. The discriminatory justice model may also rely on psychological factors such as motivation and intent as a way to assign offenders to different categories of culpability. The following example for Texas illustrates how degrees of mental culpability may be used to discriminate between different cases as more or less deserving of legal sanctioning: "Assume that a defendant strikes a pregnant woman in the abdomen and as a result the baby dies shortly after birth. In a homicide prosecution the evidence might show any of the following: (1) If he struck the woman knowing she was pregnant and for the purpose of killing the child, his conduct was intentional; (2) if he knew she was pregnant and that his blows were likely to cause the death, his conduct was knowing, even if his only purpose was to cause her pain; (3) if he knew she was pregnant and knew that death of the baby might result, but did not care, he was only reckless; (4) if he knew she was pregnant but did not think his blow was hard enough to hurt the baby, or he did not advert to the fact that she was pregnant although it was plainly observable, he acted with criminal negligence; or (5) if he did not know she was pregnant, and to the ordinary observer she did not look pregnant, he did not have any culpable mental state, at least with respect to the baby's death as a result" (Bubany, 1974: 306).

This example illustrates how judicial officials may determine the degree of culpability on the basis of an offender's purported mental state. The person found to have acted intentionally, knowingly, and even recklessly is put into a different category from the person who has merely acted in a negligent manner. Offenders, in other words, are processed through different categories of culpability on the basis of psychological discriminants. The discriminatory justice model also incorporates the idea that offensive acts per se may be categorized on the basis of relative seriousness. Here, again, I will rely upon an example from the Texas Penal Code. Texas homicide statutes clearly define homicide as the destruction of the life of one human being by the act, agency, procurement, or culpable ommision of another. A further, and critical, distinction is then made between non- criminal homicide and criminal homicide. Noncriminal homicide, which is not punishable, includes a variety of homicides that are classified as justifiable; e.g., killing in self-defense, killing to protect one's property or the property of others, killing in the performance of a public duty, or killing another as a matter of necessity to avoid harm.

Criminal homicide is sub-divided into five major categories. Each statutory category or degree of criminal homicide is associated with specific minimum and maximum forms of punishment: (1) murder may be punishable by a minimum prison sentence of five years, life imprisonment, or a maximum 99 year prison sentence, (2) capital murder, which specifically applies to anyone who kills a public official such as a police officer or a fireman, is punishable by life imprisonment or death by execution; (3) voluntary manslaughter imposes a minimum sentence of two years and a maximum sentence of twenty years; (4) involuntary manslaughter limits the maximum prison sentence to ten years; and (5) negligent homicide is trated as a misdemeanor punishable by a fine not to exceed $2000, imprisonment for one year or less, or a combination of imprisonment and a fine. All other things being equal, the person who kills a public servant stands to loose his own life whereas the person who kills a private citizen may end up by paying a small fine (Lundsgaarde, 1977).

Third, homicide is, of course, also a kind of economic behavior. The act of killing somebody else, unless by pure accident, confers some benefit upon the offender. The reciprocal costs of homicide are borne by the victim, victim survivors, and ultimately by society at large (see, e.g., Hellman, 1980, and Posner, 1981). The value of any human life may be assessed legally either in terms of the victim's social status (the Anglo-Saxon approach) or in terms of the offender's state of mind and social behavior (the modern approach). Since the modern approach to punishment formally omits the elements of revenge, reciprocity (an eye for an eye), and restitution from the sanctioning equation, we are left with social cost as a factor that best explains empirical patterns of differential punishment. This model therefore enables us to predict that killings that involve low social costs will be less severely dealt with by the public authorities than killings that involve high social costs. Punishment that enhances the goals of public orderliness (either to minimize the economic costs of adjudication or to maximize the preservation of social order) is more highly valued than punishment that only has marginal utility.

It is now possible to hypothesize that the differential punishment of known homicide offenders in contemporary American society is a function of the social costs and benefits associated with the taking of a human life. The estimation of the relative social costs and benefits associated with each act of homicide may be determined empirically by comparative analysis of case histories.

In a recent study of homicide offenders in Philadelphia, a team of criminologists concluded that "the strong relationship between the type of adjudication and subsequent punishment level suggest that there are two styles of homicides in the Philadelphia system--wholesale and retail. Most killings do not involve collateral felonies, high status or particularly vulnerable members of the community, or more than one victim--these are the wholesale cases. The prosecutor has a strong incentive to dispose of the case quickly but no pressure to press for severe penalties. The result is that the prosecutor allows the defendant to plead guilty to a lesser offense or stipulate to a trial without jury, and a minimum sentence of two years or less is imposed.

An important minority of killings--the retail cases receive more attention, more complete due process, and penalties close to an order of magnitude higher than the low visibility wholesale cases. These retail cases are more likely to involve collateral felonies and other circumstances that the community and the prosecutor see as aggravating the seriousness of the offense. In addition, of course, a fair proportion of cases will come to trial because the defendant feels he has a good chance of being acquitted. But we believe that the decision to go to trial in the majority of the jury trial cases is made because of a prosecutorial refusal to bargain down the consequences of an offese" (Zimring et al., 1976: 237-8). These researchers also concluded that their sample of felony killings shows that "...similar cases being treated differently: the hallmark of non-felony killings is that somewhat different cases are punished with grossly different measures" (Ibid., p. 233).

In my own study of Houston homicides, it was possible to group all homicides into three nominal relationship categories: (1) relatives or individuals who may be classified as either consanguineal or affinal kinsmen; (2) associates or persons who prior to a killing have known each other in some informal or formal capacity such as, for example, paramour, neighbor, co-worker, or business acquaintances; (3) strangers or persons who prior to the killing had neither encountered each other previously or otherwise known each other. Empirical data on 204 Houston homicide cases from 1969, in which both offender- victim relationships and judicial outcomes are known, show that relational distance is the best predictor of final judicial outcome. While interracial killings may result in more severe punishment for offenders, the available case data do not allow any generalization about the effects of offender-victim racial attributes on case outcome. The available data suggest that whites and nonwhites are equally likely to receive light legal sanctions if the offenders and victims share similar social class attributes. This finding is discussed at length in Chapter 6 of **Murder in Space City** (Lundsgaarde, 1977).

It is of interest, however, to point to a few unusual aspects of Texas criminal statutes pertaining to homicide and to indicate something about the effects of the almost casual evaluation of routine homicide cases by Houston grand jury members. The Texas Constitution explicitly and unamiously provides that "every citizen shall have the right to keep and bear arms in the lawful defense of himself or the State." The Texas Penal Code (revised in 1974) further allows both private citizens and public officials wide latitude in the use of lethal force. A homicide is non-criminal or justifiable, for example, if the act arises out of (1) necessity or the use of force to avoid harm, (2) self-defense, (3) defense of third person, (4) protection of property, and (5) protection of third person's property. Prior to the 1974 revision of the Texas Criminal Statutes it was also permissible for a husband to kill both his wife and her paramour if the "offended" husband could catch his wife and her paramour *in flagrante delicto*. Although the equivalent right on the part of a man's wife was not specified in the criminal statutes, it would not be difficult for a woman to create justifiable circumstances for a similar response. It is of particular interest to mention in passing that this so-called adultery statute is the only criminal statute that to my knowledge ever explicitly mentions the killer and victim relationship.

The various articles of the Texas Penal Code pertinent to the lawful killing of others in defense of either person or property, while undeniably intended to help private citizens in a frontier society protect themselves against rapists, intruders, or armed robbers, often may be applied to excuse killings under such ambivalent circumstances as public brawls, self-defined life threatening situations, or the forceful protection of property rights. The ambivalence of these situations is further complicated if the actions and events that precede a killing are not witnessed by anyone other than the two principals.

The social and legal problems of an official penal code that explicitly sanctions private citizens to use deadly force under a variety of circumstances are further compounded by a procedural system designed to view every person as innocent until proven guilty of a crime. The distinction between having done an act, something that many Texas killers readily admit to, and having done something that is illegal recalls the significance of the dictum that without law there is no crime.

Once a homicide victim has been discovered it is up to various officials to determine whether the case should be treated as the result of lawful or unlawful behavior. If prosecutors believe, on the basis of preliminary police and medical evidence, that they can establish probable cause against a particular suspect, the District Attorney will present the facts to a grand jury. The grand jury is the on-off switch of the judicial system; it is formally empowered to establish probable cause and issue a bill of indictment against the person who now officially becomes a defendant. This action initiates the prosecutorial process. If, however, the grand jury fails to find probable cause against a particular suspect it may issue a so-called "no bill" which removes the suspect from further legal liability. The odds of indictment are very much in favor of the homicide suspect. Consider, for example, the following observations by a political scientist who actually served on a Houston grand jury: "...the never-ending flow of cases with which grand juries are daily bombarded places another obstacle in the path of a full and fair hearing for all those accused of felonies. Given the generally vague and inaccurate nature of the police reports and of the district attorney's file on the accused, five minutes per case is certainly not enough time to spend on the determination of probable cause... Besides the fact that only a small percentage of cases (probably no more than 5 percent) are examined with any care at all by the grand jury, the evidence suggests that even the selection of that 5 percent is an arbitrary process reflecting the bias of the upper-middle class grand jury composition. The evidence reveals that the vast majority of these cases includes the bizarre, unusual, or important cases that are covered by the news media and that frequently involve the names of well- known local personages, businesses, and organizations. Murder of a prominent socialite, corruption in the local fire department, and alleged immoral conduct by professors at a local state university have all been subjects of extensive grand-jury investigations... Such cases are regarded as significant by upper- middle class grand juries, because the subject matter has a special appeal to the moral, ethical, or even salacious instincts of the middle-class mentality. On the other hand, the stabbing death of a derelict in a ghetto bar, and the forgery of a credit card tend to be regarded as routine, boring cases by most grand jurors" (Carp, 1974: 119). It is obvious, from these and other observations made in Carp's study, that the wholesale/retail model used to explain differential judicial outcomes for homicide offenders in Philadelphia also helps to explain the situation in Houston, Texas.

SOCIAL IMPLICATIONS OF HOMICIDE

Homicide has been aptly characterized as "the most definitive of social relationships" (Bohannan, 1960). An act of homicide, by definition, always embraces two or more persons. The actual slaying may either represent a surprise attack by the killer or result from the social interaction of the killer and his or her victim. Homicide thus serves to terminate a relationship between two persons involved in some kind of dyadic or reciprocal social relationship [1] assasination, contract murder, and organized combat exemplify homicidal acts that require neither interaction nor any form of communication between the principals (see e.g., Zimbardo, 1973: 1976-238).

The magnitude of the social problem has been summarized by Rose (1979: 1-2) who says: "The dyadic interaction that leads to death imposes a variety of costs upon society. These costs are social psychological, and economic. There have been few efforts to measure the costs of these tragic events. Nuclear families are dissolved, siblings are lost, and dependency is intensified. Offenders are charged, convicted, and imprisoned at public expense...the number of potential working years lost is high. Thus, the psychological trauma resulting from the sudden and unexpected loss of a loved one, the possibility of increased economic dependency, and the resulting stress associated with these acts suggest that we take a new look at this phenomenon."

Although homicide traditionally has been viewed as one of the least preventable crimes, particularly the kind of homicide that involves persons who are relatives or associates and who tend to kill each other in the privacy of the home, it may well be possible to identify more precisely the modal social characteristics of potential killers and victims by directing more attention to the kinds of persons, their socioeconomic circumstances, and the general factors in their social environment that appears to foster violent behavior (see e.g., Earls, 1979: 51- 67; Allen, 1980). By learning more about the individual and social characteristics of killers and victims in the different relationship categories it may be possible to (1) identify relationships and environments that promote homicidal acts and (2) predict how different official reactions to such homicides may, in fact, promote attitudes that condone the use of personal violence.

In a recent study of interspouse homicide, Chimbos (1978: 74-75) concludes that "...anyone who is aware of a family rife with drinking, quarrels over moral issues wherein one or both adults have experienced previous marriages (official or common- law) and violent childhoods, and where the situation of social isolation exists, can predict that the situation will worsen and that the spouses will not seek help...Threats to kill should especially not be dismissed as 'empty bluffs' or 'drunken ravings'."

On the basis of his study of 6389 homicides in Detroit during 1926-1968, Boudouris also concludes that "...the problem of homicide is related, in large proportion, to problems in marital and family relationships...(and)...the establishment of family- problem centers in the community could make a significant contribution to the reduction in homicide" (1974: 539). This viewpoint finds additional support in the work by Gelles (1972) and others who have focused their research on domestic violence.[2] To take the life of a relative, for example, is theoretically and by statutory law equivalent to taking the life of a complete stranger. Yet, as was noted above, th final legal disposition of a homicide case significantly correlates with the type of social relationship between the killer and victim. The closer the relationship the less likely it is that the killer will be severely penalized for the act. Although official legal punishment, or its absence, may vary from one case to another within any given offender relationship category, there is a certain uniformity to the final disposition of similar and analogous cases.

The differential legal treatment accorded killers in Houston may at first glance seem unique to that particular setting. However, evidence from other jurisdictions, in both the "Violent South" and elsewhere in the nation, at least suggest that such patterns may be more widespread than is commonly assumed. The importance, both theoretical and practical, of further investigative efforts into this discriminatory aspect of the judicial system is adumbrated by Swigert's and Farrell's (1976) study of homicide offenders in a northeastern state. They propose a concept of "the criminal stereotype" to explain observable differences in the disposition of killers from different socio-economic classes. Nevertheless, the analysis focuses almost exclusively on the social status of killers and their purported membership in the so-called "subculture of violence." They thus fail to simultaneously treat the victim's socio-economic status as a variable that may have predictive value for determining legal disposition and sentencing (cf., e.g., Wolfgang and Ferracuti, 1967; Black, 1976: 1-59).

Swigert and Farrell also state that "...those defendants whose personal or social characteristics suggest their participation in a culture where violent response is said to be appropriate, are denied the presumption of innocence constitutionally guaranteed to all. The determination of membership in such a culture involves an assessment of the offense and offender for characteristics thought to typify criminality. The appearance of nonrespectability, defiant demeanor in official encounters, and association with deviant or criminal groups provide the kinds of information on which these judicial assessments may be made (1976: 93).

The Houston data, however, indicate that homicides involving persons who fit Swigert's and Farrell's conceptualization of the "criminal stereotype" in fact receive a minimum of official attention. Furthermore, it was found that the penalties exacted against lower class offenders convicted by a jury were comparatively mild. Nevertheless, if a killing involves an ancillary offense (e.g., rape or armed robbery), if the killer and victim are strangers, or if the principals represent different races, the likelihood of severe punishment for the convicted killer is indeed very great.

To resolve such different findings and interpretations it seems essential to study simultaneously the killer and the victim (a procedure most explicitly developed in Wolfgang's seminal study of homicide patterns in Philadelphia) and to examine the relationship between the constituents of this dyad in terms of their socio-economic and relational distance. In other words, final case disposition is hypothesized to be a function of personal attributes of both the killer and victim and of the social distance between them. This hypothesis can be derived from the economic justice model. The model also helps to explain why homicide offenders, at least in Philadelphia and Houston, may find themselves processed as either wholesale or retail goods in the marketplace of social justice.

CONCLUSIONS

Homicide is a cultural universal. No known society escapes violent forms of human interaction and no society can insure complete personal safety for its members. It is also evident from the ethnographic literature, which is replete with descriptive examples of different forms of interpersonal violence, that the relative level of such violence is a function of the "cultural guidelines" that specify the exact circumstances under which violence may or may not be used to achieve some end. In modern complex societies we can look directly to the social policies embedded in various legal codes and court decisions to learn how society balances the personal freedom to use violence with the societal need to maintain order. It is also true to generalize and say that the complex relationships between individual social conduct and institutional mechanisms for the regulations of such conduct remain central to any theory about the effects of social policy on

204

differential punishment.

According to a recently published tabulation of homicide statistics by the FBI, "Law enforcement agencies' reports disclose that 55 percent of all adults arrested for murder in 1975 were prosecuted during the year. Fifty-four percent of the adults prosecuted were found guilty as charged, and 14 percent were convicted of some lesser charge. The remaining won release by acquittal or dismissal of the charges against them (FBI, 1976: 20). The FBI further reports that the clearance rate for homicide cases, nationwide, has decreased from 86 percent to 78 percent since the year 1970. The official and national homicide rate in 1975 rose to an alltime high of 20,510, or 9.6 known victims per 100,000 population. This by itself represents a 125 percent increase in homicide over the year 1960. The U. S. Department of Justice, Bureau of Justice Statistics, provides further evidence that the number of persons who commit homicide and go unpunished not only remains at a high level but that assailants are becoming more numerous in the population as a whole (Brown et al., 1984).

Despite these facts, which have contributed to recent proclamations about homicide as a public health problem, there still is no clear consensus among behavioral scientists or policy makers on the reasons why so many Americans annually kill each other and what, if anything, needs to be done to address the problem of interpersonal violence. Different explanations of the nation's high homicide rate have traditionally been attributed to a variety of factors: the continuation of the frontier mentality into the twentieth century, the discrimination against racial minorities and disadvantaged socioeconomic minorities, or the psychological frustrations of life in large and depersonalized cities. The federal government, state governments, and citizens have been equally frustrated in both explaining violence and designing effective social policies that may stop the exponential growth of interpersonal violence.

Application of the economic justice model to data on the differential treatment of homicide offenders helps to expose how social policies work to balance individual freedoms with the necessities of social order and restraint. By scaling official sanctions in response to the private and public interest in punishing persons for a particular act, or by processing cases on a wholesale or a retail basis, society manages to negatively sanction those acts that most visibly threaten public order while upholding the individual's right to enjoy property with a generous allowance for the free exercise of legal self-help to protect these rights. I leave it for others to speculate if this is the best way for intelligent policy makers to ensure the achievement of the common good.

NOTES

1. The early contributions by Ruesch and Bateson (1951) to human interaction and communication theory, together with E. T. Hall's (1964: 154-63; 1966) work in human ethology, emphasize how even trivial forms of human social interaction may in reality be the product of complex cultural rules. Frake's (1964: 127-32) explication of Subanun patterns of drinking behavior and Murphy's (1964: 1257-73) analysis of Tuareg social distance setting mechanisms further exemplify both the theoretical and practical importance of explaining both explicit and implicit cultural rules. It is assumed that different individual and collective manifestations of violent behavior are transmitted through culture.

2. Previous studies of homicide patterns in the United States show that we are looking at social phenomenon that is predominantly but not exclusively associated with urban life (see e.g., Curtis, 1975, for a recent description and overview of national patterns of interpersonal violence). Empirical studies of homicide patterns in such major U. S. metropolitan cities as, for example, Atlanta (Fisher, 1976: 387-400; Munford et al., 1976: 312-32), Chicago (Block and Zimring, 1973: 1-12; Voss and Hepburn, 1968: 499-508), Cleveland (Bensing and Schroeder, 1960; Rushforth et al., 1977: 531-44), Detroit (Boudouris, 1971, and 1974: 525-40; Fisher, 1976: 387-400; Zimring, 1977, 317-32), Houston (Lundsgaarde, 1977, and 1979: 69-82; Pokorny, 1965: 479-870, Milwaukee (Carideo, 1977), and Philadelphia (Wolfgang, 1958; Zimring et al., 1976: 227-51), demonstrate that urban homicide is predominantly but not exclusively an intraracial, intrafamilial, and lower social class form of behavior. The continuing rise in the nation's homicide rate also means that the risks of victimization are becoming significantly greater for persons who reside in the largest cities.

REFERENCES

Allen, N. H. 1980. Homicide: Perspectives on Prevention. New York: Human Sciences Press.

Bensing, R. C. and O. J. Schroeder. 1960. Homicide in an Urban Community. Springfield: Charles C. Thomas Company.

Black, D. 1976. The Behavior of Law. New York: Academic Press.

Black, R. and F. E. Zimring. 1973. "Homicide in Chicago, 1965- 1970." Journal of Research in Crime and Delinquency, 10: 1- 12.

Bohannan, P. (ed.). 1960. African Homicide and Suicide. Princeton: Princeton University Press.

Boris, S. B. 1979. "Stereotypes and Dispositions for Criminal Homicide." Criminology 17: 139-58.

Boudouris, J. 1971. Trends in Homicide, Detroit: 1926-1968. Unpublished Ph.D. dissertation. Wayne State University.

Boudouris, J. A. 1974. "Classification of Homicides." Criminology, Vol. 11: 525-540.

Brown, E. J. et al. (eds.). 1984. Sourcebook of Criminal Justice Statistics - 1983. Washington, D. C.: U. S. Department of Justice, Bureau of Justice Statistics, U. S. Government Printing Office.

Bubany, C. P. 1974. "The Texas Penal Code of 1974." Southwestern Law Journal 28: 292-339.

Carideo, T. 1977. "Murder in Milwaukee." Insight, Sunday Magazine of the Milwaukee Journal, May 1.

Carp, R. A. 1974. The Harris County Grand Jury - A Case Study. Houston Law Review 12: 90-120.

Chimbos, P. D. 1978. Marital Violence: A Study of Interspouse Homicide. San Francisco: R & E Research Associates, Inc.

Curtis, L. A. 1974. Criminal Violence: National Patterns and Behaviors. Lexington, Mass.: D. C. Heath and Company. paEarls, F. 1979. The Social Reconstruction of Adolescence: Toward an Explanation for Increasing Rates of Violence in Youth. In, Rose (ed.) Lethal Aspects of Urban Violence. Lexington, Mass.: D. C. Heath and Company.

Federal Bureau of Investigation. 1976. Crime in the United States: Uniform Crime Reports: 1975. Washington, D. C.: U. S. Government Printing Office.

Fisher, J. C. 1976. "Homicide in Detroit--The Role of Firearms." Criminology, Vol. 14: 387-400.

Frake, C. O. 1964. "How to Ask for a Drink in Subanun." American Anthropologist 66: 127-32.

Gelles, R. 1966. The Violent Home: A Study of Physical Aggression between Husbands and Wives. Beverly Hills: Sage Publications, Inc., 1972.

Goldschmidt, V. 1966. "Primary Sanction Behavior." Acta Sociologica 10: 173-190.

Hall, E. T. 1964. "Adumbration in Intercultural Communication." American Anthropologist 66: 154-63.

Hall, E. T. 1966. The Hidden Dimension. Garden City, N. Y.: Doubleday and Co., Inc.

Hellman, D. A. 1980. The Economics of Crime. N. Y.: St. Martin's Press.

Hart, H. L. A. 1961. The Concept of Law. London: Oxford University Press.

Iuul, S. 1949. Kong Christian Den Femtes Danske Lov af 15. April 1683. Copenhagen: G. E. C. Gads Forlag.

. 1969. Lov og Ret I Denmark. Copenhagen: G. E. C. Gads Forlag.

Lundsgaarde, H. P. 1977. Murder in Space City: A Cultural Analysis of Houston Homicide Patterns. New York: Oxford University Press.

. 1979. "Cultural Sanctions in Urban Homicide." In, Rose (ed.) Lethal Aspects of Urban Violence. Lexington, Mass.: D. C. Heath and Company.

Maine, H. S. 1963 [1861]. Ancient Law: Its Connection with the Early History of Society and its Relation to Modern Ideas. Boston: Beacon Press.

Munford, R. S. et al. 1976. "Homicide Trends in Atlanta." Criminology 14: 213-21.

Murphy, R. F. 1964. "Social Distance and the Veil." American Anthropologist 66: 1257-74.

Pokorny, A. 1956. "A Comparison of Homicides in Two Cities." Journal of Criminal Law, Criminology, and Police Science 56: 479-87.

Posner, R. A. 1981. The Economics of Justice. Cambridge: Harvard University Press.

Rose, H. M. 1979. "Lethal Aspects of Urban Violence: An Overview." In, Rose (ed.), Lethal Aspects of Urban Violence. Lexington, Mass.: D. C. Heath and Company.

Ruesch, J. and G. Bateson. 1951. Communication: The Social Matrix of Psychiatry. New York: W. W. Norton and Co., Inc.

Rushforth, N. B. et al. 1977. "Violent Death in a Metropolitan County: Changing Patterns in Homicide (1958-74)." New England Journal of Medicine 297: 531-8.

Sutton, L. P. 1978a. Federal Criminal Sentencing: Perspectives of Analysis and a Design for Research. Washington, D. C.: U. S. Department of Justice.

    . 1978b. Federal Sentencing Patterns: A Study of Geographical Variations. Washington, D. C.: U. S. Department of Justice.

    . 1978c. Variations in Federal Criminal Sentences: A Statistical Assessment at the National Level. Washington, D. C.: U. S. Department of Justice.

    . 1978d. Predicting Sentencing in Federal Courts: The Feasibility of a National Sentencing Policy. Washington, D. C.: U. S. Department of Justice.

Swigert, V. L. and R. A. Farrell. 1976. Murder, Inequality, and the Law. Lexington, Mass.: D. C. Heath and Company.

Taswell-Langmead, T. P. 1946. English Constitutional History. London: Sweet and Maxwell, Ltd. Voss, M. and J. Hepburn. 1968. "Patterns in Criminal Homicide in Chicago." Journal of Criminal Law, Criminology, and Police Science 59: 499-508.

Weiner, N. 1954. The Human Use of Human Beings: Cybernetics and Society. N. Y.: Doubleday and Co., Inc.

Wolfgang, M. E. 1958. Patterns in Criminal Homicide. Philadelphia: University of Pennsylvania.

Wolfgang, M. E. and F. Ferracuti. 1967. The Subculture of Violence: Towards an Integrated Theory in Criminology. London: Tavistock Publications.

Zimring, F. E. et al. 1976. "Punishing Homicide in Philadelphia: Perspectives on the Death Penalty." The University of Chicago Law Review 43: 227-51.

Zimring, F. E. 1977. "Determinants of the Death Rate From Robbery - A Detroit Time Study." Journal of Legal Studies 1: 317-32.

Zimbardo, P. G. 1973. "The Human Choice: Individuation, Reason and Order vs. Deindividuation, Impulse and Chaos." In Urbanman: The Psychology of Urban Survival, T. Helmer and N. A. Eddington (eds.). New York: The Free Press, 196-238.

BLACK HOMICIDE: THE ADEQUACY OF EXISTING RESEARCH FOR DEVISING PREVENTION STRATEGIES

Darnell F. Hawkins

Within the last five years federal health agencies have taken the unprecedented step of identifying violent death as a major public health concern (cf. **Health United States: 1980**). This has resulted in efforts to devise treatment and preventive policies that are more systematic and effective than the perennial, but inconsistent, responses of politicians, public officials, and criminal justice personnel to the deterrence of violent crime or other forms of violent life-threatening behavior. Recent government reports and social scientific investigations have shown that homicide currently ranks among the top five causes of death for every age group in the United States population from ages one through forty-four (**Health United States: 1980 and 1981; Justice Assistance News**, Vol. 2, No. 8, 1981; Dennis, 1977, 1979; Farley, 1980; Centers for Disease Control: Homicide Surveillance, 1970-78, 1983). In addition, so significant are the effects of race (and sex) in determining the likelihood that one will be a victim of homicide the Department of Health and Human Services has specifically targeted young black males between the ages of 15 and 24 for homicide reduction programs.[1] Efforts are now underway to identify aspects of black homicide that may be susceptible to professional intervention aimed at its prevention and incidence reduction.[2]

Despite the fact that this public attention to the relationship between race and homicide has come after more than fifty years of social scientific and governmental documentation and analysis, existing studies of black homicide are inadequate in many ways. This inadequacy is apparent for both basic (academic) and applied research traditions within social science as well as within governmental record keeping.[3] In this paper the most recent findings on black homicide, especially among young black males are examined.

Race and Homicide: Past and Recent Findings

As noted in an earlier article (Hawkins, 1978) the possibility of applying a given body of research to the solution of "real world" problems exposes many of the limitations (and sometimes the strengths) of that research. For example, many of the metatheoretical assumptions that underlie social theory are not explicitly stated. The attempted application of theory and postapplication evaluation often bring these assumptions to the fore where they can be examined and debated. Such assumptions may have to do with conceptions of human nature, or the linkages among race, culture, social structure and human behavior. The attempted application of research may also raise questions of the adequacy of empirical research for the development or testing of theory or sometimes for so simple a task as fully describing a given social phenomenon. I believe that applied research represents the ultimate test of social theory.

Many of the problems inherent in the application (or anticipated application) of social research are evident in current efforts to use research on black homicide to devise intervention strategies. On the one hand, it would appear that racial difference in homicide offending and victimization is one of the most well documented and least controversial findings within

211

American criminology. Since 1930, many local, regional and national studies have been conducted. All of such studies have shown consistently higher arrest and victimization rates of homicide among blacks than among whites (Brearley, 1932; Lottier, 1938; Henry and Short, 1954; Wolfgang, 1958; Pokorny, 1965; Voss and Hepburn, 1968; Boudouris, 1970; Block, 1975; Munford et al., 1976; Lundsgaarde, 1977). Further, recent data show that the black homicide rate is also substantially higher than that of other disadvantaged minority groups such as Hispanics (Pokorny, 1965; Lundsgaarde, 1977; Silberman, 1978). Most of these studies have found the black homicide arrest rate to be between five and six times greater than that of whites.

These were essentially case or short term studies and they left unanswered the question of the temporal patterning of black and white homicide rates. Two recent studies examine such patterning through an examination of national vital statistics. Shin et al. (1977) report that historically not only homicide rates but also trends in rates have been very different for blacks and whites. From 1910, when the first national data became available, until the 1930s, the white rate remained relatively unchanged. Until 1930 it remained at around four or five per 100,000 population. During the Great Depression, it declined to around two and remained at that level in 1940. However, they report that for blacks the rates during this period were more irregular. In 1910 the black rate was 22. It rose sharply toward the beginning of World War I and reached a high of 43 in the middle 1920s. Afterwards, the rate declined and by 1940 it was down to 26.

Between 1940 and the late 1950s there was a downward trend in the rates for all race-sex groups except white females whose rate remained constant. Black males experienced a major decrease during this period. Around 1955 the downward trends showed a reversal. By 1974, when they ended their study, they report that "...the rate for white males had increased by about 170 percent over its low point, and that for white females had more than doubled. For blacks the proportional increases were much less, about 90 percent for males and 50 percent for females" (p. 401). Yet, the gap between blacks and whites was larger in 1974 than it was in 1910. In 1974, the black male rate of 77.9 was slightly more than 8 times the white male rate of 9.2 The black female rate of 15.5 was five times more than the white female rate of 2.9.

Farley (1980) uses essentially the same data as that used by Shin et al. (1977) to further analyze race, sex, and age differences in homicide victimization. He compares homicide to other leading causes of death and concludes: (1) between 1940 and 1977 the age-standardized homicide death rates for all race and sex groups rose while those from all other causes generally moved in the opposite direction (p. 179). (2) Homicide accounts for a significant component of the current racial and sexual differences in life expectations (p. 180). (3) At the young adult ages (25 to 35), homicide is the leading cause of death among nonwhites and is the second leading cause of mortality for white men (p. 186, citing U. S. National Center for Health Statistics, 1979). (4) Homicide has a greater impact upon the life expectations of nonwhite men than all but three ailments--heart diseases, malignant neoplasms and cerebrovascular diseases (p. 186). For all groups except nonwhite men, the effects of homicide are small compared to those of cancer, but in 1975, the elimination of homicide would have added about

212

half as many years to the life span of nonwhite men as the elimination of cancer deaths (p. 179).[4]

The role of homicide in decreasing life expectancy, especially for black males, has also been discussed by Dennis (1977, 1979). That work along with the work of Farley (1980) and the earlier work of Shin et al. (1977) have fully documented at an aggregate level the heavy toll that homicide extracts among blacks. A study prepared by a recently established homicide surveillance unit within the Public Health Service provides other useful information on black homicide victimization. It found that between 1970 and 1978 the racial profile of homicide victims changed considerably despite the continuing black-white gap. During 1970, 7,803 (46%) of victims were white and 9,045 (54%) were black or of other races. In 1978, 11,200 (55%) were white and 9,232 (45%) were nonwhite. They report that the increase in the percentage of white victims occurred among both males and females. Age-adjusted rates for blacks and other minorities decreased from 41.3 per 100,000 to 33.4 while the rates for whites increased from 4.7 to 6. Despite these changes the risk for nonwhite males in 1978 was 6.3 times the risk for white males, while the nonwhite female risk was 4.2 times that for white females. In addition, the age- adjusted rate for black females during this nine-year period was greater than that of white males (see Centers for Disease Control: Homicide Surveillance, 1970-78, 1983: 12-13, 22).

Offense Rate Differences

Since homicide is primarily an intraracial phenomenon, racial differences in victimization reflect similar differences in offending. But since offense data come from different sources than victimization data and because the study of each represents distinct research traditions, let us now consider previous studies of racial differences in offense rates. The work of Wolfgang (1958) is considered to be a pioneering study of homicide offender characteristics. He analyzed both offender and victim characteristics for almost 600 cases of homicide in Philadelphia between 1948 and 1952. He reported that 75% of offenders were black while blacks comprised only 18% of the city's population. The black male rate of 41.7 offenders per 100,000 was 15 times that of white males. The rate for black females was three times that of white males for both victims and offenders. In addition, although he found that whites and blacks were similar in terms of the age patterning of homicide, black males 60-64 years old killed as frequently as white males in their early twenties.

Many, including Wolfgang himself, have questioned the generalizability of these rate differences. A number of studies have reported smaller black-white differences in other localities or during different years. But in general, the disproportionate rates of black homicide offending have been documented in several studies that have replicated the Wolfgang analysis. Similar patterns have been noted for Houston by Pokorny (1965) and Lundsgaarde (1977); for Chicago (Voss and Hepburn, 1968; Block, 1975); Detroit (Boudouris, 1970); and Atlanta (Munford et al, 1976). National Uniform Crime Reports also provide recent data that illustrate these race differentials.

Table 1 illustrates the disproportionate rate of black arrests for murder and nonnegligent homicide between 1973 and 1982. In addition to the racial

213

disproportions, it shows the increasing incidence of homicide in the United States, especially after 1976. In 1973 blacks comprised nearly 60% of homicide arrests. Between 1978 and 1982 the rate seems to have stabilized somewhat at around 49%. Of course, this pattern of decline parallels that reported earlier for victimization during this period. Despite the recent decrease, blacks were committing from 5 to 6 times as many homicides as expected given the size of the black American population during this period. Since 1970, Uniform Crime Reports have provided race-, age-, and sex-specific data for homicide victims but comparable data are not provided for persons arrested for homicide. For example, we are not able to ascertain the age ranges or sex of black and white arrestees. Thus, the kind of findings reported by Wolfgang (1958)--e.g. a high rate of older, black male offending--cannot be corroborated or refuted. Of course, national crime data sources also do not fully probe racial differences in the various situational and circumstantial correlates of homicide such as those discussed by Wolfgang (e.g. spatial and temporal patterning). These and other limitations of available data and research on black-white homicide differences raise questions of their usefulness in devising reasonable and effective homicide reduction policies. These limitations and their implication for governmental policies to reduce black homicide are discussed below.

Limitations of Past Research

Past research on black homicide, like earlier social scientific investigations in other areas of study, have certain conceptual and methodological limitations in comparison to present standards. Past studies were essentially descriptive and did not utilize multivariate analytic techniques. In addition, criminological investigators have been less likely than researcher in some other areas to adopt modern techniques of data analysis. Greenberg (1979) and McDonald (1976) have noted that quantitative research in criminology dates from the 1820s when researchers explored the link between crime and poverty utilizing spatially aggregated data for countries or for regions within a country. A second research tradition also appeared during this same time. It entailed the study of personal attributes of criminals. Most quantitataive research in criminology has been carried out within these two traditions. Greenberg suggests that much of the research within these two traditions is seriously flawed either because the data were of poor quality or because of the meager mathematical tools available to researchers.

But while some of the limitations of past research on black homicide may be attributed to limitations of criminological research in general, others appear to reflect a kind of selective inattention (Dexter, 1958) to the investigation of black homicide in particular. Given the consistently high rate of black homicide in comparison to that of whites, one might expect that past researchers would have paid more careful attention to the temporal, spatial, and other dimensions and correlates of homicide within the black community. Such studies need not, of course, be exclusively noncomparative in their focus; rather they would provide a more in-depth look at the dynamics surrounding black offending and victimization. However, as documented earlier (Hawkins, 1983, 1984), this type of study has been a rarity.[5] The major forms of inattention or underinvestigation evident in studies of black homicide are discussed below.

Table 1

Race Differences in Arrests
Murder and Nonnegligent Manslaughter, 1973-82

Year	Total	Whites	Blacks	All Others*
1973	12,913	5,236 (40.5)	7,478 (57.9)	199 (1.5)
1974	12,464	4,897 (39.3)	7,122 (57.1)	445 (3.5)
1975	13,743	5,967 (43.4)	7,464 (54.3)	312 (2.3)
1976	12,875	5,792 (45.0)	6,886 (53.5)	197 (1.5)
1977	17,122	7.866 (45.9)	8.731 (51.0)	525 (3.0)
1978	18,698	8,703 (46.5)	9,243 (49.4)	752 (4.1)
1979	18,238	9,010 (49.4)	8,693 (47.7)	535 (2.9)
1980	18,729	9,480 (50.6)	8,968 (47.9)	281 (1.5)
1981	20,404	10,129 (49.6)	9,998 (49.0)	277 (1.4)
1982	18,475	9,008 (48.8)	9,174 (49.7)	293 (1.6)

*Source: Uniform Crime Reports

Inattention to the Patterning of Black Homicide

Few existing studies or data sources have gone beyond a mere documentation of comparatively high rates of black homicide. These are generally calculated in percentages or rates per 100,000 population. Researchers often have not utilized even those spatially aggregated data analysis techniques that characterized 19th century studies of crime. Thus, there is a paucity of even descriptive studies of black homicide or of homicide in general. In addition, most researchers who have studied black homicide within this limited analytic framework have been primarily interested in black-white comparisons and have seldom examined the patterning of this phenomenon within the black community itself. Consequently, quite apart from the more theoretical question of the reasons for generally high rates of black homicide, a number of empirically-based questions remain unanswered. Which segments of the black population have

215

the highest rates? Is the social patterning of homicide within the black community similar to that found among whites or among other groups? If not, what are significant areas of difference? What is the link between social class and homicide among blacks? Answers to questions such as these must be provided before serious preventive strategies can be considered.

Wolfgang (1958) attempted to address some of these questions, but many could not be considered because his study was confined to one city and utilized basically bivariate analytic techniques. Pettigrew and Spier (1962) probed some of these questions through a multivariate, ecological analysis. They found that black homicide rates differed by regions of the country. They conclude that a ranking of states on the basis of black homicide rates is similar to a ranking based on white rates. Brearley (1932) and Lottier (1938) had earlier reported similar findings. In fact, regional comparisons of this sort led to the promulgation of the widely accepted explanation for high rates of southern and black homicide, southern subculture of violence (see Hackney, 1969; Gastil, 1971). But as critics of this theory have noted, it is based upon limited empirical evidence, including relatively few regional or black- white statistical analyses (Loftin and Hill, 1974).

Even more underresearched than the question of regional differences in black or black-white homicide is the question of social class variations. Although the problem of data availability is a major factor accounting for this failure of past researchers, it may also be attributable to selective inattention on the part of those analysts. It is generally assumed that crime, including homicide, is a lower class phenomenon. Such assumptions may be plausible but will not suffice when the desired goal of the researcher is homicide prevention. Researchers must empirically assess the social class patterning of homicide. For example, while the black rate of arrests for all crimes is higher than the white rate, residential patterns are evident. These residential patterns may reflect social class differences in some instances. Uniform Crime Reports (UCR) data for 1975 show that blacks living in rural areas constituted 10% of the rural population and made up about 10% of arrests for all types of crimes. The black suburban population was 15%, while only 12% of all suburban arrestees were black. A large discrepancy between population figures and arrest rates was evident only in urban areas. UCR data for other years show similar patterns. While this was not an analysis of homicide rates, a further examination of homicide statistics may yield similar findings.

Absence of studies of social class and homicide for blacks and whites prevents us from evaluating the relative contributions of race, socioeconomic status, and subculture to the production of high rates of the offense among blacks. In a study of 5,183 male homicide victims in the United States, Lalli and Turner (1968) found the homicide rates for both blacks and whites to be considerably lower for higher level occupational groups than for laborers. However, higher occupational level blacks still had rates higher than those for whites in similar occupations. On the other hand, in a recent analysis of homicide rates in Atlanta, Centerwall (1982) found blacks and whites of similar socioeconomic status to have similar rates of family and acquaintance homicide.[6]

The importance of these kinds of approaches to the analysis of black homicide and black-white homicide differences is further illustrated by a recent study of regional differences in the ecomomic correlates of urban homicide rates. Messner (1983) critiques the findings of Blau and Blau (1982) and reports that the proportion of the population below the poverty line has a significant, positive effect on the homicide rate only in his sample of non-Southern cities. No such effects were found for Southern cities. Do other correlates of homicide show regional differences? Such findings also raise the question of whether the disaggregation of the black homicide rate might produce similar or different regional variations. It must be noted that few of these questions have been fully probed in the study of black or white homicide. But given current efforts to intervene to reduce black homicide, these deficiencies of past research become more problematic. Such empirical investigations are needed to help us fully describe the phenomenon of black homicide and also to help us to identify etiological factors that may contribute to the disproportionate rates of homicide among blacks.

Another illustration of the extent to which many of these kinds of questions remain largely unexplored is found in a paper prepared by the federal homicide surveillance unit. Mercy et al. (1984) analyzed homicide rates for nonwhite males between the ages of 15 and 24 by geograqhic regions for 1970 through 1980. They found that while among all homicides the South has the highest rates, among this age and race group the North Central states had considerably higher rates than the other three regions (Northeast, South, and West, in order of rates). There was some convergence of rates between 1970 and 1980 but the rates for the North Central states in 1980 were still twice the rates for the West and much higher than the South. This contradicts some of the southern subculture of violence notions of homicide etiology. Such differences may be attributable to urban-rural residence differences, socioeconomic inequality, or a number of other unexamined factors.

Inattention to Etiological Factors

Despite the extensive documentation of a disproportionately high rate of black homicide, researchers have provided surprisingly few explanations for this phenomenon. Brearley (1932) offered one of the earliest attempts at explaining this difference. In a chapter on "The Negro and Homicide" he notes that many attempts have been made to find a satisfactory explanation for the high rate of black homicide and that these have ranged from more credible ones to those based on prejudice or hasty generalization. Yet, Brearley himself concludes: "there is some evidence, however, that the Negro is lacking in power to control himself in accordance with the requirements of others" (p.112). He goes on to suggest that the higher rates of manslaughter as compared to premeditated murder among blacks is proof of their impulsiveness. On the other hand, he suggests the possibility that the high homicide rate of blacks may be more apparent than real. He speculates that "If interracial slayings were eliminated and a careful study made of comparable groups of whites and Negroes having the same economic, educational, and social status and the same inability to secure justice except by a resort to deeds of violence, there is the possibility that approximately equal homicide rates might be found for the two races" (p. 115-116). Similar need for caution in linking race and crime was later expressed by Bonger (1943) and Wolfgang (1964).

Meanwhile, cartodemographic researchers such as Lottier (1938) were devising another form of explanation, one based on both black-white and southern-nonsouthern differences in the rate of homicide. In summarizing these earlier studies Harries (1974) observed that when one considers regional geographies of crime in the United States during the 1930s, 1950s and 1960s, the most striking finding "...is the persistence of high homicide rates in the South" (p.16). In seeking to explain high rates of black violence, he concludes that "Black violence seems to be but a special case of white southern violence, in the sense that white homicide rates in the South are higher than white rates elsewhere" (p.34).

Wolfgang (1958) devotes surprisingly little attention to explaining the extremely disproportionate rate of black homicide in Phildelphia. However, after cautioning researchers aganst making hasty judgements about the link between race and crime (1964), he proposed an essentially subcultural explanation for the high rate of black and lower class white homicide (Wolfgang and Ferracuti, 1967). The ideas of Wolfgang and Ferracuti (1967) and the cartodemographic researchers were summarized by Gastil (1971) into what had been called a "subculture of violence" explanation for high rates of southern violence and (more or less) for high rates of black violence. This subcultural theory has become the most widely proposed explanation for regional and racial differences in homicide.

Analysts in the subcultural tradition appear to have proceeded on the basis of two rather plausible assumptions. First, they have noted that criminal homicide statistics in contrast to data for other types of crime are less subject to distortion by police and other criminal justice officials, e.g., by differing patterns of detection and prosecution. There are also high clearance (arrest) rates for homicide cases in comparison to other crimes. Thus, they conclude that consistently high rates of black homicide represent a **real** phenomenon. Further, to the extent that whites and other racial groups do not display similar levels of violence, the cause of homicide does not lie within the whole of American culture.

Wolfgang and Ferracuti (1967) argued that certain subgroups in America live in a cultural and social milieu which encourages physical aggression, or at least does not actively discourage it. They noted that on the basis of an awareness of social, economic and political disparities between whites and blacks, any diligent researcher would propose that the black crime rate would be higher than the white rate and that there would be a "larger spread to the learning of, resort to, and criminal display of the violence value among minority groups such as Negroes" (1967: 264).

I have previously suggested (1983) that there are several major limitations of subculture of violence theory, many of which are relevant for the present discussion of the adequacy of past research for devising policies to reduce black homicide. Among the major weaknesses of the theory are: (1) There is an extreme emphasis on mentalistic value orientations of individuals--orientations which in the aggregate are said to produce a subculture. (2) The theory lacks empirical grounding and indeed is put in question by some empirical findings. (3) Much of the theory has tended to underemphsize a variety of structural, situational and institutional variables which affect interpersonal violence. For blacks, these variables range from historical patterns developed during slavery to the immediate racialist social context of an individual homicidal offense to the operation of the criminal justice system, past and present. (4) Subcultural theory underemphasizes the effects of law and law enforcement on patterns of criminal homicide (e.g.

218

deterrence effects). (5) There are other plausible ways apart from the inculcation of pro- violence values by which the economic, political and social disadvantages of American blacks may produce high rates of homicide. It is the lack of a full consideration of economic factors that constitutes a crucial idealogical bias of subculture of violence theory. Though economic factors are said to determine the contours and boundaries of a given subculture, subcultural theorists have seldom attempted to link such conditions to homcide as Bonger (1943,1969) proposed in his Marxist analysis. Both the lack of attention to economic correlates of black (and white) homicide and the failure to fully explore situational factors are features of existing theoretical analyses of homicide that raise questions about their adequacy for developing strategies of reduction.

Homicide is primarily a problem of the poor and disadvantaged, although as previously noted the relationship between socioeconomic status and murder has not been thoroughly documented. Consequently it may be argued, as Allen (1980:50) does, that successful prevention must involve not only changes in attitudes and behavior but also "through improving the human condition: better housing, employment, education and health." Indeed, available evidence is sufficient to suggest that black homicide is concentrated in what Glasgow (1980), Wilson (1978) and others have called the "black underclass." This segment of the black population has not benefitted from the civil rights gains of the last twenty years and recent studies report that their economic condition is worsening rather than improving. Such worsening of conditions is especially evident among urban black youth. For example, Mare and Winship (1983:39) found that "an important exception to improvements in the relative socioeconomic status of blacks during recent decades is increased levels of joblessness among black youths relative to whites.... Although racial convergence on school enrollment and educational attainment had reduced other socioeconomic inequalities between the races, it had widened the employment difference."

Recent crime statistics (to the extent available) show that it is among unemployed and underemployed black youths and young adults that the highest rates of homicide in the black community are found. Thus, it is obvious that prevention and intervention strategies must be developed to remedy these larger, macro-level conditions as well as the more situational and immediate determinants of black homicide. While it appears to be a generally accepted social fact among social scientists that economic factors influence homicide rates, they have conducted relatively little research that explores the dynamics of that influence. Still left unresolved are questions of absolute versus relative deprivation, economic condition versus cultural context, etc. For example, Henry and Short (1954) and numerous other researchers have suggested that unemployment and worsening economic conditions lead to increases in the rate of violent crime, but a recent study by Cook and Zarkin (forthcoming) finds that homicide rates in general are largely unaffected by the business cycle. They do not provide race-specific analyses and are not able to test Henry and Short's (1954) proposition that blacks are more affected by such economic trends than are whites. Researchers must also seek to explain why homicide rates decline during severe downturns in the economy and why many of the poorest among rural blacks have comparatively low rates of homicide.

Inattention to the Situational Correlates of Homicide

Although the macro-societal level etiological factors discussed above are of importance for social scientists and must be considered when devising sound homicide reduction strategies, the inattention of past researchers to the more immediate, situational determinants of homicide may be more problematic. It is at least arguable that homicide, like other problems of the poor, can be successfully remedied only through major political and socioeconomic changes. On the other hand, the kind of social reform sentiments that underlie current homicide reduction efforts are not necessarily compatible with the advocacy of such major changes. At best, major changes in the socioeconomic status of the black poor will be cited as a long term goal and prevention efforts will be targeted at perceived short-term solutions. It is also true that acts of homicide are relatively rare even among the poorest segments of the population. These two factors--the unlikelihood of major changes in the socioeconomic status of poor blacks and the relative rareness of homicide--have caused many prevention advocates to focus on situational determinants of homicide rather than on larger societal causative factors.

With these kinds of considerations as an organizing perspective, Wolfgang and Ferracutti (1967); Allen (1980), Hawkins (1983, 1984) and a few other researchers have proceeded to identify several forms of potential intervention. In general, these may be said to be targeted at either the individual criminal or at the larger community from which homicide offenders are likely to come. Each of these efforts usually considers both victims and offenders. Among the various areas of prevention and intervention discussed are:

1.The identification of high risk groups (both offenders and victims).
2.More effective and rapid police and medical personnnel response to pre- homicide behavior, e.g., assaults, verbal threats, murder attempts, and so forth.
3.Gun control.
4.Educational programs, especially those targeted at the young.
5.Community organization and education, including the physical rehabilitation of blighted neighborhoods.
6.Mental health centers for counseling and other forms of intervention for offenders, victims and their families.
7.Social scientific studies to help identify the social interactional clues to homicide, e.g. verbal and noverbal behaviors, threats, social histories of hostilities. etc.
8.More effective control and rehabilitation of potential and actual offenders by the various agencies of the criminal justice system.

Most researchers and other analysts of homicide agree that very few of these intervention efforts have been implemented. They also agree that there are very few social scientific investigations of the effectiveness (or potential effectiveness) of these various strategies. There is also the expression of doubt concerning the potential effectiveness of some intervention strategies. For example, Allen (1980:62) cites the earlier work of Bromberg (1961) who emphasized that it is questionable whether the homicidal acts of specific

220

individuals can be regularly predicted even if all of the personality variables correlated with homicide were known. This reinforces Wolfgang and Ferracuti's (1967) suggestion that predicting rare events such as homicide is extremely difficult. The difficulty of such a task has led many to deemphasize the more individual, especially psychological-psychiatric approaches to homicide intervention, and to advocate either more group or law enforcement oriented prevention including such strategies as gun control and preventive detention of aggressive criminals.

Yet, whatever the approach taken, such efforts must be informed by careful studies of the situational and individually-based determinants of homicide. For example, before counseling, educational, pre- rehabilitation, preventive detention, or similar programs can be effectively applied, we must be able to identify high-risk groups. Current research and statistics identify young, black males as having an extremely high risk of homicide. But such a broad categorization of risk identifies too large a population to be useful for implementing any but the most general preventive programs. In fact, even more detailed sociodemographic groupings of that population (through the use of such measures as income, employment status, urban-rural residence, education, etc.) may not prove very useful for precise risk calculation efforts and resulting intervention. As earlier noted, previous research and data sources do not allow policy makers to go beyond these general categorizations to identify various levels of risk within the young, black male population. For example, while it has been shown that black males in 1978 had a homicide risk rate around six times that of white males, certain segments of that population may be shown to have rates exceeding that rate. In addition some segments of the young black male population may have rates lower than the overall rate for white males. How can these groups be identified? Can they be identified with the kind of aggregate-level, sociodemographic analyses generally used by researchers?

At the purely descriptive level, some previous investigations have analysed various situational and individual level correlates of homicide. For example, Wolfgang (1958) considered such factors as the time of day, week, month and year of the homicide act; site of the act (within or outside of the home); victim- offender relationship; level of violence used in committing the act; alcohol use, and so forth. What is needed, however, are studies that go beyond mere description to discuss the various ways in which these and other factors "cause" a given homicide act. Studies such as that of Athens (1977) which use a symbolic interactionist approach may be more useful for analyzing the dynamics of the interpersonal encounters that are likely to lead to homicide. Such studies consider not only personal traits but also the processes that lead to acts of aggression. Concern for the situational correlates of homicide and their impact on the effectiveness of prevention efforts has led Jason, Strauss and Tyler (1983) to argue that primary (family, acquaintance) homicides may be more preventable than secondary homicide (those involving strangers). On the other hand, some researchers have argued that secondary homicide offenders may be more paresponsive to efforts at legal deterrence such as swift prosecution and conviction.

Summary and Conclusions

In this paper I have suggested that efforts at black homicide prevention will be impeded by the inadequacy of basic research on the phenomenon of homicide itself, including a paucity of studies on black homicide. In reviewing existing research on homicide it is evident that there are several major shortcomings. First, most of the research does not go beyond a mere calculation of rates for various racial groups, usually at the state or national level. Even if multivariate techniques are used, the focus is on the magnitude of rate differences rather than other aspects of the patterning of homicide that are correlated with rate differences. Second, few studies have specifically analyzed the variation and patterning of homicide within the black community. Third, studies that do attempt to examine the patterning of homicide (black or white) most often utilize a limited range of variables. Certain of the more situational correlates of homicide are never fully analysed. This may be largely a consequence of the limited data on homicide collected by law enforcement or health agencies and the difficulty researchers encounter when collecting these data themselves. For example, socioeconomic status data for offenders and victims are seldom available. But there also appears to be a kind of selective inattention by researchers to the non-aggregate-level correlates of homicide. That is, existing empirical research has been cast within a theoretical framework that limits the range of variables considered.

In many ways the work of criminologists and social scientists who have studied homicide has not lived up to Marvin Wolfgang's pioneering expectations. Echoing the earlier comments of Morris (1955) he suggested that:

"if the criminologist is to acquire general principles that are essential to effective control, prevention and treatment, he must seek patterns, similarities and repetitions that can become the basis for classification and generalization.... Analysis of a particular type of crime, the individuals who commit it, and those who are victims of it, is relatively rare. Such analysis, provided it is as detailed and specific as the best available data permit, may produce insights into etiology, prediction and control as yet unknown and unexplored" (Wolfgang, 1958:3-4)

Without insight into the phenomenon of homicide such as that described here, goals of reduction will be largely unrealized. For example, agreed upon preliminary steps toward intervention--identification of high risk groups apart from race, identification of the social interactional clues, etc.--depend upon the availability of sound empirical and theoretical work on homicide. Many observers have questioned the extent to which the devising of social policy is dependent upon the availability of research data. Policy decisions, sometimes sound ones, are made even in the absence of reliable data. On the other hand, even sound research findings are not always easily translated into specific policies. Despite these observations, sound empirical and non-empirical social science research is an asset for the policy maker.

The following kinds of studies are needed to begin to provide a basis for the kind of intervention efforts currently proposed by the federal government:

1.More detailed analyses of the sociodemographic characteristics of homicide victims and offenders. These should include such previously underanalyzed characteristics as socioeconomic status (absolute and comparative), residence (within and across

222

regions), and intercorrelation among various sociodemographic variable.

2.Improved studies of the individual-level and situational correlates of homicide. These studies should be geared toward not only identifying high risk individuals or circumstances but also toward identifying those conditions and persons for whom intervention might be possible and effective.

3.Beyond basic research, there is a need to conduct studies that evaluate intervention efforts. Only through such application and evaluation of existing knowledge will researchers be able to identify successful forms of intervention.

Finally, researchers must seek to more carefully define what is meant by intervention and prevention. They must also determine which kinds of interventions work most effectively with which types of homicide. There is also a need to evaluate the impact of intervention efforts on those persons involved and on the larger society. Homicide prevention may be accomplished by direct intervention with high risk individuals or groups. Such direct intervention may be more effective than the post facto, exemplary deterrence assumptions currently underlying criminal law and law enforcement. It is possible that these kinds of strategies may be more effective but they also pose the greatest risk of violating the rights and dignity of those targeted for intervention. Crime prevention efforts, perhaps more so than other forms of applied social science, have the potential for abuse. In the words of Wolfgang and Ferracuti (1967:284) we must ask "to what extent are we willing to change the traditional democratic constraints that normally function to restrict society's manupulative control over bahavior, even the conduct of criminals, in order to reduce crimes of violence?" A major task of social researchers will be to devise prevention strategies for homicide that do not contribute further to the victimization of the American underclass.

Notes

1.In the 1981 **Justice Assistance News** report (Vol.2,No.8), excerpts were taken from a recent speech by Horace G. Ogden, Director of the Center for health Promotion and Education, Center for Disease Control, U.S. Department of Health and Human Services. After stressing that homicide prevention must become a major public health concern, he listed the following goals set by federal government health experts: (1) By 1990, the death rate from homicide among black males ages 15 to 24 should by reduced to below 60 per 100,000. The 1978 rate for that group was 72.5. (2) By 1990, injuries and deaths to children inflicted by abusing parents should be reduced by at least 25 percent. (3) By 1990, the rate of suicide among people 15 to 24 should be below 11 per 100,000 compared to a 1978 rate of 12.4 (pp2-3). Each of these has emerged as major federal governmental agenda items during the last three years, although it may be argued that black homicide reduction has received much less media attention than the other goals.

2. Much of the impetus for the current prevention efforts has come as the result of two conferences convened by the National Institute of Mental Health. The first was held May 12-14, 1980 and the second, June 14-16, 1984. A summary of the proceedings of the first meeting can be found in **Public Health Reports**, Vol. 95, No.6, pp.549-561. Results of the second conference are to be published in late 1984 or 1985.

3. Although the focus of the current analysis is on black homicide, noted criticisms are applicable to studies of homicide among all groups. Studies of homicide in the United States have inevitably had to address the issue of the disproportionate rate of homicide among blacks. Thus, the limitations of past research represent problems in the study of homicide in general. The same deficiencies in available information of homicide exist for blacks, whites and other groups in the United States.

4. These findings, while useful, further illustrate the limitations of previous data and research on homicide. For example, categorized as nonwhites in such analyses are blacks, Asian Americans, Native Americans, including Alaskan natives, etc. Included among whites are Hispanics. Asian Americans have much lower rates of homicide than blacks or Native Americans, while Hispanics have rates higher than those of many other white ethnic groups.

5. A notable exception is Rose (1978,1981), who analyzes black homicide rates and patterning in several urban areas.

6. For one of the few studies of social class variations in the patterning of homicide see Green and Wakefield (1979).

References

Allen, Nancy H. 1980. **Homicide: Perspectives on Prevention.** New York: Human Sciences Press

Athens, Lonnie H. 1977. "Violent Crime: A Symbolic Interactionist Study." **Symbolic Interaction** 1: 56-70

Blau, Judith R. and Peter M. Blau. 1982. "Metropolitan Structure and Violent Crime." **American Sociological Review** 47(February): 114-129.

Block, Richard. 1975. "Homicide in Chicago: A Nine Year Study (1965-1973)." **Journal of Criminal Law and Criminology** 66 (December):496-510

Bonger, Willem. 1943. **Race and Crime.** New York: Columbia University Press.

-----. 1969. **Criminality and Economic Conditions.** Bloomington: Indiana University Press.

Bourdouris, James. 1970. "Trends in Homicide, Detroit, 1926-68." Ph.D. Dissertation, Wayne State University, Detroit, Michigan.

Brearley, H.C. 1932. **Homicide in the United States.** Chapel Hill: University of North Carolina Press.

Bromberg, W. 1961. **The Mold of Murder--A Psychiatric Study of Homicide.** New York: Grune and Stratton.

Centers for Disease Control: Homicide Surveillance Summary: 1970-78. 1983. Violence Epidemilogy Branch, Center for Health Promotion and Education. Public Health Service. U.S. Department of Health and Human Services. Atlanta, Georgia.

Centerwall, Brandon S. 1982. "Race, Socioeconomic Status, and Homicide: Atlanta, 1961-62, 1971-72." Paper presented at annual meeting of Southern Sociological Society, Memphis, Tenn.

Cook, Phillip and Gary Zarkin. Forthcoming, 1985. "Crime and the Business Cycle." **Journal of Legal Studies,** January.

Dennis, Ruth E. 1977. "Social Stress and Mortality among Nonwhite Males." **Phylon** 38 (September): 315-328.

-----. "The Role of Homicide in Decreasing Life Expectancy." In Harold M. Rose (ed.), **Lethal Aspects of Urban Violence.** Lexington, MA: D. C. Heath.

Dexter, Lewis Anthony. 1958. "A Note on Selective Inattention in Social Science." **Social Problems** 61 (Fall):176-182

Farley, Reynolds. 1980. "Homicide Trends in the United States." **Demography** 17 (May): 177-88.

Gastil, Raymond D. 1971. "Homicide and a Regional Culture of Violence."

American Sociological Review 36 (June):412-427

Glascow, Douglas G. 1980. **The Black Underclass.** San Francisco: Jossey-Bass.

Green, Edward and Russel P. Wakefield. 1979. "Patterns of Middle and Upper Class Homicide." **Journal of Criminal Law and Criminology** 70 (2):172-181

Greenberg, David F. 1979. **Mathematical Criminology.** New Brunswick, N. J.: Rutgers University Press.

Hackney, Sheldon. 1969. "Southern Violence" in H. D. Graham and T. R. Gurr (eds.), **The History of Violence in America.** New York: Bantam.

Harries, Keith D. 1974. **The Geography of Crime and Justice.** New York: Mcgraw-Hill.

Hawkins, Darnell F. 1978. "Applied Research and Social Theory." **Evaluation Quarterly (Now Evaluation Review)** 2 (February):141- 152

-----. 1983. "Black and White Homicide Differentials: Alternatives to an Inadequate Theory." **Criminal Justice and Behavior** 10 (December):407-440.

-----. 1984. "Sociological Research and the Prevention of Homicide Among Blacks." Paper prepared for the Black Homicide/Mental Health Workshop. Washington, D. C., June 14-16.

Henry, Andrew F. and James F. Short, Jr. 1954. **Suicide and Homicide.** Glencoe, IL: The Free Press.

Jason, Janine, Lilo T. Strauss, and Carl W. Tyler, Jr. 1983. "A Comparison of Primary and Secondary Homicides in the United States." **American Journal of Epidemiology** 17: 309-319

Lalli, Michael and Stanley H. Turner. 1968. "Suicide and Homicide: A Comparative Analysis by Race and Occupational Levels." **Journal of Criminal Law, Criminology, and Police Science** 59 (June): 191-200

Loftin, Colin and Robert H. Hill. 1974. "Regional Subculture and Homicide: An Examination of the Gastil-Hackney Thesis." **American Sociological Review** 39 (October):714-722.

Lottier, Stuart. 1938. "Distribution of Criminal Offenses in Sectional Regions." **Journal of Criminal Law, Criminology, and Police Science** 29:329-344.

Lundsgaarde, Henry P. 1977. **Murder in Space City: A Cultural Analysis of Houston Homicide Patterns.** New York: Oxford University Press.

Mare, Robert D. and Christopher Winship. 1984. "The Paradox of Lessening Racial Inequality and Joblessness Among Black Youth: Enrollment, Enlistment, and Employment, 1964-1981." **American Sociological Review** 49 (February):39-55.

McDonald, Lynn. 1976. **The Sociology of Law and Order.** Boulder, CO: Westview Press.

Mercy, James A., Jack C. Smith and Mark L. Rosenberg. 1984. "Monitoring of the 1990 Objective for Preventing Homicide Among Black Homicide Mental Health Workshop, Washington, D. C., June 14-16.

Messner, Steven F. 1983. "Regional Differences in the Economic Correlates of the Urban Homicide Rate: Some Evidence on the Importance of Cultural Context." **Criminolgy** 21 (November):477- 488.

Morris, Albert. 1955. **Homicide: An Approach to the Problem of Crime**. Boston: Boston University Press.

Mumford, Robert S., Ross S. Hazer, Roger S. Feldman and Robert R. Strivers. 1976. "Homicide Trends in Atlanta." **Criminology** 14 (August):213-232.

Pettigrew, Thomas F. and Rosalind Barclay Spier. 1962. "The Ecological Structure of Negro Homicide." **American Journal of Sociology** 67 (May):621-629

Pokorny, Alex D. 1965. "A Comparison of Homicide in Two Cities." **Journal of Criminal Law, Criminology, and Police Science** 56 (December):479-487.

Rose, Harold M. 1978. "The Geography of Despair." **Annals of the Association of America Geographers** 68:453-464.

------. 1981. **Black Homicide and the Urban Environment**. United States Department of Health and Human Services, National Institute of Mental Health.

Shin, Yongsock, Davor Jedlicka and Everett S. Lee. 1977. "Homicide among Blacks." **Phylon** 38 (December):398-407.

Silberman, Charles. 1978. **Criminal Violence-Criminal Justice: Criminals, Police, Courts, and Prisons in America**. New York: Random House.

United States Department of Health and Human Services. 1981. **Health-United States: 1980** DHHS Publication No. (PHS) 81-1232. United States Department of Health and Human Services, Public Health Services. Office of Health Research, Statistics and Technology. National Center for Health Statistics. National Center for Health Services Research. Washington, D. C.: Government Printing Office.

-----. 1981. **Public Health Reports**. Washington, D.C.: Author.

United States Department of Justice (1974-83). **Uniform Crime Reports 1973-82** Washington, D. C.: U.S. Government Printing Office.

-----. 1981. **Justice Assistance News**. Washington D.C. : Author

United States National Center for Health Statistics. 1979. Vital Statistics of the United States: 1975. Vol. II, Part A.

Voss, Harwin and John R. Hepburn. 1968. "Patterns in Criminal Homicide in Chicago,: **Journal of Criminal Law, Criminology and Police Science** 59 (December):499-508.

228

Wilson, William J. 1978. **The Declining Significance of Race: Blacks and Changing American Institutions.** Chicago: University of Chicago Press.

Wolfgang, Marvin. 1958. **Patterns in Criminal Homicide.** New York: Wiley.

-----. 1964. **Crime and Race: Conceptions and Misconceptions.** New York: Institute of Human Relations Press.

-------------- and Franco Ferracuti. 1967. **The Subculture of Violence: Towards an Integrated Theory in Criminology.** London: Tavistock.

HOMICIDE PREVENTION WITHIN THE BLACK COMMUNITY: PUBLIC HEALTH AND CRIMINAL JUSTICE CONCERNS

Robert Davis and Darnell F. Hawkins

As the articles in this volume well document, homicide within the black community represents a formidable challenge. Homicidal violence affects the lives of offenders and victims, their families, and the well-being of the entire community. Losing a family member at a relatively productive age has both financial and nonfinancial costs. Data on black homicide show a significant loss of life for persons even to the age of 45. That is, while homicide is highest among those persons in their teens and twenties, its incidence among older blacks is still greater than that found among whites. In addition, black women are involved in homicide at higher rates than white men. The black community's economic productivity, its childrearing and family patterns, and its reproduction potential are severely limited by these losses. In most instances of homicide, society loses two potentially productive members--the person killed and the person arrested. To a large extent, despite extremely high rates of black homicide, it has been viewed as primarily a problem of law enforcement. In this concluding contribution to the volume, we propose that homicide among blacks must also become a significant public health concern with the accompanying focus on publicly funded prevention and treatment strategies such a label implies in modern American society. We also advocate increased emphasis within the criminal justice system on homicide prevention.

Articles within this volume and numerous documents prepared by federal health agencies have shown the extent to which the life expectancy of blacks, especially black males, is affected by homicide. Nevertheless, most current public health programs do not emphasize primary prevention in the area of homicide and until relatively recently most public health officials have argued that solving such problems goes beyond their mandate. It has been proposed that homicide, including its prevention, is largely a concern for the criminal justice system. But even a cursory examination of criminal justice practice in the United States reveals that there has been little concern for homicide prevention, especially its prevention among blacks.

The result is that homicide prevention is a neglected area of concern for both public health and law enforcement agencies, two potential front-line intervenors in the effort to reduce the homicide rate among blacks. A number of political and socioeconomic considerations have influenced past efforts (or lack of effects) at violence prevention among both blacks and whites and these will likely influence future developments. First, Americans have never shown a great willingness to use public funds for crime control or prevention, but more particularly the latter. Even within the context of the modern welfare state with its expanded array of social services, politicians have had to resort periodically to various scare tactics (crime wave predictions) to garner public support. When funds are made available through such efforts, they have been spent largely on social control efforts rather than on the prevention of crime.

There are several other reasons for the lack of attention by criminal justice officials to the problem of black homicide: (1) Because of perceptions of the nature of homicide itself, many within the criminal justice system tend to view it as a largely unpreventable crime. It is seen as an act of passion or such an aberrant event as to have few anticipatory "markers" that might aid intervention efforts. (2) The view of blacks as "normal primitives" fosters a perception that even if homicide is preventable, it may be less so for lower class blacks. Among them homicide is seen as a natural and normal occurrence. (3) The intraracial character of homicide has meant that blacks victimize each other. The loss of life, especially among lower class blacks, is perceived as having less political and social costs than the loss of life among other groups. In fact, the criminal justice system can be said to have an interest in the prevention of only one category of homicide--those involving white victims. Many policemen and other criminal justice officials focus their prevention and punishment efforts primarily at felony-murder cases that involve white victims.[1] (4) Finally, the numerous crime prevention projects that have appeared over much of the country during the last twenty years most often concentrate their efforts on preventing property crime rather than crimes of violence. This is due both to the high value placed on property in American society and a view that property crimes are more preventable than most violent crimes against the person.[2]

There are also other somewhat less ideologically- based reasons for the past and continuing lack of official attention to homicide prevention among blacks. The prevention of acts of violence is not easily accomplished for any individual or group regardless of race, socioeconomic status, sex, or age. As Wolfgang and Ferracuti (1967, 1982) have noted, predicting relatively rare events such as homicide is extremely difficult. In addition, they suggest that research is needed to determine the most effective, efficient, rapid and enduring methods of reduction and prevention. They pose three other fundamental questions: (1) How much cost are we willing to tolerate for an X amount of reduction of violent crime? (2) What do we consider a "significant" reduction of violent crime, whatever the cost? and (3) To what extent are we willing to change the traditional democratic constraints that normally function to restrict society's manipulative control over behavior, even the conduct of criminals, in order to reduce crimes of violence? (p. 284).

Given such considerations and the multiplicity of competing social needs identifiable in contemporary American society, neither whites nor middle class blacks have shown a great interest in using their political leverage to fund programs aimed at homicide prevention. Recently, however, there are some indications that the federal government may be willing to consider homicide and other forms of violence as a major social and public health concern. The 1980 annual report on the health of the nation by the United States Department of Health and Human Services reports that homicide should be given a priority in expending state, local and federal public health prevention funds. Homicide was said to have emotionally stressful antecedents and consequences and is further described as the ultimate antithesis of health promotion and human resource development.[3]

There is also evidence of concern in other governmental and non-governmental sectors. In 1980 and 1984 the National Institute of Mental Health sponsored symposia on homicide among black males.[4] But despite these developments and despite the fact that the President appointed in 1983 a special task force on family violence, law enforcement and other federal

232

government funds do not yet appear to be targeted toward efforts to prevent violent crime or homicide.

In view of the possibly increasing willingness of all levels of government to invest greater resources in a variety of illness and death prevention programs, we ask: (1) Why are not more of existing prevention programs aimed at homicide in view of recent public announcements? and (2) Given the disproportionate rate of this phenomenon among young blacks, why are not more existing prevention programs and strategies directed at the black community? Patterns of institutional racism, the political powerlessness of blacks, and a general sense of the futility of intervention in instances of potential homicide likely account for much of the continuing neglect of the black community by public health and law enforcement officials. Partly as a consequence of such neglect homicide continues to take its greatest tolls among blacks and affects disproportionately the poorest and the most powerless of blacks. Homicide may be a relatively rare phenomenon, but it is currently the tenth largest killer in the United States and considerably less rare in the black community than among whites, as the articles in this volume well document.

Several articles in this volume have noted that technological or purely legalistic controls such as handgun regulation and police intervention may provide some reduction in rates of homicide. It is commonly hypothesized that much criminal violence, especially homicide, occurs simply because the means of lethal violence (handguns) are readily available. It is further suggested that many deaths from homicide would not occur without such easy accessibility of guns. Approximately 30,000 deaths occur annually as the result of accidental, homicidal, or suicidal uses of guns (Wright et al., 1981). Wright et al. also report that so far the effects of gun laws on violent crime are modest or nonexistent. Advocates of gun control offer evidence to the contrary or cite the inadequacy of present laws.

More effective governmental control of access to weapons is important. But, it may be that neither more effective handgun regulation, swifter arrests, nor other forms of intervention by already overburdened police are longterm solutions. As a recent study by a retired police officer proclaims, policemen are "damned if they do and damned if they don't" (Klein, 1968). That is, increased police intervention is both requested by the public and also often questioned as overzealous law enforcement. Nevertheless, the police must play a vital role in any coordinated effort to prevent homicide in the black community. Along with various improved law enforcement strategies police must use their personnel and resources to direct efforts at the prevention of these behaviors among blacks through the expansion of existing crime-prevention/educational programs. The police and criminal justice system role must also be augmented by a full array of community service centers and public health facilities.

Several of the articles in this volume have also reported that homicide is a social process which has somewhat predictable behavioral and situational antecedents. As a result, the crucial question for most current analysts of this phenomenon is not whether intervention and prevention are feasible but rather what constitutes the most effective forms of official response. We believe that public health education may represent the most important component of all prevention endeavors. Effective health education directed at the individual or community level is primary prevention of the kind that may impact successfully upon black homicide rates.[5]

Public health education cannot change attitudes and behavior overnight, hence education-for-prevention programs must be planned as a long term endeavor that eventually will result in the reduction of homicide within the black community. Primary prevention should also focus on community organization as well as communication of information. Both are needed to enable persons to receive, accept, and act on practical wisdom that can save many, especially youth, from untimely deaths. The black community must be fully involved before information will be used. The community itself should also be used to disperse data on homicide and its prevention. Such educational programs used in conjunction with other strategies, such as counseling and improved law enforcement practices, would likely produce the best results.

Efforts to translate factual information acquired from homicide education and prevention programs into life saving behavior is the goal. If such efforts are to be effective they must be applied on a large scale. Health officials must determine what type of services work best for specialized groups, such as teenagers and young adult males. Then efforts must be made to organize the community, to provide the needed services, and educate the potential consumer about the availability of services that would best suit his/her needs.

The homicidal individual and his/her potential victim need to internalize the knowledge that he or she needs help before action will be taken to overcome a pre-homicide crisis. So it is with the larger community. There is a need for increased efforts to create a homicide prevention awareness at all levels-- individual, community, state, and national. We need to develop homicide/prevention education programs in schools, industries and neighborhood groups. These should be designed to educate people to recognize homicide as a national health problem, as well as a problem for their own communities. People also need to be educated to the fact that something can be done to reduce the number of deaths by homicide; that is, homicide is not an unalterable fact of life.

As implied in the discussion above, our focus on health education does not mean that other intervention and prevention tactics should not be implemented. Varying approaches should be utilized. Since law enforcement officials, public health agencies and local community groups may be effective at different stages of intervention, we propose that the following strategies should be used in a coordinated effort to curb the tragically high rates of homicide among blacks.

1) Law enforcement prevention programs that are now directed primarily at the reduction of property crime among the affluent and within industry and business should direct more of their preventive efforts toward the problem of violent crime, especially violent crime among blacks. These also should include law enforcement-oriented educational programs and the funding of research to develop effective and efficient forms of prevention and intervention by law enforcement personnel.

2) Public health agencies in concert with mental health agencies should begin to support and sponsor research, demonstration projects, and workshops designed to develop and disseminate information related to the problems of

234

homicide among blacks. Currently existing programs are not occurring with enough frequency and focus to impact to any large extent upon appropriate target groups, i.e. youths and young adults in large urban communities.

3) Local voluntary groups within the black community should sponsor more programs and activities designed to provide non-law enforcement, non-government agency forms of prevention and intervention. These could include mediation centers designed to intervene and mediate instances of violent behavior, especially violent behavior that might lead to homicide; and educational programs designed to make the black and white public more aware of the tremendous loss of life due to homicide yearly within the black community; and similar efforts. Government agencies should be encouraged to fund such locally operated projects where necessary.

4) Government and private research funding agencies should be encouraged to fund more research, both basic and applied, on the etiology of homicide among blacks and strategies for reduction. Recent conferences convened by the National Institutes of Mental Health and other agencies show some initial steps in this direction. Research funds have not been readily available in the past to investigate this significant social problem.

The scholarly study of crime does not preclude efforts to apply knowledge to help solve the social problems associated with it. Indeed the application of scientific knowledge has been a major goal of criminologists since the inception of the discipline. Unfortunately it has become popular in recent years to propose that questions of the etiology of crime have no answers and in a nonsequitor to suggest that researchers should instead turn their attention to efforts at social control. We believe that researchers and policy makers cannot ignore questions of crime causation. There are identifiable social conditions that contribute to the currently high rates of homicide among blacks. Prevention efforts must ultimately be aimed at modifying these conditions, including poverty and the persistence of racism. More effective law enforcement is important but will not substitute for careful attention to the other social conditions that produce the disproportionate levels of homicide among blacks in the United States. We are suggesting, however, that an awareness of the larger structural causes of disproportionate rates of black homicide need not lead to a conclusion that the kind of intervention tactics discussed in this chapter will not be effective. Both short and long-term solutions are needed. Changes in structural conditions must be accompanied by changes in the behavior of public officials who might successfully intervene in specific circumstances that could lead to homicide. The full acceptance of homicide as a public health concern is one step in achieving these long and short-term objectives.

235

Notes

1. It has been noted that one feature of racism in the United States is a devaluation of the person and life of blacks. This set of societal values has an impact on the views of public officials, such as law enforcement personnel, who might be in a position to intervene and prevent violence among blacks. For example Banton (1964: 173) quotes a southern captain of police detectives as saying "In this town there are three classes of homicide. If a nigger kills a white man, that's murder. If a white man kills a nigger, that's justifiable homicide. If a nigger kills a nigger, that's one less nigger." The institutionalization of this form of racist bias is evidenced in numerous investigations which have reported that blacks and whites receive less punishment for the killing of blacks than for the killing of whites, even after controlling for legally relevant factors. It also appears that the police and other potential intervenors are less likely to intervene in black intraracial violence than in those instances of black-on-white or white-on-white violence.

2. Police departments in many parts of the country have recently instituted large scale crime prevention programs. In cities such as Detroit, these are a well budgeted and important part of the department's operations. However, most of such programs concentrate on the prevention of property crime rather than crimes of violence.

3. See **Health United States** for 1980. The position of the Department of Health and Human Services was made even more explicit in a speech given by Horace G. Ogden, Director of the Center for Health Promotion and Education during a violence prevention forum at the Kennedy Library in Boston in early 1981. He argued that all forms of violence, including suicide and homicide, are public health problems of the first magnitude. He emphasized the need for the development of prevention strategies. See **Justice Assistance News** (1981), Vol. 2, No. 8, pp. 2-3.

4. These symposia were sponsored by the Alcohol, Drug Abuse, and Mental Health Administration (ADAMHA). The first was held May 13-14, 1980. For a summary of the proceedings, see **Public Health Reports** (1981), Vol. 95, No. 6, pp. 549-561. The second was convened June 14-16, 1984. Summaries of its proceedings may be obtained from the National Association of Social Workers, which co-sponsored the meeting.

5. Public health education programs are provided for under federal law. Such programs are currently used to make the public aware of risks and sources of treatment for a number of illnesses. Programs that are now specifically targeted at the black community--hypertension and sickle cell anemia awareness projects--may serve as models for homicide prevention efforts.

References

Banton, Michael. 1964. **The Policeman in the Community.** London: Tavistock.

Health-United States: 1980. 1981. DHHS Publication No. (PHS) 81-1232. United States Department of Health and Human Services, Public Health Service. Office of Health Research, Statistics and Technology. National Center for Health Statistics. National Center for Health.

Justice Assistance News. 1981. Public Information Office, Office of Justice Assistance, Research and Statistics, Bureau of Justice Statistics, Law Enforcement Assistance Administration. Washington, D. C.

Klein, Herbert T. 1968. **The Police: Damned if they do-Damned if they don't.** New York: Crown Publishers.

Public Health Reports. 1981. United States Department of Health and Human Services. Washington, D. C.

Wolfgang, Marvin E. and Franco Ferracuti. 1967, 1982. **The Subculture of Violence: Towards an Integrated Theory in Criminology.** Beverly Hills, CA: Sage Publications.

Wright, James D., Peter H. Rossi, Kathleen Daly, Eleanor Weber- Burdin. 1981. **Weapons, Crime and Violence in America: A Literature Review and Research Agenda.** Washington, D. C.: National Institute of Justice, Department of Justice.